THE
EARLY ISLAMIC
ARCHITECTURE
OF THE
EAST AFRICAN COAST

PETER S. GARLAKE

Memoir Number 1
of the
British Institute of History and Archaeology
in East Africa

Published for the Institute by the
OXFORD UNIVERSITY PRESS
NAIROBI   LONDON
1966

© *British Institute of History and Archaeology in East Africa 1966*

British Institute of History and Archaeology in East Africa
P.O. Box 7680, Nairobi

Oxford University Press, Ely House, London W.1

GLASGOW NEW YORK TORONTO MELBOURNE WELLINGTON
CAPE TOWN SALISBURY IBADAN NAIROBI LUSAKA ADDIS ABABA
BOMBAY CALCUTTA MADRAS KARACHI LAHORE DACCA
KUALA LUMPUR HONG KONG

Oxford University Press, Church House, Government Road, Nairobi

Made and printed in Great Britain by
William Clowes and Sons, Limited, London and Beccles

CONTENTS

FOREWORD

by

The President of the British Institute of History and Archaeology in East Africa

The publication of this first Research Memoir of the British Institute is an occasion to say something of the Institute which sponsored this work. It is appropriate the first Memoir should be concerned, geographically, with the coast of Tanzania. It was at the capital of the Republic of Tanzania, Dar es Salaam, that the Institute was originally founded in 1960, under the aegis and through the endowment of the British Academy, and it owes not a little of its early success to the help and hospitality of the then government of Tanganyika. It is a pleasure therefore in introducing this Memoir to acknowledge this indebtedness, and to acknowledge also the assistance of the succeeding government of Tanzania. President Nyerere's government continued the former government's grant to the Institute until quite recently and it still continues to facilitate and to encourage the Institute's work in its territory.

This indebtedness happily has not gone entirely unrepaid, for the excavations at the great trading coastal city of Kilwa conducted by Mr. H. N. Chittick, Director of the Institute from 1961, have revealed a Muslim town which attained a high level of civilization, with mosques and palaces of remarkable historical interest. They have also provided Tanzania with a potential tourist attraction, less than 200 miles south of Dar es Salaam, which of its kind is unrivalled in East Africa, and a rich collection of objects for the newly extended National Museum in the capital. Kilwa's cultural and trade contacts stretched out to Arabia and Persia, India and the Far East. The architecture at Kilwa naturally has its place in Mr. Garlake's Memoir. A full-scale work by Mr. Chittick on the Kilwa excavations will appear in this series when he has completed his excavations there.

But the Institute's work has by no means been confined to Kilwa or to Tanzania, or to the coast. Inland, in Uganda and Kenya, whose governments have in turn provided grants to the Institute and much other generous help besides, important excavations have been carried out on sites of the Early Iron Age, of vital significance because it was then that the foundations of modern tribal society were being laid. This work, some of it directed towards the great unsolved problem of Bantu origins, will form the subject of future Memoirs in this series.

Nor have research and field work been the Institute's only activities. In 1962 it became a "Connected Institute" of the University of East Africa. This involves the Director and his staff in obligations in the educational and training field, over and above those of supervising the Institute's own students. The Vacation Course held at Makerere College, Uganda, drew students from many parts of East Africa, and led to the publication of the lectures then given under the title "Prelude to East African History", edited by Dr. Merrick Posnansky. A training course in archaeological techniques has been held at Kilwa and British and African students have worked together on the excavations there and in Kenya and Uganda. With this same need in mind to contribute to higher education in East Africa in the field of pre-European history and archaeology, the Institute offers two Gulbenkian studentships for African students from the Commonwealth, preference being given to those prepared to sit for the University of East Africa's higher degrees.

For such students, and for the growing number of universities throughout the world now promoting African studies, memoirs like this Memoir by Mr. Garlake, and the Institute's journal *Azania* will provide the raw material for study.   They are addressed to them no less than to the professional scholar—historian, archaeologist, anthropologist —concerned with special aspects of the ancient and mediaeval heritage of East Africa.

L. P. KIRWAN

PREFACE

This paper is the result of research work carried out in East Africa between July 1962 and March 1964 under a research studentship financed by the Nuffield Foundation and awarded and administered by the British Institute of History and Archaeology in East Africa, which also bears the cost of publication. The work was supervised by the Director of this Institute in East Africa, Mr. H. N. Chittick. Grateful acknowledgements are therefore due to both these bodies and to the Director.

The author is not in any way a specialist in the history of the East African coast, the dating of Islamic and Far Eastern ceramics or in the architecture of Islam and was, indeed, a complete novice in these fields before starting this research work. All material concerning these has been drawn from published sources noted in the bibliography.

Extensive use has also been made of the published works of H. N. Chittick and J. S. Kirkman on the coastal archaeology, and of unpublished information given to the author by them.

With three exceptions all plans are the author's, from complete new surveys carried out by him. Although in many cases other plans are in existence, and several have been published, these do not, in most cases, carry the detail considered necessary to a study of this type. The plans of the mosques of Sanje Majoma and Mgao Mwanya are copied from sketch plans and photographs in the files of the Antiquities Department of Tanganyika, and the town and Palace plan of Gedi from originals of plans surveyed and published by J. S. Kirkman. The author is indebted to them for permission to do this. The photographs are by Mrs. R. M. Garlake or the author. Mrs. Garlake also made the model illustrated in Plates XIV and XV.

Extensive excavations were initiated at the Kilwa sites in 1958, and since 1961 have been carried on by the British Institute of History and Archaeology in East Africa. These have not yet been completed and will form the subject of a separate monograph by H. N. Chittick, to be published by this Institute. Therefore, while work on the architecture of the Kilwa sites is included here, and use has been made of archaeological reports already published, only minimal information can be included on the recent specifically archaeological evidence now being obtained at the Kilwa sites.

Finally, the author would like to thank Mr. J. S. Kirkman for his advice, assistance, hospitality and encouragement during the periods spent in Kenya.

London   P. S. G.
June 1964

LIST OF PLATES

LIST OF FIGURES

The figures of mosques, their mihrab details and plans are followed by those of domestic buildings and certain decorative details. The figures are arranged as far as possible in approximate chronological order of architectural style.

On the map of the East African coast (Fig. 1) all illustrated sites have been given a number. These numbers run from north to south along the mainland, followed consecutively by those of sites on the islands of Pemba, Zanzibar and Mafia, again running from north to south. Thus, Pate, a site on the northern mainland, is numbered 4, Kilwa in southern Tanganyika 42, Msuka Mjini in northern Pemba 46, and Jibondo, off southern Mafia, 56. These same numbers are also found adjacent to the title of each figure. Reference to this number on each figure will thus give directly an indication of the approximate position of the site on the East African coast.

CHAPTER I

INTRODUCTION

History

Traditionally, the Islamic colonization of the East African coast started in the eighth century A.D., and local histories record various Arab immigrations in the subsequent two centuries. Certainly, by the early tenth century, when Masudi visited the island off the East African coast of Qanbalu, probably Pemba, Islamic settlers were established. Before this, there are only the brief references of the first century Periplus of the Erythraean Sea and the fourth century Geography of Ptolemy to show that trading voyages were taking place even then to the coast of Azania or Zanj.[1] But archaeology has yet to confirm these facts. The earliest unarguable confirmation of this history remains the Kufic inscription dated A.H. 500/A.D.1107 in the mosque of Kizimkazi, Zanzibar. However, the archaeological contents of basal levels of excavations at Kilwa and Husuni Kubwa in Tanganyika, and Gedi, Ungwana and Kilepwa in Kenya, coupled with inscriptions from graves and mosques in Mogadishu, show that by the thirteenth century there were established centres all along the coast. These flourished through the fourteenth and fifteenth centuries, and are described at first hand by travellers as various as Ibn Battuta in 1331 and the Chinese voyagers of the early fifteenth century. The arrival of the Portuguese at the start of the sixteenth century did much to disrupt the trade and prosperity of the towns, but they had little positive influence on the culture of the coast and left no deep mark on it. Building works apparently continued through the sixteenth century in the north at least, and not only among the allies of the Portuguese. A new, and apparently more disastrous, threat to the coastal prosperity arose with the southward spread of the nomadic Galla from what is now Somalia who, in the late sixteenth and early seventeenth centuries, drove out the inhabitants of the mainland towns and reached almost as far south as Mombasa. Archaeological evidence shows that the sites of Ungwana, Gedi, Kilepwa and Mnarani were all abandoned finally during this period. At the same time the barbarous Zimba pillaged up the coast from Kilwa to their defeat before Malindi. With the rise of Omani power in the Indian Ocean in the mid seventeenth century, and their immediate participation in the undermining of Portuguese power on the coast, a true and positive new influence on the culture grew, at first in alliance with, but later hostile to the older order, the chief representative of which at this time was Pate. By the early eighteenth century Portuguese control of the coast had ceased and by the end of this century many towns, particularly in the south, enjoyed a revival of the prosperity and independence they had last known two centuries before. In the early nineteenth century Omani ascendancy over the mainland was strong and direct enough for the mainland towns to be considered for the first time no more than colonies of an external ruler—a process completed when the Sultan, Sayyid Said, moved his capital from Muscat to Zanzibar in 1832.

The coastal towns and settlements were always completely dependent on the trade of the Indian Ocean. Provincial, and with their destiny always finally decided by outside powers, until the nineteenth century they nevertheless always retained their own internal

[1] The Periplus is now maintained by some authorities to date from the third century.

independence except for brief periods, not only from abroad, but from each other. Pate appears to have attempted to expand and conquer her rivals in the fourteenth century, while Kilwa enjoyed an economic supremacy, with her control of the gold trade of Sofala, in the fifteenth century. In general, however, there was never any permanent policy of territorial expansion or domination; warfare took place to solve a specific and limited problem and the results had little permanency. Each town or city was a centre of trade and their fortunes fluctuated with their trade—they had no control over the sources of trade, or even of the trade routes, and did not want or need it. Indeed, it will be seen that the sites of the majority of the towns were poorly placed to exert any influence outside their restricted boundaries, and defensive works beyond poorly constructed town walls were non-existent until the late eighteenth century. Natural resources were unexploited (though iron was smelted in the early fourteenth century and earlier at Kilwa (near Husuni Kubwa) and Gedi, but in no large quantities) and agriculture played little part in the siting or planning of the towns. They were entirely dependent on the goodwill and cooperation of the inhabitants of the hinterland —a policy that succeeded and lasted. A natural corollary and extension of this policy was that the population and, as a result, the culture of the settlements was a mixture of native African and Arab elements. The religion was Islam and the fundamental bases of the culture came from abroad. In language and the materials of everyday life local African influence was stronger. The standing architecture however reflects little African influence and its forms are entirely alien to those of the hinterland—its origins were outside East Africa and it is present fully fledged in the earliest known buildings. If anything, only a slow subsequent decline can be traced in both design and technique. Nevertheless, the resulting style is individual to the coast and homogeneous throughout its length. The culture was provincial—initiative was always from abroad—but its standards of comfort and amenity were high, even luxurious, especially in the minor arts. It was in no way impoverished or impermanent. Until the coming of the Portuguese, and the subsequent incursions of the hostile Galla and Zimba tribes, the pressures and tensions enforced from outside were minimal. When they came, however, many centres crumbled rapidly and the whole structure of the culture entered a slow but sure decline. The internal self-reliance and human resources of the coastal culture were too weak to meet the challenge of determined antagonists or to respond with initiative of their own.

Buildings

The earliest settlements were, as pioneering enterprises are everywhere, poor and controlled by the immediately available local resources. At Kilwa there are some 7 m. of successive levels of occupation deposit and red earth with traces of post holes, representing the earliest building fabrics. The first buildings were for a long time only of mud and wattle, with open hearths, and storage pits dug below the floor within them. They appear, indeed, entirely African, but for the rare imported pottery of the Near East. In the lowest levels of Ungwana, dated to the end of the twelfth century, traces of burnt bricks, 5 cms. thick, on a plastered stone foundation, were revealed, but these remain unique. The standing remains of the coast take several forms. Stone-lined wells are frequently found in isolation. Single tombs or groups of tombs of characteristic construction, with a tall, masonry pillar at their head and surrounded by walls, whose façades are partly, or completely, decorated with panels formed in dressed stone, frequently stand isolated on the edge of the sea shore, with no further trace of settlement beyond scatters of sherds. They will be discussed only incidentally in this paper. However, they frequently adjoin the remains of stone-built mosques. The

Islamic mosque is not only a religious building but the focal point of the whole community—it may fulfil the functions of refuge, court, school and treasury. It is not unexpected that on the coast it should often have been the only building of stone, while mud and wattle served for the rest of the buildings. Ruined mosques may only survive as traces of foundations, but often fragments of wall stand even to roof height. The mihrab, an apsidal recess indicating the direction of Mecca (in East Africa this is due north, and the mosques are therefore always orientated northwards) and focal point of the mosque, forms a strong projecting buttress on the exterior of the north wall of the mosques—so this wall is usually found in a much less ruinous condition than the remainder of the mosque. The mosques, and more particularly the mihrabs, also owe their survival to the fact that in Islamic law the materials of a mosque may only be reused in another religious building. The mosques are the structures most worthy of study for not only are there many more of them than any other stone buildings, but their importance naturally means that the best techniques, and most carefully made and elaborate decorative elements, were used in their construction. The normal minor settlement contained, besides the mosque, only one or two stone-built houses. The few major towns however have several mosques besides the Jamia[1] or main congregational mosque, used for the Friday prayers. They may have up to 30 or 40 large stone houses, one of which is usually several times larger than the rest, and no doubt formed the palace of the ruler. The whole town may cover up to 50 acres, and a wall frequently surrounds it. No true secular public or non-residential buildings are anywhere discernible, in even the largest towns, with the probable single exception of Husuni Ndogo on Kilwa, until the building of forts in many towns in the nineteenth century. It is the stone buildings that form the subject of this paper. They were obviously the most important buildings, and are the only structures that now survive and the only ones that can truly be considered architecture in the fullest meaning of the word, though they were not the only buildings and were surrounded by the impermanent dwellings of the major part of the people and often, no doubt, themselves had subsidiary elements of similar impermanent materials.

Siting

The East African coast (Map, Fig. 1) is on the whole low lying, with many creeks and inlets, and with a gradually shelving shore, frequently fringed by mangroves. With a tidal range averaging only some 3 m., the sea may retreat more than a quarter of a mile. Offshore, the coral reefs never form a continuous barrier, but everywhere they prevent the penetration of ocean swells—the shore itself is calm. There are very few true deep water harbours or anchorages—Mombasa and Dar es Salaam are two of the few exceptions—but this was no hindrance in the past. The shallow draught and resilient construction of all the early vessels enabled them to be brought close inshore on the high tide. When the tide retreated they would rest on the sandy sea bed supported by a simple timber cradle and could then be unloaded without difficulty. This procedure is followed today, and early graffiti and written records show that it was the universal practice in the past. All the sites of settlements are found right on the edge of the shore. Only the great city of Gedi, four miles from the open sea and two miles from Mida Creek, is an exception. Naturally the individual sites vary a great deal, but perhaps the most typical is on the shore of a low peninsula or sand-spit backed, and so separated from the mainland proper, by a very shallow tidal creek, filled only at high spring tides (e.g. Ndumi, Dege, Mtitimira, Ras Mkumbuu, Utondwe). This may be

[1] The correct transliteration of the Arabic word for a congregational mosque is Jami^c. Jamia has, however, been used throughout this paper.

varied either by sites situated on the higher ground of fossil dunes and backed by seasonal swamps, or rivers, running parallel to the coast behind the old dune until they break through to the sea (e.g. Kunduchi, Kaole, Kimbiji, Sala, Kutani) or by sites, on small offshore islands, often so close to the mainland as virtually to form part of it, but permanently separated from it (e.g. the Kilwa and Songo Mnara sites, Mombasa, the Lamu Islands, Toten Island, Kilepwa). In all these cases there is a barrier between settlement and mainland, easily penetrated when desired, but still creating a certain obstruction or even only a sense of apartness from the mainland—a no man's land. The links are all with the sea. Seemingly advantageous or more easily defensible sites on inland bluffs overlooking the sea and dominating the foreshore were often ignored in preference to low-lying ones closer to the shore (e.g. Kaole).

The Kilwa Chronicle[1] records how the founder bought the island, then joined to the mainland at low tide, from an infidel; he was then warned that the infidel would return to the island and reclaim it, killing the immigrants. "So they set themselves to work and dug out the creek across which in former times men passed at low tide between the mainland and the island.... The infidel came ... he saw the tide was up and waited in the usual way for it to ebb until he could cross; but the water remained up.... Then he despaired of seizing the island.... He went home full of remorse and sorrow". This legend must have been echoed many times at many sites. The security (largely illusory against a strong enemy, as the subsequent history of Kilwa proved) of the swamps or creek between settlement and mainland was felt to be a sufficient hindrance to satisfy the inhabitants and is a feature of the majority of sites.

Small mosques are frequently found in isolation on a cliff or headland, or very close to the shore, in positions where they were easily visible to passing vessels. Such mosques, probably buildings of special veneration to seafarers, no doubt intentionally symbolize the close association of the inhabitants with the sea and their trade across it. They probably never formed part of a settlement, or certainly were not the main mosque of a settlement. Today in Zanzibar there is at least one such mosque, close to the sea and outside the town, opposite which sailors place offerings in the sea as they sail past, as thanks for a safe landfall. In the past, the small mosque at the entrance to Mida Creek, the Mvinje mosque on the north-east tip of Kilwa Island, and probably the small mosque, called "the Mnara", at Songo Mnara (actually built in shallow water some 15 m. off the shore) and the mosque on the beach at the foot of the headland of Husuni Kubwa (if this is a mosque, see p. 98) no doubt fulfilled similar purposes.

Site List

Not all the sites of the coast have been visited in the course of preparing this paper. No sites north of the Lamu Islands or in Somalia (except for Mogadishu and the nearby towns of Merca and Brava) have been visited, nor any south of the Kilwa Islands, though sites belonging to the East Coast sphere probably extend as far as the Comoro Islands and Sofala. Comprehensive site lists, including the standing remains, of Tanganyika and Mafia have been compiled by H. N. Chittick[2] and G. S. P. Freeman-Grenville[3] and list some 46 sites containing the standing ruins of 69 mosques, of which 49 have been visited. In Kenya 31 sites contain the standing ruins of some 53 mosques, 36 of which have been studied. These are listed by A. J. H. Prins[4] and J. S. Kirkman.[5]

[1] G. S. P. Freeman-Grenville: East African Coast, p. 37.
[2] Annual Report, Antiquities Division of Tanganyika, 1958.
[3] Mediaeval History of the Coast of Tanganyika.
[4] Swahili Speaking Peoples.
[5] Antiquaries Journal, Vol. XXXVII, April 1957, and S.A.A.B. Vol. XI, No. 44, Dec. 1956.

J. S. Kirkman,[1] L. A. C. Buchanan[2] and F. B. Pearce[3] list altogether some 15 pre-nineteenth century mosques on the islands of Zanzibar and Pemba, of which 7 have been planned. These lists, taken together, are almost certainly practically complete and comprehensive and the discovery of further major monuments is unlikely—though new minor sites will no doubt be found. No attempt was made to search for new sites and only one previously unknown mosque was found and that at a known site. All the major sites have been included in this paper, and photographs of the remainder indicate that their inclusion would add little further information—many are so ruined that no details are visible and even major elements of the ground plans are entirely destroyed. Work on domestic buildings has been limited to a study of the major sites of Gedi, Mtwapa, Kua, Kilwa and Songo Mnara. Very few complete house plans are recoverable outside the main sites and the major elements still visible in the incomplete plans are so similar to each other as to be valueless in a typological study. Decorative details are largely absent in all domestic buildings, and in the absence of these it is only in minor planning details that valid comparisons can be made.

A résumé of the coastal sites running from north to south along a coastline of 1000 miles will indicate more clearly the scope of the subject (Map, Fig. 1). From Kismayu in Somalia, south of the Juba River mouth, a string of low, scrub covered, offshore islands runs south almost as far as the Lamu group. This is the Bajun coast and the islands form a barrier reef to the navigable and protected coastal lane between them and the dune lined mainland. One would expect these islands to be rich in remains of the early sites. V. L. Grottanelli[4] records ruins from all the larger inhabited islands of this group but most appear to be only of the eighteenth and nineteenth centuries. One earlier mihrab, that of Rasini, called by him "one of the most perfect monuments of Muslim art in East Africa", is reproduced here (Fig. 62).

Kenya

In northern Kenya, on the mainland itself, the sites of Ishikani, Kiunga, Mwana Mtama and Omwe contain mosques, but are not included here. The three low-lying islands of Pate, Manda and Lamu lie close together and close offshore and together form an extremely complex indented coastline—the submerged delta of a former Tana River. The town of Pate, whose traditional history is recorded, was one of the most important of the coast under its ruling Nabhan dynasty and at times its influence spread as far as Kilwa. Protected by the sea from the Galla invasions it retained its importance in the seventeenth century. On the same island there are also extensive remains in the towns of Faza and Siu and, of lesser importance, Tundwa. The ruined towns of Takwa,[5] Kitao and Manda are found on Manda Island. Lamu today dominates the islands, but little remains of its pre-nineteenth century past. Southward, on the northern shores of Formosa Bay, the present mouth of the Tana (Ozi) River, stands the large, 45 acre, walled town of Ungwana, the Portuguese Hoja (excavated by Kirkman, unpublished) with the subsidiary settlements of Shaka (Jaca of the Portuguese), and Mwana on the headland at the entrance to the bay. The even, southward sweep of Formosa Bay contains no sites, neither does the mouth of the Sabaki River. Malindi, 50 miles to the south of Ungwana, was of great importance particularly in the early sixteenth century when it was a loyal ally of the Portuguese, but it declined

---

[1] Unpublished report on the ruins of Zanzibar and Pemba.
[2] Ancient Monuments of Pemba.
[3] Zanzibar.
[4] Pescatori dell' Oceano Indiano, p. 76.
[5] J. S. Kirkman: Ars Orientalis II, 1957.

in the late sixteenth century with the transfer to Fort Jesus and the Galla invasions. Little early building remains. Round Mida Creek, however, there are the remains of many sites. Here, the sea shore is lined by vertical coral cliffs 2–6 m. high, whose flat tops mark an early high sea level, which are characteristic of much of the coast especially from south of Mida Creek to the Tanganyika border. On the cliff bordering the shore is the small mosque of Kiburugeni, and another stands on the northern head-land marking the entrance to Mida Creek itself. On an island within the creek is the site of Kilepwa, and on the creek shores that of Mgangani, while two miles from the creek head is the major walled town of Gedi.[1] The coast south of Gedi as far as Mombasa is, even today, virtually uninhabited with the exceptions of the two steep-sided major creeks which provide sheltered deep water anchorages. The three sites of Kilifi, Mnarani and Kitoka formed the "city state" of Kilifi, known to the Portuguese. Of these, the ruined town of Mnarani, on a steep bluff dominating the south shore of Kilifi Creek, has been excavated.[2] Kitoka lies three miles to the south, on the open shore of the mouth of the minor Takaungu Creek. Fifteen miles south, on the north bank of Mtwapa Creek, a very large settlement existed, exceeding Gedi in extent, while on the open shore just north of it are the ruins of Jumba la Mtwana. The island of Mombasa lies only twelve miles south—its deep water harbour of Kilindini is un-equalled on the coast and here the only remaining early mosque on the island is found. The old town (rebuilt in the nineteenth century) and harbour, dominated by the Portuguese Fort Jesus, lie on the other side of the island to the north. At the mouth of the Mwachema River, a short distance south of Mombasa, stands the mosque of Tiwi and, a little further south, that of Diani.

Tanganyika

None of the sites in the vicinity of Vanga Bay (Muungi, Gazi, Wasin Island and Vumba Kuu) have been visited. This is an area very like the Lamu area, and itself a maze of creeks and islands formed by submerged deltas. The two nineteenth century mosques of Toten Island, in the large creek that now forms Tanga harbour, have not been visited. On a creek on the coast south of Tanga harbour is the site of Ndumi. Tongoni—a site noted for its fine cemetery of panel tombs, and known to the Portuguese as Mtangata, is at the mouth of the next estuarine creek 15 miles south of Tanga. The coast south of Tanga as far as Dar es Salaam is hardly broken by bays or headlands but is well watered by many small streams and the major Pangani River, on the low lying silts of whose estuary the nineteenth century town of Pangani lies. On a steep bluff overlooking the flats of the town is the extensive earlier site of Muhembo with two mosques, while on the opposite bank is the much more recent mosque of Bweni Kuu, still in use. Mnarani, a tiny mosque, lies alone with a pillar tomb on a small, steep headland between Muhembo and Tongoni. South of here there are the many mosques of the early nineteenth century—some still used—relics of the many little eighteenth century states known as the Shirazi confederacies, which survived into the twentieth century. Of these, Kisikimto, Mkwaja, Mafui and Kipumbwe are included here. The site of Utondwe, on the sea-arm of a very extensive shallow creek, was probably in existence earlier, as the Otondo of the Portuguese. The still earlier sites of Kaole or Pumbuji (Pamboga of the Portuguese), Mbweni, Ukutani and Kunduchi, all at the mouths of seasonal rivers, continue the series to Dar es Salaam. On the large headland stretching from Dar es Salaam for 40 miles south to Kisiju, are many minor, post Portuguese, sites—Mjimwema, Mboamaji, then Dege and Bandarini together on a

[1] J. S. Kirkman: Gedi, The Great Mosque, 1954, The Palace, 1962.
[2] J. S. Kirkman: Ars Orientalis III, 1959.

large tidal bay, Sala, Kutani, Kimbiji and others still more minor. Beyond this are the vast swamps of the Rufiji delta, stretching for 50 miles. Indeed, no further mainland sites are known until one reaches Kilwa itself 160 miles south of Dar es Salaam—with the single exception of Mtitimira 10 miles to the north of Kilwa. Kilwa—yet another typical offshore island—within a reef and with a fine anchorage, is the most famous site of the coast. The Kilwa Chronicle, written about 1520, the copper coinage minted there, the Portuguese records, and the extensive excavations now being undertaken by the British Institute of History and Archaeology in East Africa, combine to make it of crucial importance to coastal research. Besides the ruins of the mediaeval town, there is an eighteenth century palace and enclosure to the west, and to the east, on a steep sandstone headland, the complex of Husuni Kubwa, probably the largest pre-colonial structure south of the Sahara. Across a gully from Husuni Kubwa stands the large rectangular enclosure of Husuni Ndogo. South of Kilwa, the island of Songo Mnara has the most substantial standing ruins of any mediaeval town in Tanganyika, with its subsidiary settlement of Sanje Majoma. Between Songo Mnara and the mainland lies Sanje ya Kati, whose standing ruins belong to a period earlier than those of Kilwa or Songo Mnara. No further important remains are known to the south, but the cultural area extended beyond the Ruvuma River and Cape Delgado into Mozambique and beyond the Zambesi delta, probably as far as Sofala, and included a string of offshore islands (the Kerimba Islands) and also the Comoro Islands.

Mafia

Mafia, off the great Rufiji delta, is only 10 miles from the mainland and separated from it by a shallow, shoaly channel. No doubt it owed much of its importance to trade coming down the Rufiji from the hinterland as well as to its dominant position on the coastal sea lanes. Kisimani, at the south-west end of the island, lies on a point governing a deep water channel close inshore—a coastal shipping route. The other sites are found on small islands a mile or so offshore to the south-east of Mafia. The ruins of Chole, capital of Mafia until 1916, are mainly of nineteenth century date, but on Juani Island, the town of Kua (Coa of the Portuguese) with five known mosques and many houses (the majority of which are late eighteenth century) was one of the major sites of the coast until destroyed by Sakalava raiders of Madagascar in 1820. Jibondo, the most southerly of the inhabited offshore islands, has a further early site.

Zanzibar

Zanzibar is 20 miles from the mainland. It contains few pre-nineteenth century remains, though the mosque of Kizimkazi on the south-east contains an inscription of A.D. 1107—perhaps the best known relic of the entire coast. The old capital of Zanzibar, Unguja Kuu, has no standing remains. Tumbatu, a waterless island at Zanzibar's north-east tip, separated from the main island by a narrow strait which forms one of the main coastal shipping routes, has one of the major pre-Portuguese town sites. On the main island opposite it are the isolated fortified houses of Mvuleni.

Pemba

Pemba differs from both Zanzibar and Mafia in that it does not lie on the continental shelf, but is a true oceanic island. It contains many more ruined sites for its area than any other part of the coast. Its western coastline is extremely indented—a long series of sounds, peninsulas and tiny islands. On one of these, Ras Mkumbuu, lies a major early site. Most sites on Pemba, unlike those of Mafia and Zanzibar, lie along the eastern shore, facing the open Indian Ocean, though protected from it by

2

reefs. Msuka Mjini, Chwaka and Shengejuu are illustrated here, but the "fortified citadel" of Pujini (from all descriptions quite unlike any other building, but probably late in date) has not been visited.

Previous work

The many ruins of the coast have attracted the attention of travellers, anthropologists and colonial administrators since the earliest days of European colonization. Many have left accurate descriptions of sites visited by them; collected, studied and dated the imported sherds found on the surface nearby; and drawn on oral traditions and ethnographic parallels to elucidate the origins and dates of the sites. This work has been incorporated in many descriptive or anthropological works written on the coast and its cultures, and is of great value. Much however suffers from the fact that the authors were unaware of the extent and variety of the ruined sites outside the limited area with which they were acquainted, while no serious archaeological work or excavation was undertaken. However, Major F. B. Pearce, the British Resident in Zanzibar, not only called attention to, and described, the ruins of Pemba extremely accurately in 1920, but was able, from the knowledge gained from this limited area alone, to describe the characteristic and significant features of the early architecture extremely accurately—a description that can hardly be bettered today.[1] "The chief characteristics of their architectural style are the pointed arch, the free employment of dressed coral for the edgings of pillars and doorways, the utilization of squared roof and floor beams, the rectangular wall recess as distinct from the rounded or pointed recesses of the Arabian style, the rectangular window and the peaked and divided keystone—a very distinctive feature. It may be noted also that the stone mouldings of their doorways and arches are invariably cut at less than a right angle—generally 85°. Apart from these, refinement of design marks the…work as different from all other styles." No more succinct or accurate description of the truly significant features of the classic architectural styles is possible.

A further extremely valuable work is the survey and planning of the ruins on Kilwa and Songo Mnara by M. H. Dorman in 1938.[2] The Kilwa plans made by him were only superseded in 1957, and his plan of the whole town of Songo Mnara, based on a rapid chain and compass survey, though inaccurate in detail, was a valuable foundation on which to base the town plan published here. His descriptions of the ruins are also accurate, though his conclusions, untested by excavations, have now been largely superseded.

With the appointment of J. S. Kirkman as Warden of the Coastal Historical Sites of Kenya in 1947, serious and large scale archaeological excavation became possible, and commenced with work on the town of Gedi. The results of this work, expanded and tested by smaller excavations at several other sites and published in several articles and two books, provides the foundation of all coastal dating, based on the pottery found, especially imported Near Eastern and Chinese wares. The dating evidence used in this paper is predominantly that obtained from these works. Ten years later in 1957, H. N. Chittick was appointed Conservator of Antiquities in Tanganyika, and later Director of the British Institute of History and Archaeology in East Africa. Archaeological work then became possible on the coastal sites of Tanganyika. This work has been concentrated on the sites on, and in the vicinity of, Kilwa. The results, which await definitive publication, may well alter the Kenya dating in detail, for there appears to be a general tendency for the dating of imported ceramic wares in the Kilwa

[1] Zanzibar, p. 351.
[2] T.N.R. 6, 1938.

area to be earlier than the corresponding wares of Kenya by approximately half a century. The significance or validity of this discrepancy is outside the scope of the present paper—nor does it significantly affect this paper, where it is relative rather than absolute dating that is important.

Previous to the start of archaeological excavation in Tanganyika, extensive exploratory work had been undertaken from 1950, notably by Dr. G. S. P. Freeman-Grenville and Rev. G. Mathew. The results of Dr. Freeman-Grenville's work were published in his "Mediaeval History of the Coast of Tanganyika" in 1962. In this work, the brief description of all known sites, the work on the coinage of Kilwa and the study of the Kilwa Chronicle are of major importance. However, in the discussion of the architecture, this work takes no account of any of the recent archaeological work and is unsupported by any plans or sections. Its conclusions on the architecture of the coast and its development have largely proved untenable and, in many cases, the views expressed differ widely from those of the present author. This is largely due to the knowledge now available from archaeological evidence. In particular, the building sequence of the Great Mosque at Kilwa that is followed here, is one amplifying, but based on, that published by H. N. Chittick in Tanganyika Notes and Records No. 53, 1959, and not that of Dr. Freeman-Grenville. A detailed discussion on these particular divergent views hinges finally on archaeological, not architectural, evidence and is therefore not appropriate to this paper. The same applies to certain articles on Songo Mnara and Kilwa by Rev. G. Mathew.[1] While his descriptions of the visible remains on these sites are completely accurate, many of the tentative conclusions drawn regarding the function or date of many of the buildings have been superseded by evidence from excavation or complete clearance of buildings and the detailed study of the plans—evidence obviously not available earlier. It is not felt necessary, therefore, to refute specifically these earlier conclusions.

Dating

There are four basic approaches possible to the dating of the buildings of the coast. These are, firstly, the written and traditional oral histories and the descriptions and records of outside travellers and administrators; secondly, archaeological excavation; thirdly, the inscriptions (or dateable decorative insets such as imported ceramics) set into the fabric of the buildings, and fourthly, an analysis of the typology of the architecture.

Written records

The Kilwa Chronicle, written in the early sixteenth century, and now known in a version of the Portuguese de Barros, written in 1552, and from a nineteenth century Arabic copy of the original, is the most authoritative traditional history. But Pate, Lamu, Tumbatu and other towns also had extensive traditional histories which were recorded in the late nineteenth century or later. Travellers from the time of Ibn Battuta in 1331 have left detailed descriptions of many towns and the Portuguese administrative records, besides those of her travellers and missionaries, are particularly detailed. Up to the end of the nineteenth century explorers or traders, such as Morice at Kilwa in 1776, Prior in 1811, and subsequently Burton and Guillain have all left records of things seen on the coast. However, there are many strange lacunae and errors in even the most reliable account. To give only two examples: Gedi, one of the largest towns in existence on the coast in the sixteenth century is never mentioned in Portuguese records. Ibn Battuta, the great Arab traveller of the early fourteenth century, has left descriptions

1 T.N.R. 53, 1959, and East African Annual 1951–2.

of the East African coast, notably of Kilwa, but there his description of the buildings is at complete variance with the archaeological record—he states that Kilwa was built entirely of wood and roofed with reeds, whereas it is certain that many houses were of stone with "coral concrete" roofs supported on rafters. Freeman-Grenville's emendations of this text in an attempt to reconcile the two views[1] have not proved acceptable.[2]

Excavation

Archaeological excavation in the last 15 years has yielded the most reliable evidence regarding date. It is sufficient to say here that the basic dating evidence is obtained from the imported glazed wares of the Near East, the celadons, porcelains and stonewares of the Far East and, after the arrival of the Portuguese, from Iberian imitations of these wares. Locally made unglazed wares occur in abundance at every site but they vary almost completely from zone to zone and, while of considerable value in clarifying relationships within a limited locality, they cannot of their nature provide absolute dates of the same order as the imported wares. Copper coins were minted at Kilwa in the fourteenth and fifteenth centuries and used only there and on Mafia—they give the sultan's name but no date, and their chronology depends, therefore, on correlating these sultans with those of the Kilwa Chronicle. The recent excavations at Kilwa show that the dating of the Chronicle's list of sultans from the length of their reigns is at variance with the archaeological evidence.

The standing buildings so far excavated on the coast are: Husuni Kubwa—late thirteenth century; the Great Mosque of Ras Mkumbuu—end of the fourteenth century; Mnarani—early to late fifteenth century; Kilwa and Songo Mnara Palace, mosques and adjoining buildings—mainly mid fifteenth century; the minor Gedi mosques—fifteenth century. The final forms of the Double Jamia at Ungwana, the mosque of the Domed Mihrab at Ungwana and the small mosque at Mnarani are all early sixteenth century; while the Great Mosque of Gedi and Takwa mosque are mid sixteenth century—the latter with additions of the end of the seventeenth century. The evidence for these dates, which are in all cases the dates of the surviving structures as seen today, will be discussed in Chapter V.

Inscriptions

Dated inscriptions are rare in the mosques of the coast: most famous is the Kufic inscription of the mihrab of Kizimkazi, Zanzibar, recording its building in A.H. 500/A.D. 1107, while an adjacent inscription records its rebuilding in A.H. 1184/A.D. 1772/3. In the Jamia of Mogadishu, the inscription over the entrance to the tower records the start of construction on 1 Muharram A.H. 636/A.D. 1238. The nearby mosque of Arba Rukn has an inscription recording the death of a Shirazi, Khusrau ibn Muhammed, in A.H. 667/A.D. 1269. In the mihrab of the mosque of Fakhr ad Din there is a marble relief carved also in A.H. 667/A.D. 1269. In the nearby town of Merca, an inscription in the Jamia gives its date of construction as A.H. 1018/A.D. 1609, while one of the minor Merca mosques has an inscription dated A.H. 1185/A.D. 1773 incorporated in the mihrab decoration.

In Tanganyika, the poorly constructed mosque at Utondwe, north of Bagamoyo, has a carved coral plaque to the east of the mihrab with a dedicatory inscription and date which is variously read as A.H. 1116/A.D. 1700 or A.H. 1196/A.D. 1782. The mosque, still in use, in the village of Mboamaji, just south of Dar es Salaam, had a date alone, A.H. 1017/A.D. 1608, carved on the lintol over the door. This date is said by the elders

1 East African Coast, p. 31.
2 H. N. Chittick: T.N.R. 61, 1963, and others.

of the village today to refer to the first Arab settlement in the area, and not, as previously supposed, to the building of the mosque which they say was built about 1870[1]—a date much more in accord with its style. Of extremely doubtful value are the rudimentary graffiti scratched in plaster on the mosques of Tongoni (variously read as A.H. 609/A.D. 1213 and A.H. 817/A.D. 1414) and Msuka Mjini, Pemba (read as A.H. 816/A.D. 1414). Most authorities now deny these latter readings and consider the graffiti as insufficiently clear to be read at all coherently.

The value of these inscriptions for dating purposes is very variable. There is no reason to doubt the value of an inscription such as that of the Mogadishu Jamia tower where it forms the architrave, and indeed the major part, of the design of the tower entrance door, and is obviously in its original position in a fabric that is a homogeneous whole (Fig. 67). The same reasoning applies to the inscription in the small eighteenth century mosque at Merca. However, in other cases (such as the inscriptions in the Mogadishu mosque mihrabs of Arba Rukn and Fakhr ad Din and in the mihrabs of the Jamia of Merca and Mogadishu) the inscriptions are separate entities and sufficiently valuable decoratively, intrinsically and historically, to be incorporated in fabrics that, stylistically, are obviously several centuries later than the date of the inscriptions. The gap between style and inscription date is so wide, and the inscriptions in several cases so ill adapted to their present positions, that there is little danger of confusion in the dating. The Kufic inscription of Kizimkazi is a similar case as Freeman-Grenville has shown.[2] It, like other elements of this mihrab, has been reused in the eighteenth century, or even subsequent, rebuildings. Once it is realized that inscribed plaques and blocks are preserved and incorporated in rebuildings several centuries later, as is so obvious in the Somali examples, all inscriptions must be used with reserve, except where it is clear that they are an integral and dominant part of their surrounds. The latter test only succeeds certainly in the tower of the Mogadishu Jamia.

Architectural analysis

The architecture will be separated for analysis and comparison into five basic elements—techniques of construction, ornamental and decorative detail, the composition of mosque mihrabs, mosque planning, and the planning of domestic buildings.

The whole basis of construction depends on the complete mastery of working coralline limestone which was already fully exploited in the earliest buildings. Coral rag is used for all masonry and the outstanding quality possible in the finished work is shown in the fine dressed coral blocks used for all mouldings, arches, salient angles and, in fact, wherever precision is required. Lime mortar, and plaster, derived from burnt coral, is used on floors and walls. Fine concrete, whose coarse aggregate is coral rubble, is used for vaults and roofs. A slow deterioration in the standards of workmanship is discernible, particularly in the use of dressed coral. There is only a limited repertoire of decorative mouldings. Examples are the carved cable pattern or the simpler incised herring-bone mouldings, and the curious ogival or keel-shaped nick at the apex of many arches. All may be found identically in buildings of various dates and regions—they are not limited in time or space. The composition of these various elements in the design of the mihrab, focal point visually and functionally of the mosque, shows a slow development from a uniform basis. Detailing becomes progressively less visually effective as it becomes more elaborate. The planning of every building is restricted by the span of the timber rafters—which never exceeds 2·80 m. This places the plans in a dimensional "strait jacket", so restrictive that it is a universal feature of every space—even the vaulted buildings conform to it. As a result all building plans are

1 H. N. Chittick: Annual Report of the British Institute of History and Archaeology in East Africa, 1963.
2 Unpublished report in files of the Antiquities Division of Tanganyika.

aggregations of narrow rectangles—a monotonous geometry with little regard to visual or spatial variation or excitement.

Style

From this brief summary it can already be seen that there is a basic unity, a homogeneity in all the elements, that combines to form an individual architectural style common to the whole coast—present in thirteenth century Husuni Kubwa and lasting into the eighteenth century, if not beyond.   Slow change there is, in every aspect, as standards apparently decline or as new elements of detail are introduced, but there are no radical or basic changes.   This is perhaps typical of the Islamic world.   A. U. Pope says of Persian architecture,[1] "The evolution of Persian architecture and ornament is deliberate and decorous.   It is doubtful if there are any sudden outbursts or swift revolutions in taste.   The aesthetic sophistication of the designers and principal patrons was such as to maintain for long periods any values that were gradually discovered. The passionate revulsions too frequent in the history of taste in Europe would be thought a display of gauche immaturity in the Orient, always scornful of change as such." Nevertheless, the continuity of style in East Africa for some five centuries is remarkable. Its position on the perimeter of the Islamic world and the basic inability of the culture that evolved on the coast to respond with initiative, or to originate its own individual solutions to its problems (already noticed in the political history of the coast), help to explain the static quality of the architectural style.   This is not to imply that the architecture of the coast is stagnant—minor change and modification certainly take place and there is never sterile imitation of the past.   In every period the architecture is alive, but there are no manifest or basic advances (in technique especially is this true) or any forms of basic experiment or search for better answers to the problems posed— especially by the limitations of the plan dimensions.   There is throughout a complete acceptance of the tenets present at the start of building on the coast.

Use of an Architect

It is basic to the understanding of the coastal architecture to see the difference between the architecture of an "architect" and that of a "master builder" or competent artisan. To over-simplify cruelly, it is the difference between "art" and "folk art" or "peasant art".   If architecture is "firmness, commodity and delight", the first two qualities are those provided by a master builder, and are outstanding attributes of the coast, but the latter—delight—is only truly possible by creative design and is missing in all the coastal architecture.   For a building to have an architect by no means implies the use of paper plans.   The architect does, however, impose a visual discipline; an aesthetic unity and regularity thought out beforehand, with foresight; a regard to organizing the various elements of the design into a single whole.   The limitations of the site and of constructional techniques are accepted but used and modulated.   They are not allowed to dominate the initial conception.   Architects, as so defined, may well work in completely traditional methods and the individuality of the designer may or may not show through.

In contrast, the artisan or master builder, while a complete master of structural techniques, will normally allow them to control the architecture.   There is no seeking after new solutions or experimentation.   Tradition is always the strength of the craftsman who is therefore conservative by nature and unlikely to initiate change himself, and only likely to accept it and use new methods when there is a considerable body of precedent already established.   This precedent, in a provincial society, must normally

[1] A Survey of Persian Art, vol. VI: The Architecture of the Islamic Period, p. 1089.

come from outside.   Site and structure rule the building, visual and aesthetic considerations are secondary.

A comparison of the fifteenth century extensions to the Great Mosque at Kilwa (Fig. 15), typical of the finest achievements of the coastal builders, with the mosque of Fakhr ad Din (Fig. 66) in Mogadishu, which seems clearly to have had an architect, will illustrate this contrast.   The domes and vaults of the extensions to the Great Mosque are, structurally, masterpieces of the coastal architecture.   Five aisles wide and six bays deep, the thirty bays cover one of the largest areas of building on the coast—yet this space is not articulated or modulated in any way.   The alternation of plain dome, fluted dome and barrel vault, each technically highly competent, have, due to their height and the bay proportions, no visual impact on the space they cover.   The earlier chambers and corridors at either side, and the original mosque to the north, admittedly pre-existing, have in no way been incorporated into a unified final design.   This is a conjunction of a series of independent units, not a unified whole.   Comparison with nearly contemporary vaulted buildings at Kilwa show that a dimensional system had been evolved whereby column, arch and bay dimensions increase in strict proportion.   This is a technically proficient solution and typical of the artisan.   Yet roofing the large area of the Great Mosque additions evokes none of the experiment in solving the unique problems posed that one would expect.

In contrast, the main hall of the mosque of Fakhr ad Din is a building clearly designed by an architect.   By the style of the squared masonry used in its walling, the conical dome shape, and other minor architectural features, this mosque will be shown to date, almost certainly, from the thirteenth century.   An inscription of that date is incorporated in the later mihrab.   The mosque suffers from the limitations of the possible rafter spans common to all coastal architecture.   Yet the nine roof bays necessitated by these restrictions are supported by only two columns, through adopting a novel system of main roof beams.   A single visually unified space results—further emphasized by using a single central dome.   The secondary beams of the corner bays are placed diagonally, and the axes of the rafters alternate from bay to bay, purely for aesthetic "delight".   The entire plan is modulated to form a single unity—through the monumental doorways leading from an open court, one enters the low roofed, arched portico, with the main entrance axis emphasized by a unique, octagonal, conical, tent-shaped dome, whose decoration and form are individual, and quite different from the central dome of the main hall.   Here a designer's individual taste was allowed to express itself.   The roof of the main hall is considerably higher than that of the portico—sensibly so, for it is the largest and most important space.   Two completely symmetrical side rooms occur, one on either side.   Each part of the design is subordinate to the whole and consciously related to it—yet in technique or detailing it is no different or more advanced than the Kilwa Great Mosque

A brief study of Husuni Kubwa (Figs. 68 and 69), the largest and most complex building of the coast, further illustrates the deficiencies of the master builder as opposed to the architect.   Husuni, a late thirteenth century building, is only slightly later in date than the mosque of Fakhr ad Din.   The numerous complex vault and dome forms, the elaborate geometry of the octagonal pool, the advantage taken of the fine site, the symmetry and the use of the axial vista in the Palace Court, all would seem to point to the presence of an architect.   It is clear that, at Husuni Kubwa, an overriding concern with strict axial planning dominated the layout of every element of the complex.   Yet, the main axis of the most important part of the building, running from north to south from the north end of the site through the Palace court and the domestic quarters of the owner, is interrupted and marred by the transposition of the northern domestic building one metre to the east of the axis.   This is forced on the layout by the shape of the head-land on which the buildings lie, but could have been very easily and simply avoided if foresight had been used in laying out the plan before building commenced.   Similar dimensional irregularities abound—the four sides of the great South Court (each identical in layout and function) were intended to form a perfect square, yet they differ in dimensions by 8 m. in 50 m.   These, and other less important irregularities are entirely due to the fact that major or minor elements have been added together as work progressed, but with no detailed overall concept of the whole present before the building started.   The missed opportunities of controlled visual excitement and an overall articulation of the space are only partly compensated by the one or two cases where these opportunities have been exploited.   Husuni Kubwa had an enlightened patron, sensitive to the potentialities of the site and with a conscious aesthetic sense.   It also had highly competent builders, but it did not have an architect capable of welding the disparate elements into a unified whole, greater than its parts.   Nevertheless, Husuni Kubwa and the mosque of Fakhr ad Din—the earliest remaining major buildings of the coast—come nearer to having an articulated plan than any subsequent buildings.

The architecture of the coast has as its basis a rigid rectangular geometry, yet small dimensional irregularities are characteristic of every building on the coast.   Where dimensions are, by necessity, governed by a structural rule of thumb, as in the vaulted buildings of Kilwa, this rule is followed, but where there is no such limitation (as even in the overall bay dimensions of these vaulted bays) discrepancies in measurement of up to 10 per cent are normal.   Because of the impossibility of taking all dimensions in incomplete and ruinous buildings and allowing for movements of walls and columns, a rectangularity has been assumed in most plans illustrated here which did not in fact exist.   This does not, however, affect the final analysis.   Once it is realized that irregularity exists, it is of no consequence in the conclusions drawn from analysis.

Methods of Analysis

It is only by an exhaustive comparison of the most minor elements, by isolating each feature of decoration, plan and construction and then tracing the combinations and composition of each separate item as they are joined to form larger and broader design entities, that a sequence of development is traceable.   Each combination inevitably becomes more and more individual and so proves more and more difficult to relate to a spatial or temporal grouping.   Throughout such an analysis the greatest weight should be placed on similarities of minor details—these are the elements least governed by exigencies and problems specific only to the building in question.   They are the elements most governed by tradition and sufficiently minor to survive the attention of innovators.   The greater the number of detailed correspondences, the more reliable the comparison, though it is believed that even two or three correspondences in rare minor details will make a comparison valid.   However, individual human idiosyncrasies will always occur and the resultant anomalies in the designs we study today will inevitably be difficult to explain.   Furthermore, regional variations must be recognized and separated from variations due to a development in time if the conclusions are to be valid.   An analysis such as this, and the resultant typological sequence, can only give a relative idea of date—especially as influence from outside East Africa is rare, and the place and date of origin can in no case be pinpointed with accuracy.   The fixed "datum points" of the typological framework are those buildings accurately dated by archaeological excavations and are the only means available to establish an absolute chronology.   To this framework the complete typological sequence must be related—in itself it is only a sliding scale or a relative chronology.

CHAPTER II

MATERIALS AND TECHNIQUES OF CONSTRUCTION

It is characteristic of Islamic architecture that in every region local building materials are exploited and architectural style adapted to them. As Islam expanded, it occupied countries with very varied resources available for building. Each had its influence on building methods and modified the architectural style.

Coral

In East Africa, one material completely dominated the buildings—coralline lime-stone, or simply, coral. There are two basic types of coral—a fine-grained "reef" coral, cut from the present offshore coral reefs, which is used particularly in all work requiring a finely dressed finish and which weathers to a grey colour; and a coarse-grained, vesicular, ochre-coloured "fossil" coral cut from the fossil reefs which form the basal rock of most of the coastal foreshore. The latter cannot be dressed to a smooth finish, although it may be cut with precision. Coral forms an ideal building material—its cellular, vesicular nature makes it light in weight, easily transported and handled, yet surprisingly strong. It is readily available everywhere and, when fresh, is easily cut and worked. It does not deteriorate with weathering but rather hardens and improves with exposure. When dressed, the fine-grained coral can be given an almost marble-like finish. There is no grain or cleavage plane, so it may be cut and carved without any likelihood of splitting—a particularly important factor in arch construction where large curved pieces can be used. Although normally used in small blocks, it was also possible to obtain large blocks, as the octagonal monolithic columns of "fossil" coral, 140 cms. tall and 40 cms. square, of the Kilwa Great Mosque illustrate. Pearce explains the advantages of reef coral as a building material thus:[1] "Coralline limestone has a marked propensity to harden with age and exposure to elements. When excavated from the quarry, the stone is soft, but after some years it becomes extremely hard. Continual wetting by spray or rain and drying under the tropical sun has a very marked effect on hardening and consolidating elevated coral or coral sand. The upper parts are dissolved, and as the water sinks into the porous corals and becomes super saturated with lime the latter is crystallized out, thus filling all cavities with crystalline limestone. Thus in the end the highly porous, heterogeneous limestone becomes a rock of exceeding hardness, crystalline and homogeneous." This process of hardening limestone by exposure is so well known in Zanzibar that it was the custom among the Arabs to spread the building of their houses over a period of years, in order to ensure that the foundations especially should remain exposed to rain and sun for at least one season.

Stone was not readily available. A hard, calcareous sandstone does occur on the coast and, where available, as at Kilwa and the neighbouring sites, is used for flag-stones, external steps or seats, in irregular slabs 5 cms. thick, laid to form a continuous edging in a position where a permanent, hard-wearing surface is needed. It may also, at such sites, be haphazardly incorporated in walls or roofs in small quantities. At sites such as Gedi, where sandstone is not available, steps and seats are quite satisfactorily made in the normal coral. A soft sandstone is also present on the coast

[1] Zanzibar, p. 348 in part quoting Crosland: Desert and Water Gardens of the Red Sea, 1913, p. 111.

but was not exploited. It has been used, and delicately carved in fluted shafts, on the tomb of Sayyid Said bin Sultan in Zanzibar, built in 1856, but there has weathered and flaked so badly and is so badly worn, even by the hands of pious passers-by, that the results in 100 years have been disastrous. Sensibly, it had previously been neglected as a building material.

Mortar and Plaster

Coral provides not only the basic building material, but from it lime for mortar can be obtained. Lime burning at Kilwa is described by a member of the expedition of d'Almeida in 1505:[1] "Lime is prepared here in this manner: large logs of wood are piled in a circle and inside them coral limestone is placed; then the wood is burnt. The process after that is the same as in Portugal." This process can be seen today along the length of the coast. Firewood is cut and placed in a circle about 5 m. in diameter and 1 m. high, stacked extremely regularly and sloping towards the centre of the circle. On this, cut "dead" coral is stacked until it reaches about 1·50 m. above the wood. The wood is then fired and allowed to burn until it is entirely consumed. This may take up to four weeks. After this period lime remains and is ready for use. Coral burning normally takes place on the foreshore where the coral is quarried but firewood may have to be brought considerable distances by boat to the site.

A chemical analysis of the plaster used in the early mosque at Kaole[2] has shown that it consisted of a mixture of 50% lime: 50% "burnt" gypsum (i.e. "Plaster of Paris"). This mixture was also used for the mortar, with the addition of sand in the normal proportions of 1 lime:2 sand. Gypsum plasters were probably used for the finest plasterwork elsewhere also. There is no known source of gypsum readily available on the coast, nor is there any evidence of early gypsum working in known deposits. However, a very thin, fine, smooth, pure white, plaster skim coat is characteristic of the finest finished work in the earlier buildings. It was a quick setting plaster, and indeed there is often evidence that this plaster had set before it had been completely smoothed —preserving irregularities and tool marks.

The concrete used for the flat roofs and the vaults of all buildings had broken coral chips or rubble for its coarse aggregate, plus sand and coral lime. A basically red earth mortar, though no doubt containing lime, was used at Gedi and elsewhere in Kenya. This survives just as well as the pure lime mortar which is used in conjunction with it, round openings and for the upper 50 cms. of walls supporting rafters. It was covered with a normal lime plaster.

Walls

Practically all walls are random rubble, of coral rag. The blocks are completely irregular, have no regard to coursing or bonding and are set in a thick mortar. Walls vary rationally in thickness from 30 to 56 cms. in proportion to their height and load bearing function, though the normal wall is between 44 and 48 cms. thick, until the late eighteenth century when the normal thickness increases to 52 cms.

There are rare examples of walls built of very roughly squared coral blocks, laid in regular courses about 22 cms. in height, often with a packing of spalls to form a regular top to each course or even a thin intermediate course. In the thirteenth century tower of the Jamia of Mogadishu, and in the doorway of the mosque of Fakhr ad Din (Plate VIII), the blocks are particularly well cut and squared and originally the courses were extremely regular, 22 cms. in height. Such coursed rubble walls form the original walls

1 G. S. P. Freeman-Grenville: East African Coast, p. 107.
2 Annual Report, Antiquities Division of Tanganyika, 1958, p. 46.

and the later inner wall lining of the earliest Great Mosque at Kilwa (Plate I), and the walls of the early mosque at Kisimani Mafia. They are found everywhere at Sanje ya Kati including the mosque. All are associated with archaeological levels containing sherds of Islamic sgraffiato ware as the only imported ware, dating from the thirteenth or early fourteenth century. These coursed rubble walls thus themselves become valuable evidence of a date of the thirteenth century or possibly even earlier. At Gedi, the masonry of the earliest walls has some slight indication of coursing, and the coral used is finer grained, smaller and better set than in the subsequent rebuildings. This technique survives at Gedi from the thirteenth century up to the early fifteenth century. Cut, coursed, rectangular blocks offer little advantage; in fact, squaring blocks in this way is a technique alien to coral. Coral is not laminated or bedded, nor has it a cleavage plane, nor, of course, does it split or exfoliate in layers as does granite, whose rectangular blocks are so characteristic of African Iron Age coursed stone walling. Squaring coral would seem, therefore, to have been abandoned early and is not found at Husuni Kubwa at the end of the thirteenth century. There, the massive, 84 cms. thick, walls of the store rooms of the South Court and elsewhere have well finished horizontal plastered building levels at regular vertical intervals some 90 cms. apart. These represent a halt in building, possibly to allow a weathering and hardening of the inner coral to take place. More probably, they are halts in building at significant structural points (e.g. threshold or cill levels) designed to coordinate the work over the whole site. Similar building levels occur at other sites. All mark subsequent additions, or are due to major halts in the building of various stages of the structure. Additions and alterations to the rubble walls are rarely bonded into the original structure. Throughout, there is little concern with bonding and corners are particularly weak, structural collapse normally starting with separation at the corners.

A notable feature, only seen exposed in the walls of the later Jamia of Ungwana and of the mosque at Kunduchi, but no doubt widely if not universally applied, is the use of timber reinforcement within the thickness of the walls. Circular undressed timber poles, 11 cms. in diameter, are set horizontally down all unbroken stretches of wall at a vertical interval of 65 cms. They have no connection with door or window openings and their only purpose can be as a reinforcement. In the vaulted rooms of Husuni Kubwa, 14 cms. diameter timbers run lengthwise down the centre of the walls at cornice level (Fig. 71D), their only function being reinforcement, while in one flat roofed section a massive 21 cms. diameter pole occurs at a level in which it was probably used as a relieving beam above an opening. In the small, fifteenth century Jangwani mosque at Kilwa squared timbers laid flat act as relieving members above the squinches. Squared timbers relieve the mihrab arches in the small mosque at Ungwana and at Kisikimto. Similar timber reinforcement occurs in Byzantine buildings as a precaution against earthquake, and subsequently in Persia, and Pope notes[1]: "In many other structures in every part of the country since Seljuq times [i.e. twelfth century], beams are set horizontally in the walls, either crowning them or in intermediate courses or spanning openings. This wood is nearly always cypress and its renowned toughness and durability have made it a useful adjunct of brick building in an earthquake country for it contributes in measurable degree added coherence and resilience." East Africa is not an earthquake country, so this technique may well be a useful indication of the origin of the buildings. In the very poor stone buildings of the Swahili on the coast today, a thin upright lattice framework of timber is erected before the wall is built on either side of it—this is much closer to, and probably derived from, the wattle frame of all African mud and wattle huts rather than the early buildings.

[1] Survey of Persian Art, Vol. VI, p. 903.

Foundations

The treatment of foundations varies widely and is often perfunctory. Walls are frequently carried down only 20 cms. or so below ground level and the footing consists of one "course" of coral a few centimetres wider than the wall it supports. This may happen even where the subsoil is only beach sand—a frequent occurrence as sites are so often near the sea or on sandspits. Even where there is firm coral bedrock less than 1 m. below ground level, as in the Palace of Songo Mnara, the walls are not carried down to this, but rest on the soil or even sand that covers it. At Gedi, the walls of the Jamia are carried down to coral bedrock 1 m. below the surface, but this is exceptional. Where earlier buildings underlie the existing structures, their walls, of course, are used as foundations but the lack of concern for stable foundations is further illustrated in the south wall of the Jamia of Gedi which in part rests on an earlier south wall, but in part oversails this to rest on nothing more than an earlier plaster floor. At least one column in the later Jamia of Ungwana rests similarly on the plaster floor alone. In the Great Mosque of Kilwa, the columns supporting the vaults have an irregular, circular concrete foundation extending 30 cms. from them and resting on an earlier floor 30 cms. below the present floor. They are however connected by foundation walls between the two floors. Such connecting foundation walls below floor level also join the only piers found at Husuni Kubwa. In two of the fifteenth century houses excavated at Songo Mnara it was interesting to see that the footings were not built in foundation trenches—but that, internally at least, they lie on an original ground surface. A layer of mortar and masons' chips, found only next to the walls, and ash hearths mark the ground level existing as the walls were erected. When they reached their full height, and were ready for plastering, this level was raised with some 15 cms. of packed red earth and the walls then plastered—an irregular floor of masons' chips, plaster, thick pockets of unused plaster and pure sand mark this temporary working surface. Finally a packing 15 cms. thick of fine red earth, topped normally by a hardcore of coral rubble and chips, was added and the final plaster floor laid on this. In the early mosque at Kaole the wall footings rest directly on an early occupation level covering pure beach sand 120 cms. below the floor, the lower 60 cms. of these walls being thickened from 46 cms. to 76 cms. The material below the floor consisted entirely of artificial fill of impure beach sand, interrupted by rubble and lenses of builders' sand. This same considerable depth of sand fill, interrupted by lenses of plaster or rubble dropped during building, is also found in the later mosque at Kaole (Plate III)—both within and outside the mosque walls, which here also extend 120 cms. below floor level to rest on pure beach sand. The 26 cms. diameter timber columns of this mosque (a feature found elsewhere only in the early Great Mosque of Kilwa[1]) extended 95 cms. below the floor to rest on an irregular circular masonry base 60 cms. in diameter, built on the basal sand. A rammed sand packing held them firmly within the fill while a small octagonal collar of fitted and dressed coral blocks provided a skirting at floor level (a feature not found at Kilwa). In the earlier Kaole mosque a massive circular base 120 cms. deep and 130 cms. in diameter provided the foundations for what were masonry columns, now destroyed. The large depth of artificial fill occurs in an early (probably thirteenth century) mosque at Kisimani Mafia where the excavator notes "The building is remarkable for the fact that it is built on a sort of plinth...the earliest floor being about 1·30 m. above what must have been the ground level when the mosque was in use."[2] (There is in fact no true plinth and this refers rather to an external seat or to the

---

[1] The mosques at Kisimani Mafia (Figs. 13, 49) and Sanje ya Kati prove, on excavation, also to have had timber columns. Infm. H. N. Chittick, October 1964.
[2] H. N. Chittick: Occ. Paper, Antiquities Division of Tanganyika 1961, p. 10.

internal thickening of the foundations which occurs in an identical way to that used at Kaole.)

The absence of foundation trenches and their replacement by considerable depths of artificial fill below floor level, inserted in stages as building progressed, seems a strange and wasteful building technique necessitating considerable labour in excavation and earth moving.   The widening of foundation walls to give external plinths 15 cms. wide at floor level is frequent, especially in the rear projections of mihrabs, if not round the entire mosque as at Mnarani, Kenya (Fig. 28), and indicates that, in the lower levels, walls were deliberately thickened, where the floor level of the mosque was appreciably above normal ground level.   The lack of care taken over foundations no doubt led to frequent complications.   This accounts for the many cases in which buttress walls with sloping weathered tops have been added externally to support the lower levels of high walls (Manda, Mtwapa, Mtitimira, Kilwa South Building, Kua, Kisimani, Kaole).

Scaffolding

As the walls rose above a comfortable working height, scaffolding was erected.   In an earlier floor, 30 cms. below the present floor, of the vaulted extension of the Great Mosque at Kilwa, the 15 cms. diameter holes made for the undressed timber scaffold poles used in erecting the extension can be seen.   They are in pairs, 40 cms. apart—the width of the platform—and spaced at intervals of roughly 1 m.   Similar post holes have been found in excavations throughout this area of the mosque.

Many mosques have irregular rectangular holes (some 12–15 cms. square) partly or entirely through their walls (Figs. 20, 26).   These are not dressed, plastered or finished in any way.   They vary between 1·80 and 2·25 m. above floor level.   At Ras Mkumbuu (Fig. 4) a series of such holes 1·60 cms. apart occur at approximately ceiling level— 3·20 m. above floor level—their irregular height and spacing rule out the possibility that they held rafters.   At Shengejuu, there is a further series of round holes below such rectangular holes, and only 100–180 cms. above the floor, which obviously held undressed scaffold poles while the wall was built round them.   These unsightly and irregular niches or "portholes" cannot be due to structural collapse.   One published explanation is that they were for worshippers to spit through so that the mosque was not desecrated by spitting inside—an ingenious solution which, however, does not meet the majority of cases.   It was only when similar holes, with fragments of timber built into, and still protruding from, them were observed in a nineteenth century house in Zanzibar, and there known to be scaffolding supports, that this interpretation was confirmed and adopted.   It shows an odd lack of concern for appearances, for the holes or niches are extremely unsightly, even if of practical value in subsequent repaintings or re-plasterings.   Confirmation of this interpretation occurs in fourteenth century Persia on which Wilber comments[1] "To our modern eyes the presence of gaping scaffold holes on many of the structures seems unaesthetic, but apparently the builders and patrons of the monuments were not at all disturbed by them.   The Imamzada Jafar at Isfahan displays exterior walls...laid up with meticulous care which are marred by a single row of holes encircling the structure."   Further examples are quoted, and here too the holes are normally 15 cms. square.   In the great ranges of store rooms at Husuni Kubwa similar irregular, unfinished holes 20–30 cms. square occur immediately above a building level about 150 cms. above floor level.   Normally there are two to each wall, in line with those of the opposite wall.   They could have been simply for ventilation, but their spacing suggests that they were for horizontal beams acting as

[1] Architecture of Islamic Iran, p. 55.

shelving supports to take the substantial weight of whatever goods were stored in the rooms.

Floors

All floors are of plaster, normally laid on a hardcore of crushed coral rubble, but frequently on packed red earth alone—as in parts of Songo Mnara, Husuni Kubwa and the early Jamia of Gedi. This red earth, material of the early pisé buildings of Kilwa, and highly regarded by Africans for building in pisé today, is a pure and stable material with no organic impurities. It is the subsoil of the leached, red, lateritic soils so common in tropical Africa. A very thin (2 or 3 cms.) layer of this red earth, possibly laid as a coating of mud to prevent absorption and too rapid drying of the plaster, was frequently laid over earlier floors when new plaster floors were added (e.g. Kilwa Great Mosque). In the later mosque of Kaole the plaster floor was laid directly on the black sandy fill with no packing or other preparation (Plate III). A reason for the original internal ground level being so far below floor level (as seen above in the houses of Songo Mnara) is provided by the necessity of constructing the soakaways that occur centrally in all the larger and more important rooms of domestic buildings. These are circular pits from 80–100 cms. deep, and of a similar diameter at the bottom; their sides are of rough coral blocks laid without mortar, and roughly corbelled inwards towards the top to take a cap of sandstone or, less frequently, a coral slab (the latter occurs at Gedi) with a drainage hole 4 cms. in diameter bored in it. These soakaways provided an escape for the water used in washing down the floors of the main rooms, which could then percolate away through their bottom and sides. Such soakaways are cut into the natural decomposed sandstone subsoil in the domestic rooms of Husuni Kubwa, and are again revetted in coral blocks. Similar soakaways also occur in the unroofed entrance court of the Palace at Gedi. They are never found in mosques—an indication perhaps that the mosque floors were covered or carpeted, unlike the reception rooms in domestic buildings.

Coral working

Dressed coral is used to form the salient angles of all corners—piers, pilasters, door and window jambs and architrave projections. The mouldings of the mihrab, its recessed "orders" in jambs and arches, all capitals and frequently even the external corners of the mosque and rear mihrab projection are similarly made. All decorative mouldings are also of dressed coral as are the projecting rainspouts. At Kimbiji (Plate XII) it appears that not only was the mihrab apse constructed of close fitting rectangular dressed coral blocks curved to the shape of the apse, but the external mihrab projection was cased in dressed coral slabs. This is, however, a unique case. The use of dressed coral declines until, by the eighteenth century, it is rare and incised and moulded plasterwork replaces it. Similarly, the precision of the carving declines and, as the simpler early forms give way to an increasing complexity and elaboration of motifs, so the care taken in the carving of each element decreases (Plate VI). This steady deterioration in both the craftsmanship and use of fine coral is a good general guide to the dating of any particular building—though the technique continued to be used until the nineteenth century. The last certain example of a mosque incorporating dressed and fitted coral is probably the very late eighteenth century mosque of Kilindini, Mombasa (Fig. 59). Here it is used in conjunction with plaster mouldings, curved in section.

Mouldings with curved profiles are frequent in nineteenth century plasterwork but difficult to achieve in coral and only found in this material in the carved cable pattern coral mouldings. Fine grained "reef" coral was used for all dressed blocks. Only at Gedi, and in parts of Ungwana, was the coarser "fossil" coral used—understandably in the former case, for Gedi is four miles from the sea and the sources of "reef" coral while "fossil" coral could be cut on the spot. At Ungwana Jamia (Fig. 21) "fossil" coral is used only in the rebuildings of the early sixteenth century—and here, though the piers, pilasters and doors and even the shafts and architrave of the mihrab itself are of "fossil" coral, still the arch orders of the mihrab are made of fine-grained coral—probably blocks re-used from an earlier mihrab that existed in this mosque.

Coarser dressed coral blocks, used in doors, architraves and the corners of piers and columns, are only dressed and smoothed on their two right angled faces, and retain the basic irregular shape of the coral block. There is no attempt at standardization or further shaping—nor at bonding with transverse bonding blocks or "throughs"—though in arched doorways, where the arch profile is not broken at springing level, the impost block is always a single block running from face to face of the wall. It is rare to find further "throughs": they occur in a Husuni Kubwa door, and in columns at Mtwapa. Dressed coral is used only to obtain precision at angles and had no further structural significance. In unfinished work at Husuni Kubwa (Plate IV) it can be seen that a thin bladed metal chisel (c. 2 cms. wide) was used to shape the block to virtually the final form. It was then polished until an almost marble like smoothness was achieved.

The finer and more elaborate work of jamb shafts, arches and niches of mihrabs or monumental doorways is built up entirely with dressed coral blocks (Plate V). The face of each order is normally 8–10 cms. wide and consists of a single block. Mouldings of smaller dimensions than this (such as the very common arris rebates) are cut from the parent moulding and not formed of separate blocks. In a series of recessed orders, each block sits in a rebate cut in the block behind it (Fig. 2A). Only the visible faces, the fitted ends and the rebate are dressed—the remainder, built into the wall, is a completely shapeless block. The precision of the dressing and fitting at the joints of each block is such that no mortar is required or used.

The most notable feature of the technique is, however, the complete lack of standardization. Each block is cut for its own individual position and would fit nowhere else. The advantage of this technique is that there is no waste of raw material—each block is carved for a single position and need not be reduced to a standard size. The precision of the joints is much finer than could be achieved with the assemblage of standard units—but it also means that each mihrab or doorway can only be the work of a single, or at the most, two men. It is reasonable to assume that this skilled stoneworker was very probably not only the carver but also the designer of the work, if not of the whole building. It is natural that such a master craftsman working in a fixed tradition would work to his own design, rather than receive instructions. This supports the observations made earlier on the place of architects in the coastal buildings.

The technique is well illustrated in the series of rectangular recesses that line the lower part of the apse of a mihrab at Kua (Fig. 47). The size of each recess is the same, but the blocks that comprise them are in no way standard. The jambs of the recesses are normally single blocks, but the blocks, with the recess heads carved from them, may comprise either a head and two half jamb tops or one entire jamb top and a head, with either vertical or angled junctions between them—from the variations, it is obvious that each block was carved for one position alone. The craftsman, working alone, carved each block and then fitted it into position before proceeding to the carving of the next block. Speed of construction was sacrificed to the quality of workmanship obtainable from a single skilled carver. The method is confirmed at the small mosque at Ungwana (Fig. 29), where one entire half of the mihrab arch is a single carved block of coral—a curved block 80 × 12 × 12 cms.—while at nearby Shaka, one can see the guide lines on the inner arch marking the position of the outer one. The spandrels of the monumental Palace doors at Songo Mnara (Plate V) are, uniquely, entirely of dressed coral—each piece an irregular smooth-faced polygon cut exactly to fit its neighbour to form finally an interlocking marquetry. In fact, with this technique, it is more correct to visualize each mihrab or doorway as a single sculptured entity rather than as an assemblage of units or portion of a building.

Plaster

All stonework was covered by plaster. Even the precise mouldings and detailed carving of the dressed coral, including the virtuoso performance of the Songo Mnara spandrels—all were covered by a skim coat of pure plaster, some 2 mm. thick. It is difficult to realize, in their present weathered state, that the entire external and internal surface of every building was plastered, especially as the plaster has flaked particularly from the smooth surface of dressed coral, so that only vestiges remain. Only the most delicate ornament—such as cable pattern or herringbone mouldings—were left un-plastered. There are various forms of plasterwork often used in the same building—varying in quality in a rational way. At Husuni Kubwa, a thick lime plaster (Plate II) was applied liberally to the walls. To increase its strength, small coral pebbles or chips (c. 3 cms. in size) were set in it by hand, or alternatively, handfuls of still smaller chips were inset—each handful represented by a cluster of such chips. (This technique continued, for it is found again in the nineteenth century Palace of Mwenyi Mkuu at Dunga, Zanzibar). In rooms of lesser importance, such as servants' rooms, this thick plaster is not smoothed so the trowel strokes remain to give an irregular surface (Plate II). In the important reception rooms, however, a thin skim-coat of fine, smooth plaster was used as a final finish, often renewed. In the Pavilion of Husuni Kubwa there are several such skim-coats, and in the earlier mosque at Kaole the plaster has been renewed up to five times. Such skim-coats are the normal internal wall finish in all earlier buildings. In a fifteenth century house near the Small Domed Mosque at Kilwa, the reception rooms have such a fine finish, while the plaster of the latrine leading from them retains the rough preliminary finish and the marks of the application strokes—where appearance was unimportant, an economical lack of care was enjoyed.

The normal external wall plaster in most early buildings is a plaster up to 5 cms. thick—its final finish is usually not completely regular, no doubt due to its quick setting. This plaster decays in a characteristic circular whorl pattern, which the excavator of Gedi has assumed to be due to the circular action of the plasterer's strokes. This is unlikely, for the centre of such whorls can occur precisely on the corner of a building—an impossible centre for a plastering stroke. It is, in fact, probably due to organic impurities in the plaster initiating decay which allows moisture penetration and from which the decay spreads. Frequently, graffiti are incised in this plaster—rudimentary ships are frequent on both the external walls of mosques and in the entrance halls of houses—though nowhere else. Such engravings appear at Husuni Kubwa, Songo Mnara, Kilwa, Gedi and many other sites. To our eyes they mar the appearance of these rooms—their purpose was certainly not decorative, but this apparently did not disturb the owners. In later, post-Portuguese buildings, coarser, thicker coats of lime plaster with sand added often replace the fine pure skimcoat (Plate XII)—though in eighteenth and nineteenth century tombs moulded plasterwork with diaper

Plate I.   Coursed rubble wall of coral blocks roughly squared, characteristic of the earliest buildings of the Coast.   North wall of the original Great Mosque of Kilwa, thirteenth century or earlier.

Plate II.   Coarse wall plaster in a servants' room of the Palace of Husuni Kubwa. The trowel strokes, and the coral chips used as a coarse aggregate, remain visible.

Plate IV. Unfinished block of dressed coral from the Palace of Husuni Kubwa showing chisel marks, and the unfinished groove and nick of an arch apex.

Plate III. Evidence of timber columns, extending below the floor of the later mosque at Kaole. The octagonal dressed coral floor collar, the floor fill, the rammed sand packing round the timber column and the circular concrete column base are all visible.

patterning and of fine quality is re-introduced. Plaster mouldings at this time replace the earlier mouldings of carved coral. The finish of the plasterwork frequently degenerates as thicker plasters are used in buildings and thus sharp corners give way to rounded ones.

Rafters

The roofing of all buildings is naturally dependent on the maximum available rafter span. On the coast this fell between the limits of 1·80 and 2·80 m. There can be little doubt that mangrove poles, the only universally available structural timber of the coast, were used, and the rafter spans fall within the limiting dimensions of these poles. Today there is still an extensive export traffic in such poles to Arabia and the Persian Gulf for use in building. The side rooms of the mosque at Mnarani (Kenya), alone are exceptionally wide at 3·00 m. At Husuni Kubwa the width of domestic rooms averages 2·80 m., but the average width of rooms elsewhere is 2·40 m. This limitation governs the entire architecture of the coast and is probably the most important single factor in determining the architectural style. The rafters used in all important rooms, until the eighteenth century, were squared and dressed timbers varying between 17 × 3 cms. and 12 × 6 cms. in size (normally 15 × 5 cms.), spaced at approximately 23 cms. centres. The only certain example, until recently, of large timbers being used as columns and major beams was that of the reconstruction of the northern section of the Great Mosque of Kilwa (Fig. 15). Here nine circular timber columns, 36 cms. in diameter, supported three transverse timber main beams 47 × 34 cms. which in turn supported three secondary beams 30 × 22 cms. Above them were the normal rafters. Only the column holes within the plaster floor remain, but they clearly retain the marks of the timber, while, in the walls, the rectangular recesses which seated the beams remain. The building of this almost unique structure was sufficiently noteworthy to be described, somewhat inaccurately, in the legendary account of the reconstruction of the Great Mosque in the Kilwa Chronicle.[1] "When the mosque was being restored, they lacked wood to rebuild the pillars. For the original pillars were of cut stone, and there were now no masons who could reassemble them as they were previously. This had perplexed them and had prevented the restoration. But by Divine Providence a great tree was cast up on shore, of exactly the right length. The people recognized the hand of Divine Providence, for the tree was complete with its root and branches. They made pillars for the front part of the mosque from the root, and there were seven pillars in all. From the branches they made rafters and crossbeams for the front part and the two wings. At the back they built domes...."

There are several examples of main timber beams 15 × 40 cms. in size. These may, however, well have been composite beams and consisted of several members. At Takwa (Fig. 25) such a beam runs down the centre of the main hall to intersect cross beams of similar dimensions. At Shaka (Fig. 27) a side room has two such main beams to carry the rafters, while at Mbweni (Fig. 26) similar longitudinal main beams spanned between the columns. At Takwa, indeed, timber columns have been presumed to exist as, at the intersection of these main beams, there was no trace of a column, on the plaster floor. This is not sufficient evidence however, especially when it is seen that the timber columns of Kilwa were set into deep postholes in the floor and certainly did not just rest on it. Recent excavation of the later mosque at Kaole (Plate III) has shown that it also had timber columns, 26 cms. in diameter, set on a circular masonry base at a depth of 95 cms. below the floor, with an octagonal collar or skirting of dressed coral blocks, with mitred joints, surrounding it at floor level.

[1] G. S. P. Freeman-Grenville: East African Coast, p. 40.

3

Column spacing

The main structural timbering in almost all buildings remained the standard rafter. This means that any space of greater width than the rafter span must, in the absence of appreciably larger structural timber main beams, be columned and that the column spacing and bay dimensions will themselves fall within the limits of the rafter span in both directions and be governed by it. This occurs in the main hall of every mosque. There is a marked tendancy for the mosques to have a single central row of supports or, in the larger congregational mosques, three rows of supports. Such uneven rows of supports mean that the mihrab is obscured by the central row. To thus conceal the focal point of the mosque is a very unsatisfactory feature visually and to some extent structurally. It means that central longitudinal beams meet the end wall above the mihrab and their weight must therefore be carried eventually by the mihrab arch. Indeed, in domed buildings with this plan it is impossible for the central structural arch to intersect the mihrab and it will be seen how alternate vaulting methods, or complex structural substitutes, were evolved to escape this impasse. Yet there is a marked preference in every region and period for central supports, though a large minority of mosques do have two rows of supports, giving a central and two side aisles and an unobscured view of the mihrab.

Columns

Square or rectangular piers or octagonal columns provide the supports. These two types have an interesting distribution. The pier occurs in the fourteenth, fifteenth and sixteenth century mosques of Kenya and Pemba while in the south, in Tanganyika, after thirteenth century Husuni Kubwa, only columns are found. In the post-Portuguese periods however, the column appears in Kenya and the pier in Tanganyika. Post-Portuguese vaulted buildings are always supported on octagonal columns. An interesting method was evolved in erecting octagonal columns. At Tongoni, Bandarini and Ndumi alternate column faces are made of dressed coral panels— at Tongoni and Bandarini 20×40 cm. rectangles, at Ndumi of smaller and more irregular shapes but still close fitting. In the vaulted extension of the Kilwa Great Mosque the octagonal columns also have rectangular coral panels, averaging 34×30 cms. in size. These are also found on only four faces in any one course, but the faces chosen alternate from course to course, to give a chequerboard effect. Only the panel faces are dressed—the backs remain irregular. The reason for this construction is that by only facing alternate sides complex mitring or chamfering at the corners is avoided. Moreover, as the columns are of concrete rather than masonry, during the pouring of each "layer" of concrete the panels are self supporting and act as a permanent form-work or shuttering while the concrete is poured for each course. It was then allowed to set before the next similar course is added. Furthermore, the panels ensure sharp arrises and the correct size to each face of the column. With this technique both timber casing and complex joints are dispensed with. Freeman-Grenville in his account of the building of the Great Mosque at Kilwa has sought to prove that timber casing was used.[1] This would appear a denial of the basic purpose of the dressed panels and would make a simple and ingenious operation both complex and impractical—in fact, almost certainly, impossible for it is difficult to visualize the panels remaining in position when the shuttering was erected round them, especially as the panels of the Kilwa columns rest not on each other but on the concrete of the course below.

[1] *Mediaeval History of the Coast of Tanganyika*, p. 123.

Beams

Beams span between the columns to support the rafters. These may be either longitudinal or transverse or both may be combined. They are of various types. The earliest beam form probably consisted of three timbers only slightly larger and closer set than the rafters (averaging 20 × 8 cms. at 15 cms. centres) spanning between the columns in only one direction—transversely in the case of wide mosques such as the Jamia of Gedi (Fig. 24) and Ras Mkumbuu (Fig. 4) and longitudinally in long, narrow, single-columned mosques such as Tongoni (Fig. 5), the early Kaole mosque (Fig. 3) and Ndumi (Fig. 51). The rafters spanned at right angles to, and rested on, these triple timbers, supporting and immediately below them. More rarely, and possibly rather later, transverse and longitudinal beams divided the ceiling into bays in both directions. The rafters of such bays, therefore, could, and did, span in either direction or alternate from bay to bay to give a patterned ceiling. There is only slight evidence, however, that such beams and ceiling divisions were not employed from the start.

It was soon realized that, by casing the underside of the triple beams in planking 5 cms. thick, they would appear to be a single wide timber beam though the size of each member remained small. These were no doubt decorated and carved as a single entity. This "composite" timber beam remained in use until the nineteenth century. In the eighteenth century such composite beams were lowered and used to support a masonry superstructure—almost a masonry beam and, in fact, once hardened it no doubt acted almost as a concrete beam and served to distribute the point loads of the rafters now set in the top of this masonry. By so greatly increasing the depth of the beam the unity of the space in the mosque is considerably broken up and compartmented and, moreover, central, longitudinal beams can no longer be employed for they would now be so low as to interfere with the mihrab arch. Transverse beams therefore become normal and since, as has been seen, the main beam tends to span the wider axis of the mosque so, therefore, also do the mosques become wide in relation to their length—in fact almost square in plan.

Where there is a double row of columns lining up with the architrave framing the mihrab, longitudinal beams could still be used and they occur springing from the mihrab architrave at such sites as Kimbiji (Fig. 40) and the Bwana Tamu mosque at Pate (Fig. 32), and running the length of the mosque, which can therefore retain its normal proportions—much longer than wide. In such mosques, secondary beams of the older composite type span between columns, at right angles to the main masonry and timber beams, and so divide the ceiling into square bays, in which the rafters can again run in either direction to form a patterned ceiling. At Kimbiji, the rafters of the central aisle run transversely and those of the side aisles longitudinally, a reasonable patterning which adds an impression of width to the central aisle. But the pattern varies considerably from mosque to mosque. Late in the eighteenth century the masonry beam was replaced by arches. The transition is exemplified in the mosque of Shala Fatani, Faza (Fig. 34), where the front columns support masonry beams while the rear arcade is arched. These arches are very characteristic of the nineteenth century mosques and are always transverse (Figs. 52–56). The mosques, following the usual rule, thus tend to be as wide as they are long. The arches are supported on pilasters or engaged half columns at the side walls. Pilasters were used to support main beams in the large congregational mosques—such as Ras Mkumbuu and Gedi—from very early, but are never found in the smaller, pre-seventeenth century mosques—except, of course, in vaulted mosques where they are essential for the support of the structural cross arches. Secondary beams are never employed in conjunction with the transverse arch. Consequently, the rafters all span from north to south and the transverse bays are undifferentiated. The columns of late eighteenth century transverse arches are large, heavy octagons, their width exceeding their length, while the arch form may be stilted, stepped or lobed—often each arch differs from its neighbour. The arch spans afforded no increase in bay dimensions—if anything, the reverse occurred. The heavy, exuberant and asymetric arch forms, the compartmented space, and the poor workmanship, with increased thickness of structure and reduced spans, are all typical of the degenerate nineteenth century architecture. The unity of volume and economy of structure and crisp, emphatic workmanship of the early styles are all lost.

Ceilings

Ceilings consist of a closely fitting network of roughly rectangular coral blocks or "tiles" spanning across the rafters. Their undersides are roughly dressed. The technique used for making the octagonal concrete columns described above is repeated for these "tiles". Spanning between the rafters, they provide a permanent casing for the coral lime concrete of the flat roof, poured above them, some 30–50 cms. thick. The underside of the tiles received a thin skimcoat of plaster to form the ceiling finish while the roof itself was plastered externally to render it waterproof. This plaster often required frequent renewal to remain impervious. In part of the Palace at Songo Mnara some six or eight such renewals are visible on a section of roof within the Palace (which is, in fact, uniquely slightly double pitched, with a slope of about 1:9).

Internally, the ceiling was decorated by small, 15 cm. square, fine-dressed coral, angle brackets inserted between the rafters with a face sloping from wall to ceiling at 45°. The faces are plain and though they resemble, and can be called, "brackets", in fact they are purely decorative inserts between the rafters, forming the transition between wall and ceiling, and restricting and masking any movement of the timbers. At Husuni Kubwa alone they are larger (15 × 22 cms.) and considerably more elaborate (Fig. 72B) with a slightly concave face and a semicircular moulding below it. Below the rafters in all mosques and most domestic buildings a timber cornice, 15 × 5 cms., was built into the wall—this was almost certainly carved.

In the eighteenth century the decline in standards is reflected by the fact that brackets and timber cornices disappear and, though the cornice may be replaced by a rough moulded plaster frieze, frequently the rafters are inserted in the walls without any masking or decoration. By the nineteenth century, the rafters are, most frequently, no longer even dressed but remain as rough poles, closely set. The technique required in forming and dressing the flat coral tiles of the ceiling had been lost, and tiles are therefore absent. Only the rafters remained to provide a casing for the concrete of the roof.

Roofs

Roofs were surrounded by a low parapet wall, some 50 cms. high. Rain water was discharged clear of the building by extremely characteristic rainspouts of dressed coral. These are rectangular coral blocks, rectangular in section (about 15–25 cms. wide by 10–15 cms. deep and 45 cms. long) with a shallow rectangular channel about 7 cms. wide and 3 cms. deep cut in their top. They frequently have a semicircular head which was embedded in the fabric of the roof, and a flared lip. Such spouts are found in identical form from thirteenth century Husuni Kubwa into the seventeenth century.

The parapet walls may often have been surmounted by cresting such as the stepped pyramidal forms of Kilwa Great Mosque (Fig. 15). Though no traces of such decoration have been found elsewhere on the coast it is ubiquitous in Islamic buildings elsewhere and such buildings as the eighteenth century mosques of Merca in Somalia have identical cresting forms to Kilwa, at least at the corners of the parapets, and frequently all round.

Arches

The mihrabs, the majority of doors and windows and the structural arcades between the bays of vaulted buildings are all arched. The semicircular arch occurs in doorways at Husuni Kubwa and, indeed, appears to have been more popular there than the pointed arch. Subsequently, the arch used universally on the coast, until the eighteenth century, was the simple pointed or drop arch, struck from two centres, whose spacing apart varied from $\frac{1}{10}$ span, to give a very slightly pointed arch, to $\frac{5}{8}$ span apart. The most frequent separation of these centres is, however, just under $\frac{1}{4}$ span, approximately 1/4·25. Stilted drop arches are characteristic of the sixteenth century and later—but are only found in the mihrab. A trefoil arch, used as a purely decorative feature in mihrab design, probably dates from the late seventeenth century, with perhaps isolated earlier examples. Semicircular, elliptical, multifoil and four centred arches were introduced in the eighteenth century, formed in undressed masonry and plastered. The simple pointed arch died out with the art of fine-dressed coral and with the simple and refined early design forms. The horseshoe arch is entirely absent on the coast.

It is one of the most characteristic features of the coastal arches that they lack keystones. Until the eighteenth century two blocks of finely dressed coral form the apex of every arch and meet to form a close fitting vertical joint, laid without mortar. The great care taken with the fit of this vertical joint is apparent in every arch, whether it was subsequently intended to be visible or not. It was, however, frequently expressed in two characteristic ways. The first method was the formation of a small ogival, or keel-shaped, nick at the arch apex—achieved by giving the lower corner of the top of each apex block a very slight curve (Plate V). At Husuni Kubwa an unfinished block, still in a rough undressed stage (Plate IV) has a nick carved in its intrados with a groove rising from the nick across the face of the block. This must have been intended to be cut through to form two typical apex blocks. By so cutting a single block in two with a thin bladed saw—the only possible instrument—the close fit of the vertical joint, subsequently reassembled, could be ensured. It is hardly possible that this block was intended, uniquely, as a keystone. The arch with nicked apex continued in use throughout the coastal sites, to appear in the coarsely built four-centred and trefoil arches of the eighteenth century and later, when the structural function it expressed—the fine-dressed vertical joint—had largely fallen into disuse as technique declined.

The vertical joint was also expressed in a second way, in which the two blocks at the arch apex project from the spandrel to form a vertical panel, which continued to form a projecting archivolt to the arch. This is found less frequently than the nicked apex block but either of these features may occur at any time or in any region of the coast and are in no way diagnostic. They are simply a method of emphasizing visually the structural technique employed. Frequently neither is present—though the lack of keystones is universal.

Doorways

Doorways most frequently consist of arched openings (Fig. 84). The simple pointed arched head may be firstly, simply a continuation of the jambs with no emphasis or moulding at its springing (Fig. 84A); secondly, it may spring from an impost block, usually with three or four tiny rebated mouldings to its underside, which breaks the profile of the door by a projecting offset to the reveal alone, leaving a flush façade (Fig. 16); thirdly, by an impost block which projects forwards from the face of the arch as well as at the reveal (Fig. 84D). The form used appears to have little significance. For instance, all are present in some form in the core of the Palace of Songo Mnara.

In structural arches and small decorative recesses, the impost block frequently projects on the face alone and not on the reveal.

The square-headed door is much less frequent. The elaborate north doors of the Jamia at Ungwana are the most important example. Here the door head consists of three exposed timber rafters, separated by angle brackets (in fact a replica of ceiling construction—though here resting on a timber wallplate). But at the small mosque nearby, an ordinary composite timber beam was used as a door head. This was the normal method of spanning square-headed door openings elsewhere—though, until the eighteenth century, examples seem extremely rare. In the nineteenth century, the door heads, like the ceilings, have close-set undressed poles for their support and are universally square headed.

There is no indication in the masonry of the doorways of any building of the coast of any trace of metal fixing or fixing holes for door hinges or pivots. However, in many cases timber door frames were inserted in the doorways. As with all doors, these doors opened inwards, and like the rebate for a door leaf in a timber frame, their masonry jambs were themselves rebated, so that the timber frame could be seated and wedged behind the external masonry nib, and thus remain invisible externally and not detract from the dressed coral decoration of the external face. The presence of rebated jambs can probably be taken as an indication that doors were present. They are also a valuable indicator of room functions in a complex site such as Husuni Kubwa, for the rebate always occurs on the inner, or more private, side of the doorway—thus in long passages or hallways one can, by examining the rebates, get an indication of the normal circulation of the inhabitants, and from this, some indication of function. At Husuni Kubwa, the rebated masonry jambs of those doorways containing doors have an inverse splay (i.e. both salient angles are acute rather than obtuse) probably designed to enable the timber frames to be securely wedged behind the nib. Many of the jambs of arched doorways are not rebated. In the absence of any signs of fixing it is difficult to see how they could ever have contained timber doors or frames and it is considered that in such cases these were never present. At Husuni Kubwa such jambs also occur and there it seems clear that they only occur in positions where doors were not necessary.

Door timbers

Timber was used extensively for the thresholds of all doorways. Normally the threshold is equal to wall thickness and is raised 5 cms. above floor level, to take two timber members (each of about 12 × 8 cms.) built in along both its edges—or if only one timber occurs, on the outer edge. These form the wearing surface of the threshold step—if doors were present, they, together with the head, may very probably have taken vertical wooden pivots on which the doors swung—for this method seems more likely to have been used than metal hinges, except at Songo Mnara and Ungwana. In at least three early mosques (Tongoni, Mbweni and Gedi Jamia) massive timbers, 18–27 cms. thick, occurred at the base of the doorways firmly held at each side by two inverted L-shaped dressed coral blocks. Many thresholds at Husuni Kubwa have square coral tiles running between the doorway nibs alone, slightly raising this section of the floor from that of the timber door behind.

Timber cills occur at the inner and outer edges of most windows and also frame the outer edges of many niches. All are laid flat and held in position by being built into the walls on either side, flush with the wall surface. Many square-headed wall niches of smaller size, lacking timber cill or jambs, are supported at their head by a similar dressed timber lintol, laid flat and built into the wall on each side.

Horizontal timbers, some 12 × 5 cms. thick, are laid flat, flush with the wall surface, some 15 cms. above the apex of many arched doorways, and extending about 45 cms. on either side of the doorway. These appear to have been relieving beams performing a similar function to the timber reinforcing members described earlier. They are set above the arch to bear and spread the weight of the masonry above it, particularly during the initial setting and hardening. That they were not subsequently needed is evident from the fact that the deep grooves remaining today, now that the timbers have vanished, have only rarely collapsed. It is possible that in conjunction with the timber thresholds they afforded some means of door fixing—though this is very difficult to visualize when they occur in conjunction with openings that lack rebates. They do not project from the walls and their position is too far above the arch. Where pilasters occur, at such sites as Ras Mkumbuu (Fig. 84A) and Gedi Jamia, these timbers extend, above the door arches, from pilaster to pilaster. In the related arcade patterns of Kisimani Mafia and Tumbatu, the doorways are set in rectangular recesses and the lintols of these are supported by similar timbers, which are not therefore flush with the wall below but project forward of it and so have their underside exposed. These may therefore, have acted as door heads with doors pivoting in this head and in the threshold (Fig. 84B).

At the Palace of Songo Mnara, a recessed rectangular panel occurs in the masonry of the inner face of the doorway (Fig. 84D)—the lintol of this is the 12×8 cms. timber door head, laid flat and flush with, and built into, the wall on each side of the recess. Intersecting this with a lap joint are two timber uprights of the same size, forming the door jambs, separated by a gap from the masonry jambs. Their heads project beyond the door head to obtain a firm seating in the masonry and are likewise built into the wall flush. Their inner sides are flush with the arch reveals of the outer masonry doorway nib, and they project back from the nib the width of the doorway recess. Doors were probably hinged to these uprights. This neat piece of design leaves room for the hinged edges of the two leaves of the rectangular timber doors to swing back into the recess between the timber and the masonry door jambs. By setting the doors in a rectangular recess behind the arched masonry doorways it is possible to have a simple timber door structure, yet an elaborate decorated and arched masonry doorway. A similar principle is applied to the doors behind the elaborate doorways of the Jamia of Ungwana, which therefore probably also contained hinged doors.

CHAPTER III

VAULTED STRUCTURES

Two factors already described would seem to predispose the buildings of the coast towards the adoption of vaulted construction; firstly, the severe restriction placed on all planning by the limited roofing spans possible with available timber and secondly, the fine quality concrete easily available. It has already been seen how such concrete was exploited in columns and flat roofs. The technical skills required for vaulting were certainly familiar to the builders, who applied them in a consistent, standardized fashion in the buildings of the fifteenth century Kilwa group. They experienced no technical difficulty in vaulting and a set of fixed principles had been fully evolved. These indicate that the initial experimentation in vaulting was over and, since no buildings showing this are found in East Africa, it had presumably taken place outside the coast.

In fact, however, vaults and domes are found only at a limited number of sites. Thirteenth century Husuni Kubwa has an extraordinary variety of vault forms, never repeated but followed in the same area by the flowering of a homogeneous group of simpler domed and vaulted buildings in the fifteenth century—such as the Great Mosque of Kilwa and three smaller mosques nearby. Songo Mnara, built at the same time, had vaults to an arcade in the Palace, to a room in a nearby house and in two mosques (one there and one at the nearby site of Sanje Majoma). In Kenya, only the western room of the Jamia of Ungwana, built towards the end of the fifteenth century, and a small, possibly contemporary, mosque at Mwana, a few miles away, were certainly vaulted. These resemble Husuni more closely than the Kilwa group in their details. In the eighteenth century, isolated domed mosques appear in southern Kenya at Tiwi and Jumba la Mtwana and in the mosques of Chwaka on Pemba—though they show a lack of understanding of some of the basic principles of vault construction.

The dearth of vaulted buildings must be due to reasons other than lack of technical competence. These were probably firstly, the practical difficulty of obtaining timber suitable for planking and centring to support the vaults during construction; and secondly, the fact that the domed structures do not, in fact, represent any real advance, either practically or visually, on the normal flat roof. This is due solely to a lack of design, as opposed to technical, skills. They observe the limitations in bay dimensions derived from the rafter span, and vaulted bays do not exceed this dimensional restriction, even though there appears to be no technical reason why they should not. Only the unique dome at the south east corner of Kilwa Great Mosque departs from this, to reach a diameter of 4 m. This is no doubt the famous early fourteenth century dome of Sultan al Hasan ibn Sulaiman recorded in the Kilwa Chronicle,[1] which survived the collapse of the rest of the mosque during his reign, to become the prototype of the fifteenth century vaulted reconstruction. Visually, all vaults have a minimal effect. The small bay proportions, the effect of short columns and low structural cross arches with small vaults set high above them, the lack of real variety in either form or size, in fact in anything other than in purely surface decoration—all these factors

[1] G. S. P. Freeman-Grenville: East African Coast, pp. 39-40.

combine to dissipate the final visual and spatial effect. The repetition of a series of identical units with no significant visual differentiation or articulation leads to a monotony over a large area no different from that of the normal flat roofed columned hall. Structural expertize fails to be widely adopted if it fails to give practical or easily appreciable aesthetic benefits—it is of little use for its own sake.

Vault types

Barrel vaults

There are three main vault types used on the coast. The semicircular barrel vault is already fully evolved and widely used at Husuni Kubwa. It is ideal for roofing the normal rectangular room for there are no difficulties in adapting room shape to roof form, its only limitation being the width of the span possible. Intersecting barrel vaults, or groined vaults are unknown on the coast, though in one room at Husuni Kubwa a groined vault intersection is almost realized (Fig. 71C).

Domes

The construction of the second vault type, the true hemispherical dome, entails two structural necessities. The bay proportions must be square or nearly so, and the square of the ground plan must then be converted to a circular base on which the dome can rest. This transition can be effected by using either pendentives or squinches. The use of a true spherical triangle pendentive is the most efficient method—this is a spherical triangle of the same diameter as the dome which extends below it in each corner of the square. Four such pendentives at the corners combine to give immediately a regular circular seat on which the dome proper may rest. This pendentive type is a complex piece of structural geometry and does not appear on the coast, though the curvature and concave face of the pendentives of one room at Husuni Kubwa show that it was closely approached (Fig. 71F). The normal pendentive on the coast (strictly speaking a flat faced, false pendentive or "Turkish triangle", Fig. 71E) is a plane surfaced triangle inclined inwards from each corner, with its point low in the corner, and rising to span across the corner at 45°, and so convert the square to an octagon. The squinch is a small arch spanning across the corner of the square and again converting it to an octagon. The groined squinch is the squinch type used on the coast (Figs. 14, 15, 16) for beneath the intrados of the squinch arch spanning the corners there is a small sector of vault. The pendentive is used at Husuni Kubwa in several rooms, and subsequently at Ungwana and Mwana in Kenya, while the squinch is the characteristic form of the fifteenth century buildings of the Kilwa group. This difference between pendentive and squinch is basic, and diagnostically significant, especially when combined with the fact that the three sites using pendentives are the only vaulted buildings using the square pier. (At Husuni Kubwa, the pier is present only in another area of the building and not as a vault support, however.)

The octagon formed by squinches or pendentives must then be converted to a circle. On the coast this is simply achieved by the use of a dressed coral cornice above the octagon, whose projection is adjusted to form a circle. In the Kilwa group (Figs. 14, 16) this mode of transition becomes stereotyped—the basic cornice, a dressed coral block some 12 cms. wide, with a square rebate cut from its lower arris, surrounds the octagon of a dome and is surmounted by a second identical cornice, but now curved in plan, whose upper moulding is flush with and forms the base of the dome. This typical cornice moulding is employed also as the base of all barrel vaults (Figs. 14, 16)—though here its function is purely decorative and only one cornice is used, as there is no longer any necessity for the second.

Pendentives (though used in the side aisles) are not present in the two central bays of the mosque at Mwana (Fig. 11, Plate VII). They are replaced by blocks of fine-dressed coral, triangular in plan and 11 cms. thick, spanning horizontally across the corners and converting the square to an octagon. This is effective enough over the short span—the base of the triangle (i.e. its maximum span) measures only 50 cms. Two similar triangular slabs convert the irregular triangle of the apse of a mihrab at Ungwana to a shape closer to the circle required to support the little dome over this apse (Fig. 29). Slabs of dressed coral are thus capable of and used to support weight over very limited spans.

In the three eighteenth century vaulted mosques (Fig. 37) the pendentive and squinch no longer occur, instead an attempt is made at Chakwa and Jumba la Mtwana to modify the bay corners by an increased projection of the cornice—curved at the corners at Jumba la Mtwana and a straight splay at Chwaka. These are however, structurally insignificant and little more than decoration; this decorative element is elaborated and confused at Chwaka where a tiny bracket spans the corner and from it rises a triangular moulding (one half of which is parallel to each bay face for it does not span across the corners) to the cornice base. The idea of some decorative emphasis at the corners of the bays thus persists after the structural element previously present is no longer used. At Tiwi the irregular conical domes have a square base and rest directly on a string course with no attempt to modify the bay shape.

Cloister vaults

The third vaulting method is the irregular cloister vault (rather than circular domical vault) which can roof a rectangular bay. At Husuni Kubwa only fragments of vault above cornice level survive, attached to fallen blocks of masonry—but it is clear from these that rectangular rooms were converted by the normal pendentive to elongate octagons, and these were not further converted to a curved plan shape (Fig. 71D, E). Nor were regular curved profiles used for the vaults, but rather, the irregular straight sided vaults retained the hard angles of the octagon supporting them, to form poly-hedral tent-shaped vaults. In the thirteenth century mosque of Fakhr ad Din, Moga-dishu (Fig. 65), a vault of this type still stands over the portico—an eight sided tent-shaped cone.

The Great Mosque at Kilwa has elongate domical vaults (Fig. 15), though here the rectangular bays with squinches at their corners, surmounted by the typical double cornice, support domes with semicircular ends (though their longer sides are, of course, straight at the centre).

Profiles

The domes that survive have a variety of profiles, none of them particularly economic in material, or structurally or geometrically ideal, but all functioning satisfactorily over their small spans. The slightly stilted hemisphere is perhaps the most common form found in the Kilwa group (Figs. 14, 16), but the domes of the Great Mosque of Kilwa (Fig. 15) have a stilted four-centred curve in section with a pointed apex. The regular conical dome of Husuni Kubwa is echoed in a rougher form at Mwana and Tiwi in Kenya whose domes are closer in section to the cone than to the hemisphere. Barrel vaults are far more competently handled and are always regular semicircles in section.

Supports

The weight and thrust of the vaults is carried either by load bearing walls round the perimeter of each vault, as at Husuni Kubwa, where multiple vaults are unknown, or on a system of structural arches, supporting each vault round its perimeter and bracing between and transferring the thrust out from each bay to the perimeter walls. This system of structural arches springing from columns necessitates the use of either engaged columns at the outer side walls, or brackets corbelled from these walls to support the outer arches. It also means that if a central row of columns occurs in a mosque, a popular plan form, a different system must be evolved for vaulting the northern bays in front of the mihrab, for a central structural arch in this bay would interfere with the mihrab, and could not be supported. The same applies if a central door occurs at the south end. The transverse barrel vault is the normal solution adopted, running transversely from side to side across the northern bays of the mosque—as at Sanje Majoma (Fig. 18), Chwaka (Fig. 38) and the Ungwana side room (Fig. 23) (though there it is a central door to be avoided, not a mihrab). The barrel vault has the added advantage that the bay width can be varied from that of the remaining bays as required —at Chwaka it is considerably narrower and at Ungwana wider. This means of course that the northern columns support only east, west and southern structural arches. The asymmetry that results is accepted at Chwaka but at Sanje Majoma a pilaster rises from each capital on the north face to match the structural arches. Lintols span between these pilasters, below the cornice, to form a projecting, rectangular frame to each arch of the northern arcade. This is, therefore, a decorative substitute to match the structural arches of the remaining bays. It continues in use as a purely decorative rectangular frame surrounding each arch in a mosque at Kilwa (Fig. 18) entirely roofed by a series of transverse barrel vaults, and also on the outer face of the vaulted arcade of Songo Mnara Palace (Fig. 16) and is no doubt the source of the same frame that surrounds the arches of the transverse arcades spanning across the width of the flat roofed main mosque of Songo Mnara (Fig. 48). The latter appears to be the earliest example of a transverse arched arcade in a flat roofed mosque, possibly long antedating those of the late eighteenth century, and it is satisfying to be able to trace its origins to the arcades of those local vaulted buildings with transverse barrel vaults. It may therefore be quite unrelated to the much later buildings with transverse arcades.

Longitudinal Barrel Vaults

Longitudinal barrel vaults are used at the northern and southern ends of the central aisles of the small domed mosques of Mwana (Fig. 11) and Kilwa (Fig. 14). At Mwana the northern barrel vault is a structural necessity for the three northern bays are here much longer than the remaining bays—probably in order to obtain as much unobstructed space in front of the mihrab as possible. Here the longitudinal barrel vault was the only feasible solution to roofing the bay immediately in front of the mihrab. In the Small Domed Mosque of Kilwa however, the barrel vaults of the central aisle are employed purely as a visual variation—though of course they do give an impression of added height to the north wall immediately above the mihrab, which the normal dome could not.

In describing the vaulted buildings individually, it is convenient to use a unit of measurement varying between 44 and 50 cms. which will be called a cubit. This cannot be taken to mean that it is in any way certain that such a unit was actually used by the builders. The examination of the dimensions of all plans to see if a standard unit could be discerned leads one to the conclusion that, while a module within this range was probably employed, it was not standardized but varied from site to site. The question is discussed more fully in Chapter VII. The "cubit" is used here only because it is a helpful method of giving an easily appreciated idea of the proportions of the buildings, and probably approximates to the unit of measure used by the builders.

Husuni Kubwa

The Palace complex of Husuni Kubwa (Figs. 68, 69) consists, basically, of single storied domestic buildings on a headland at the northern end of the site and a great quadrangle of storage rooms at the south. The massive walls of these store rooms supported, in the north-west corner of the quadrangle, an upper storey of two long ranges, some fourteen rooms in all, arranged in series, seven rooms to the west range and seven to the north range. These ranges were flanked by terraces and are approached by stairs from the South Court (though possibly there was a further entrance at their north-west corner). They were probably a series of reception rooms (the living quarters are elsewhere) and their position dominates the site, overlooking all the rest of the building with fine distant views as well. These rooms were all vaulted, in many individual ways. This, and the fine decorative and surface finishes, indicates a luxury, and an exuberance of form, not found later. Here, in the thirteenth century, are many forms of decoration and construction never subsequently repeated, while those elements that do continue seldom achieve the quality of their Husuni prototypes. Yet in planning, decoration and construction this building is quite typical of the coastal architecture. In siting, complexity, variety and quality Husuni is unrivalled but not isolated.

At Husuni, columns are not used as vault supports. Each room, averaging 6 × 9 cubits, is surrounded by load-bearing perimeter walls which support the individual vaulting of that room. The monotony of the later vaulting systems is avoided—indeed, Husuni approaches the opposite extreme—each room in the range seems to differ radically from its neighbour. Further, the relatively large room sizes and proportions mean that the vault was visually effective and rightly dominated the space it roofed. The aesthetic and planning strictures applied to later buildings do not, therefore, apply to their predecessor.

The barrel is the commonest vault form at Husuni and exists in two basic forms—firstly, as an extremely thick (70–90 cms.), regular semicircle spanning the normal room width of 5–6 cubits, probably without a cornice and no more than 8 cubits in length (Fig. 71A). The second form is more delicate (Fig. 71B)—the vault is no more than 16 cms. thick with a span of three cubits and springing always from a cornice. The limitations of the latter span mean that the vault could, normally, only span across the width of the rooms. But this limitation was overcome triumphantly in one room (Fig. 71C) where such a barrel vault runs longitudinally down the length of a standard 6 × 9 cubit room and is supported by quarter vaults or quadrants 1½ cubits in radius (giving an identical curve to that of the central vault) round its perimeter, springing from the sides and ends of the room, and curving inwards to support the central barrel round its perimeter. The cross section of this vault is thus "trefoliate". One would expect the intersection of the perimeter quadrants at the corners to be groined—opening, perhaps, a new structural field. However, they are not—instead the side quadrants curve round the corners to end in a curved decorative rib in plaster before giving way to the end quadrant. Pendentives were used in at least three typical rooms. In two cases these pendentives were plane surfaced triangles (Fig. 71D, E), and in the last case concave faced, to approach the spherical triangle in form (Fig. 71F). They converted the rectangular rooms to elongate octagons at cornice level, which were then roofed by vaults whose corners were hard angles rather than curved, for the octagon was not further altered to a curved vault base. The vault sides were straight. In one of these (Fig. 71E) the cornice surmounting the octagon is replaced by a frieze of recessed rectangular panels 35 cm. high by 25 cms. wide. The intersection of the two ranges of vaulted rooms was marked by a great conical dome (Fig. 71G), 1 cubit thick, 5½ cubits in diameter and 3½ cubits in height, whose slope was thus about 60°.   The exterior is formed of twenty large convex ribs while the interior is the reverse of this—twenty concave flutes separated and defined by narrow dressed coral ribbing.   This is the only large fragment of dome that remains on the site, and the dome itself must indeed have provided a dramatic focus when seen from the shore and lower levels of the Palace (Plate XIV).

The vaulting of the remaining rooms is less certain.   A fragment of plain circular frieze, 53 cms. high and 4 cubits in diameter, would seem to indicate that a similar but smaller cone rested on it.   Several large fallen blocks of masonry indicate that widely separated rooms appear to have had apsidal recesses in their end walls, in some cases only above cornice level, in others recesses at floor level, framed by semicircular arches.   The latter may have supported four-sided (or, less likely, eight-sided) tent-shaped vaults with flat, though sloping, inner and outer surfaces.   Fragments of such flat surfaces are found which slope upwards from the attached arches at 60°—approximately the same slope as the conical dome.   What appears to be one fragment of the side of such a tent-shaped vault survives (Fig. 71H).   Like the conical dome, it has internal ribs (though now in plaster) radiating from an apex or centre point, but its internal surface is not curved to give a cone, but plane.   It seems logical to assume that it can only be from the straight sloping side of a polyhedral tent-shaped dome.   This means, in fact, that, while the barrel vault was in frequent use, the true curved dome did not occur at Husuni Kubwa, but was replaced by the conical or tent-shaped vault.   The outward thrust of such massive, straight sided structures, not deflected downwards as in a dome of more normal curved profile, could scarcely have been supported on columns—the load-bearing wall round the perimeter of each vault was a necessity.

All these structures were built of lime concrete entirely, but many dressed coral panels are found among the fallen rubble which could only have been used to line the underside of barrel vaults.   They are regular, straight edged rectangular panels 16 cms thick, a cubit long and half a cubit wide, curved in one direction only to form the arc of a circle 6 cubits (a room width) in diameter.

Kilwa Great Mosque

Moving from Husuni to the town of Kilwa itself, the first addition (beyond the inner reinforcing wall) to the original, northern, Great Mosque (Fig. 15) was a narrow corridor along its eastern side, only 110 cms. wide, roofed by a barrel vault, lined with dressed coral panels closely similar to those of Husuni.   This corridor appears to have continued southwards; for the early wall, with engaged coral monolithic columns, that now forms the outer wall of the later great southern extension of the mosque, lines up with this eastern corridor and probably formed the outer wall of a vaulted walk enclosing the irregular quadrangle of an open southern courtyard.   In the south-east corner an additional irregular space was enclosed by a splayed wall that still forms the outer wall of the mosque in that corner.   It was decided subsequently to roof this south-east corner, and to do this it was then necessary to straighten the inner splay of this wall by adding two tiny chambers, containing water tanks roofed by barrel vaults of concrete alone and without dressed panels.   This gave a long rectangle to the north, which was easily roofed with a barrel vault lined with dressed panels, but to the south of this a square, 4 m. across, received a Great Dome.   This Dome has already been mentioned as being, almost certainly, the famous Dome of al Hasan ibn Sulaiman, recorded in the Kilwa Chronicle.   This, the first and easily the largest true dome of the coast, was supported on squinches for the first time and lined with panels of dressed coral.   It has entirely collapsed and therefore its profile cannot be reconstructed, though it was certainly curved. Al Hasan ibn Sulaiman was reigning at Kilwa during the visit of Ibn Battuta in 1331 and these additions to the mosque had taken place well before that, for the Kilwa Chronicle tells that by the time of al Hasan ibn Sulaiman's death—calculated to have taken place in 1333—all of the mosque but the dome had collapsed. For a hundred years, the Chronicle relates, the mosque was in ruins until in the reign of the Sultan Sulaiman ibn Muhammed (c. 1421–1442) the great domed southern extension was added (and the northern area re-roofed with massive timber beams and columns).

In the homogeneous Kilwa group of vaulted buildings (Figs. 14, 15, 16, 17, 18), regular, hemispherical domes, of lime/coral concrete, 20–30 cms. thick, are supported on groined squinches, via a double cornice with typical mouldings, supported on simple pointed structural arches. The arches spring from square capitals supported by octagonal columns (of the characteristic construction described on page 24). Engaged columns or corbelled brackets support the arches at the outer walls. Longitudinal barrel vaults often alternate with the domes while transverse barrel vaults also occur. The interior surfaces of domes and vaults may be decorated with small, imported, Islamic glazed bowls inset in the concrete, or domes may have a triangular sectioned plaster fluting.

The fifteenth century vaulted extensions of the Great Mosque (Fig. 15) took place within the early enclosure wall already described. This wall enclosed an irregular rectangle, its sides differing by 50 cms. in 20 m. The engaged columns and walls of the original east and south sides were retained and reused, but the west wall was entirely rebuilt, for the early wall ran towards the east at too great an angle to be satisfactorily incorporated in the new structure. The irregular rectangle to be vaulted meant that the bay lengths needed adjusting. This took place in the two second and third bays from the south, with some bays 20 cms. shorter than normal as a result. Thirty vaults or domes cover the five aisles of the width and the six bays of the length. The perimeter bays are all domed, as is the central aisle. The north and south bays have noticeably shallower domes than the remainder. The remaining inner bays on either side of the central aisle are barrel vaulted, while two of the domes of the east aisle, both immediately inside entrances, are fluted. (The southern of the two entrances was the most important entrance to the mosque, used probably by the Sultan alone—it adjoins the Great South-East Dome where al Hasan ibn Sulaiman "was wont to pray", and its tiny private ablution tank could not have been used by more than one person at a time.) It has already been shown that these alternations of plain and fluted domes and barrel vaults are of little visual significance, for the bay proportions largely minimize their impact.

Kilwa Small Domed Mosque

The Small Domed Mosque at Kilwa (Fig. 14), three bays long and three aisles wide, has a central aisle somewhat wider than its neighbours while the 3 middle bays are somewhat longer. This makes the central bay slightly larger than the rest, and its hemispherical vault has inset bowls and a quadruple cornice of dressed coral (doubling the normal cornice) to reduce the dome span and add decorative emphasis to its central position. Flanking it on north and south, the central dome has two longitudinal barrel vaults also with glazed bowls inset and a cornice double that of the normal barrel vault. Flanking the central dome on east and west, the hemispherical domes of the side aisles are fluted, while those of the somewhat smaller corner bays are plain. The variety of forms thus builds up to a central climax, both in size and decoration, and shows a concern with symmetry, and with centralizing and articulating the design, but it is only apparent with close study and had little true effect.

Jangwani Mosque

At the south end of the town, near the shore of a tidal creek or *jangwa*, dry at all except high spring tides, there are the fallen remains of a third typical domed building (Fig. 17). This was almost certainly another mosque: it is correctly orientated, though no trace of the mihrab (or of the north wall) survives.[1] Like the Small Domed Mosque, it is three aisles wide and three bays deep and again the central aisle is somewhat wider than the side aisles. There do not appear to have been barrel vaults, but at least one of the nine domes was typically fluted, though the majority were plain. An interesting variation is found in the squinches of this building. Their arches are pointed, rather than semicircular, and have a nick at their apex, continued as a decorative vertical groove. A horizontal rectangular timber, laid flat, acted as a relieving member above the squinch arches, within the thickness of the fabric and not visible. This building was at some time near collapse for the two north columns have both been thickened (the west considerably more so than the east) with casing of coarse masonry, roughly plastered. This strengthening probably took place long after erection and in quality would seem to be eighteenth century work though both the square base and octagonal column shapes were retained.

It is interesting to compare the dimensions of the three domed buildings of Kilwa as shown in the following table.

	Small Domed Mosque	Jangwani Mosque	Great Mosque
Width of bay	1·92 m	2·16 m	2·38 m
Length of bay	2·12 m	2·20 m	2·80 m
Column size	54 cms	56 cms	58 cms
Arch width	32 cms	36 cms	38 cms

From this it can be seen how, as the normal bay size increased, so columns and arches increased regularly and proportionally, in response to what must have been a clearly recognized and successful rule of thumb. The builders were, therefore, in no doubt as to the structural techniques and strengths required for these buildings—all details indicate that they were working in a developed, settled tradition with none of the fluctuations and individuality of an initial experimental period. This table of dimensions also illustrates how difficult it is to discern with certainty a fixed unit of measurement or cubit. There appears to be no common multiple uniting these dimensions.

Songo Mnara Palace

At Songo Mnara the main court of the Palace has an arcade (Fig. 16) lining its southern face, with alternating dome and barrel vaults, building up to a central climax. A high central barrel vault runs across the bay fronting the monumental central door of the Palace. It is flanked on each side by a hemispherical dome with a further barrel vault, lower than the central one, ending the arcade on each side. Squinch, cornice and vault forms and sizes, the glazed bowls inset decoratively, the alternation of dome and barrel—all are typical of the Kilwa group of vaulted buildings. The only facts worthy of comment are that the supports are now not columns but wide, rectangular piers (2 × 1 cubits)—at first sight very unusual for this area at this date, but explained by the fact that they are external and take the entire outward thrust of the vaults, which cannot be further transferred to a solid perimeter wall as happens with internal columns. They should perhaps be considered as making up a perimeter wall broken by arches rather than as piers. On the inner faces, the cross arches spring from brackets not engaged columns—probably again because the arcade is only a single bay

[1] Excavation has now revealed the mihrab foundations. Infm. H. N. Chittick, October 1964.

in width.   It seems probable that the east and west sides of the court were originally lined by similar arcades.

Sanje Majoma

At the subsidiary site of Sanje Majoma, a small mosque (Fig. 18) typical of the Kilwa group in every way, has a central row of two columns, and so is two aisles wide and three bays long.   Here the mihrab and probably a central south door prevented the use of longitudinal structural arches and hence of domes in north or south bays; transverse barrel vaults replace them.   This is the building in which one can see the rectangular framing of the supporting arches of the transverse arched arcade develop in response to a particular problem, to be repeated in mosques entirely roofed by transverse barrel vaults, and then on the outer face of the Palace arcade and finally in the flat roofed main mosque of Songo Mnara where it is purely embellishment.

Barrel vaulted buildings

At Songo Mnara, the main private room of a fine house near the Palace is roofed with a typical barrel vault, inset with a grid of 121 small glazed bowls.   Two vaulted mosques entirely roofed with transverse barrel vaults form a class by themselves, due partly to this roof form, but more particularly to their extraordinary mihrab forms and plans (Fig. 18).   One is at the west end of Kilwa, now within the eighteenth century Palace precincts, and the second on the shore west of the Palace of Songo Mnara.   The latter has an extensive cemetery beside it of plain graves, marked by sandstone head and foot stones within a square enclosure.   Both are long, narrow buildings and the mihrab is not built against the north wall but is a free-standing construction flanked on each side by narrow doorways leading via a short passage the depth of the mihrab to further similar doorways which lead to a further chamber and then to an external entrance door at the north.   Both mihrabs are very tall (one over four and the other over five cubits tall), plain, and semi-cylindrical in form with no sign of a roof or semi-dome now visible.   They are framed by engaged square piers and have no further decoration.   Both mosques lack internal columns and were roofed by three transverse barrel vaults resting on the normal cornice, but in both cases this has a further timber cornice beneath—a feature found nowhere else. The sides of the barrel vaults were, at Kilwa, supported on transverse arches rising from the normal engaged column with rectangular capitals, with pilasters and lintel forming a rectangular frame to the single arch, in the way already described.   Both mosques have south doors but no side doors.   At Kilwa the mosque is 6 cubits wide and 6½ cubits high to the cornice alone—extremely tall in proportions, for the bay length is only 4 cubits.   At Songo Mnara similar proportions occur—the mosque is 6⅓ cubits wide and 5 cubits high, yet the bays barely exceed 3 cubits in length.

These two extremely unusual mosques are strikingly similar—there must be more than just visual preferences behind the unusual plan and mihrab form.   One may suppose that they were private mosques of the sultans—the Songo Mnara mosque is isolated from the town, yet near the Palace; while at Kilwa, though the site of the fifteenth century Palace is unknown, it possibly existed on the site of the much later Palace near this mosque.   The arrangement of north doors on each side of the mihrab occurs nowhere else on the coast in a comparable mosque, though there are many precedents to the Sultan's entrance to a mosque being at the northern end, outside East Africa.   This conjecture is, however, contradicted at Kilwa by the strong probability that the original Palace existed on the east of the Great Mosque—the elaborate south-east entrance of the Great Mosque lends architectural support to this.

Plate VI. Carved coral decoration typical of the Neo-Classic period, showing characteristic grooved mouldings. Mihrab jamb block, Manda Mosque, seventeenth century.

Plate V. Dressed coral mouldings and pilaster recess typical of the finest work of the Classic period. Door of the Palace of Songo Mnara, fifteenth century.

Plate VIII. Outer door of Mosque of Fakhr ad Din, Mogadishu. Note the use of squared coral blocks in both walls and arch spandrels. Thirteenth century.

Plate VII. Supporting arches, cornice and vault seating, formed of horizontal slabs of dressed coral. Central bay, Mwana Mosque, possibly fourteenth century.

Alternatively, one may suppose that the fact that there is a cemetery attached to the Songo Mnara mosque may in some way have influenced the plan form of the mosque, but there is no cemetery near the Kilwa mosque—in fact this mosque is attached to the east side of a large double-storied building, with further structures to the east of it. The chambers north of the mihrab are nothing more than entrances, in the Songo Mnara case apparently unpaved. Neither north chamber contains a tomb, as was first expected, but subsequently tested and disproved by excavation. Nevertheless, there must be a functional link between these two mosques and it remains to be discerned.

Ungwana

Excavation[1] has indicated that the vaulted western side room of the Jamia of Ungwana (Fig. 23) was built in the late fifteenth century—thus slightly later than or possibly contemporary with, the buildings of the Kilwa group. Six square piers divide the room centrally into two aisles. As it was entered by a central north door, a transverse barrel vault 6 cubits wide spanned the north bays, matched by a similar barrel at the south end. The remaining bays were covered by ten domes, 3 cubits square.

Mwana

North of Ungwana, the little mosque of Mwana (Fig. 11) is three aisles wide and four bays long. Its massive piers, 70 cms. square, support four domes, roughly conical in form, $3\frac{1}{2}$ cubits square, over each side aisle. The central aisle is narrower and only 3 cubits wide. At the north and south ends it has longitudinal barrel vaults, while the two central bays (Plate VII), rectangular in shape, are first altered to squares by projecting cornices at their north and south sides only, which support horizontal triangular blocks of dressed coral at each corner, replacing the pendentive and converting the plan to an octagon, which is then surmounted by a further cornice. All the cornices of Mwana are octagonal in plan and do not form a transition to a circle.

Mwana and Ungwana have many features in common. Both have square piers, without dressed coral corners, combined with arches formed of fine-dressed coral. In both, the arches spring from brackets at the side walls, not engaged columns. Both have plain pendentives, plain cornices without the rebated moulding of the Kilwa group, and windows set in the end wall of barrel vaults. The replacement of pendentives by horizontal slabs of dressed coral in the Mwana central domes is found, not in the Jamia of Ungwana but in the small mosque nearby (Fig. 29) where they are used to support the little mihrab dome, whose form is conical if not originally polyhedral. None of these features of detail occur in the Kilwa group, though, of course, the alternation of plain domes in the side aisles of Mwana with more elaborate central domes, flanked by longitudinal barrel vaults in the central aisle, has similarities with the layout of the Small Domed Mosque at Kilwa. Such broad planning resemblances are without great significance. It is surely natural to concentrate decoration in the centre aisle, and the longitudinal barrel vault above the mihrab is an obvious method of giving an impression of height above a major focal point, which is then matched for the sake of symmetry at the south end. The detailed correspondence between the mosques of Ungwana and Mwana and the great dissimilarity with the Kilwa group is of much greater consequence. The dome forms of Ungwana are not now recoverable, but the conical shape of the Mwana domes is reminiscent of Husuni Kubwa, and their slope, like those of Husuni, is about

[1] J. S. Kirkman: Ungwana, unpublished.

4

60°. There are further correspondences with Husuni in both pendentives and piers. These correspondences may well be significant—yet at present, they can only be noted without explanation.

The large columns and small spans of Mwana restrict the space available; this is overcome in front of the mihrab, where space is not needed, by supporting the northern domes of the side aisles not on the north wall but on a deep transverse arch or arcade. The depth of this arcade thus adds to the space available. The span of the longitudinal supporting arches of the central aisle could not be increased—they are however not supported on a pier in the normal position; instead the pier is moved north to become a pilaster of the north wall and from it springs a quarter arch or quadrant to support, in its turn, the springing of the main arch.

The much later mosques of Jumba la Mtwana, Chwaka and Tiwi do not have either pendentive or squinch, while their techniques of building, plain mihrab designs and octagonal columns (late in the northern area) would all seem to indicate an eighteenth century date.

Jumba la Mtwana

Jumba la Mtwana (Fig. 37) has deep, engaged columns round the side walls supporting, for the first time, a perimeter arcade of arches. Two central columns divide it into two aisles and three bays (4 cubits square). It is the only example on the coast where central columns are not combined with a transverse barrel vault in front of the mihrab. The results are disastrous visually and the structural complications were almost equally unfortunate. The mihrab is surrounded to form a plain rectangle which projects forward of the engaged columns into the floor space of the mosque. It is flanked by two arches of the perimeter arcade. These consequently do not span to the centre of the mosque but only to the sides of the mihrab and are so reduced in span and proportions as to become structurally meaningless and to clash with, and detract visually from, both the normal structural arches and the mihrab arch itself. The central structural and longitudinal arch has now collapsed—it must have been an incomplete or "rampant" arch supported above, and by, the mihrab projection at its north end.

Tiwi

At Tiwi in southern Kenya (Fig. 37) the barrel is the major vault form used. Three central columns divide the main hall to support two transverse barrels at the north and south ends separated by two longitudinal barrels. Continuing to the south, but as a separate room (presumably for women), a central row of columns supports two further longitudinal barrel vaults. This room is flanked by side rooms with single barrels while the main hall is flanked by side rooms each roofed by three rough conical domes, of masonry rather than concrete and irregularly curved internally, resting on square bays. This plan, with its many subsidiary rooms, would seem to be typical of the simplified classic mosques of the eighteenth century, as will be shown in Chapter VI. The economy of structure achieved in this mosque is remarkable. The columns are only 44 cms. square and the walls little thicker, yet the barrel vaults span 5 cubits and are from 10 to 12 cubits long, while the domes are 6 cubits square at their base. These large spans are largely possible because a great proportion of the weight and thrust of each vault is taken on load bearing walls, not columns. Though this mosque lacks in precision (the plan itself is notably irregular), decoration and finish, the plan evolved is most competent, both structurally and visually. A maximum visual effect is achieved with little elaboration and a great economy of materials.

Chwaka

The mosque of Chwaka (Fig. 37) has a more normal plan than either Jumba la Mtwana or Tiwi. Three central columns divide it into two aisles, four bays ($4\frac{1}{2}$ cubits wide and 4 cubits long) long. Consequent on the central columns, a transverse barrel vault, 3 cubits in span, occurs in front of the mihrab matched by a similar vault at the rear. At the side walls, plain brackets support the arches, unlike the pilasters of Tiwi and the engaged columns of Jumba la Mtwana. The north face of the arched arcade supporting the barrel vault is plain, and has not got the projecting rectangular frame which occurs in the Kilwa group and whose origin was discussed in connection with this group.

From the analysis of the vaulted buildings of the coast several points emerge. There are only a small number of such buildings, though the necessary skills and materials required to erect them are not lacking. This may largely be due to the fact that they offer little functional or aesthetic improvement on more normal structures. The variety of forms of Husuni may not have included the true dome or multiple vaults, but while most of its forms do not continue (dying out in the early forms of the Great Mosque of Kilwa) several are found again only at Ungwana and Mwana, which appear from excavation to be some two centuries later, and later than the homogeneous Kilwa group. The many domed buildings of the Kilwa area represent a restricted yet flourishing group of the fifteenth century, where vaulting techniques were so familiar as to become almost standardized. Only three vaulted buildings occur after the fifteenth century—over two centuries later—and the basic techniques of dome support have been lost. Each differs radically from the others and appears to approach the problem in a basically different manner. Only at Chwaka does a plan typical of the early periods recur.

CHAPTER IV

APPLIED DECORATION

With the complete decay or destruction of all timber, and most plasterwork, in all early buildings it is impossible to determine how much carved and painted decoration, applied to the timber cornices, beams, skirtings (an uncommon feature, but found in the mosque at Takwa, at least) and to the final plasterwork, has been destroyed. The only decorated timber work to survive, that of a late eighteenth century Mazrui house within Fort Jesus, shows that, here at least, cornices and rafters were carved with religious texts. Paintwork survives in the eighteenth century Palace and adjacent houses of Kilwa as a dark red ochre dado to several rooms, with carved plasterwork friezes picked out in a similar colour. A painted floral frieze decorates the string course within the mihrab of the fifteenth century Small Domed Mosque nearby, though this was probably added to it in the eighteenth century. A carved boss, fallen from a fifteenth century tomb near the Palace of Gedi, had a painted red ochre background to the raised pattern. There is, therefore, no reason to doubt that carved and painted decoration also occurred on the timber work, and that plaster work was probably painted in earlier periods also. Tiny scratched graffiti of a crude herring-bone pattern occur in the spandrels of the mihrabs of the fifteenth century Mosque of the Long Conduit at Gedi and the eighteenth century mosque of Kimbiji but they are too irregular and insignificant to be considered as a true decoration. The minor decorative elements that embellish both mosques and houses form one of the clearest indications of the unity of the architecture of the coast. The repertoire is limited, but it is drawn on for over five centuries and slowly but progressively elaborated. Many of these minor elements—cornices, string courses, mouldings, insets, niches, capitals, arch and door forms—form parts of varied compositions but are themselves apparently uniformly distributed in time and space, rising from a basis common to the whole coast. They probably show more conclusively than anything else that there is, on the coast of East Africa, a single clear style of local architecture—divisible in particulars, both regionally and in time, with new forms added to it; but, from the thirteenth to eighteenth centuries at least, from Lamu to Kilwa or Pemba, securely based on a common foundation.

Mouldings

The basic moulding is the square block of finely dressed coral, between 6 and 10 cms. wide (Fig. 2A). In mihrabs and doorways this is arranged in a series of recessed "orders", each set back some 6–10 cms. from its neighbour and of the same width. It is a precise, yet bold and simple shape, well made in fine coral, severe, geometric, and based on the right-angled corner and the square section.

The immediate development of this moulding is a break in the salient angle or projecting corner of the moulding, formed by excising from the block a 2–3 cms. square rebate—the "rebated arris" moulding (Fig. 2B). The precise right angle and square section is retained but the line of the outer edges is both made more delicate and more emphatic by repeating the major form in a minor key. This moulding occurred, as the main cornice moulding, from the earliest period. In such a cornice, it is the line of the lower corner of the cornice projection that is rebated. It spread, soon after, to the straight edges of façades and frames. The small rectangular recesses, that occur in pilasters or walls, are framed by this moulding while the large plane surfaces of the architraves surrounding mihrabs or doorways receive it at their salient angles or as a frame to the slightly recessed inner field that frequently breaks the surface of their upper half. Considerably later, in the sixteenth century, the rebated arris moulding is reduced in size to a rebate only 1 cm. square and applied to the projecting edge of curved arches (Plate XI). By this period it is in such general use that the clear emphasis it previously gave to the major angles and edges is reduced by its very ubiquity.

In the seventeenth century, after the rebated arris moulding had been in use some time, the plain face of the main moulding was embellished for the first time—usually in conjunction with the rebated arris. This embellishment consists of incising a deep double V-groove in the moulding face to give a moulding with a triangular section 2 cms. wide recessed 1 cm. into the face of the main moulding (Fig. 2C, Plate VI). It only once occurs singly—in the mihrab arches of Ndumi (Fig. 51), where its comparatively large size and subtle splayed terminations set it further apart from the typical form. In the mosques of the Lamu group, where it is most popular, two to four recessed grooves forming one or two recessed triangles are incised within the face of almost every moulding until they form almost a uniform surface finish to the whole façade. It is not so common elsewhere, but isolated blocks of mouldings of identical size and form are found at such widely separated sites as the mosques of Msuka Mjini in northern Pemba and Makutani at Kilwa. Thus, by this period, the plain mouldings of earlier type have not changed their basic form or technique of manufacture, but have become elaborated by the application of detailed surface decoration—the rebated arris and then the multiple recessed triangles.

In the late eighteenth century, however, there is a major break in moulding types as dressed coral mouldings are practically entirely replaced by plaster mouldings. Curved profiles to mouldings are more easily obtainable in this material but precision and crisp edges are almost impossible and scarcely sought after. This period has one ubiquitous, entirely characteristic moulding—the "half keyhole moulding" in which a projecting semicircle surmounts half a triangle (Fig. 2D). The nineteenth century mosques of the towns of the Shirazi confederacies of the Tanganyika coast, such as Kipumbwe (Fig. 53), Bweni (Fig. 55) and Mkwaja (Fig. 56), have it immediately beneath the column capitals, or as a cornice. It is characteristic of the nineteenth century architecture of Zanzibar and is found in nineteenth century Zanzibari houses on the mainland and in Zanzibari additions to Fort Jesus, Mombasa. It is one of the most diagnostic architectural features and gives a clear indication of date and origin wherever it is found.

The late eighteenth century is characterized by moulded plaster work. Rectangular panels, surmounted by polylobed arched niches, both some 2 cms. deep, and entirely formed in plaster, form a surface decoration to the eighteenth century Palace (Fig. 78), houses and mosques of Kilwa. Incised plaster friezes with curvilinear forms based on naturalistic foliage, and a characteristic, plain, embattled cornice moulding in plaster also occur there. Far more elaborate surface decoration, in moulded plasterwork, covers the entire inner walls of the houses and Palace of eighteenth century Pate and its adjacent sites—Faza and Siu. This is also the period of fine moulded plaster diaper patterning on many tombs. Earlier, much simpler incised mouldings of simple geometric shapes occur in plaster—diamond patterns in particular and often the incised or recessed triangle moulding carried over from the earlier carved coral moulding form)—for instance on the mihrab mouldings of the Kua Jamia (Fig. 43), or on the little domed tomb of Kilwa dated A.H. 1124/A.D. 1712 (Fig. 56).

Cable pattern

The moulding that runs most clearly as a theme through the entire decoration of the coast is the cable pattern or herring-bone. In its finest form (Fig. 2E), the cable pattern, carved from fine coral, stands proud of a plain edge by some 5 cms. Each element or strand of the cable is 2 cms. wide and each is deeply and individually carved to give a curved profile and curved edge. The regularity of the firm, clear, sensitively curved forms, mitred at the corners or carried round the corner in a single block is most clearly seen at Husuni Kubwa (the width of a single cable here is some 7 cms. and a double cable 10 cms.). At Ungwana, a single cable pattern of the same excellent quality is further elaborated by breaking the cable with small roundels containing interlaced palmettes at 20 cms. intervals (Fig. 82D). In the mihrab of Kizimkazi (Fig. 49), a double cable pattern, rising proud of plain borders, is of equal quality. Incorporated in this mihrab there are also unique circular shafts of coral, 10 cms. in diameter, similarly carved. Both shafts and mouldings are likely to be contemporary with the early twelfth century inscription incorporated in the mihrab of this mosque. The quality of this early workmanship is never again attained after the thirteenth century. The size of the cable moulding itself, the sensitive curves and the depth of carving (not only of the individual cable strands, but also that necessary for the cable itself to stand so far proud of its border, which is carved from the same coral block), are not subsequently repeated. Nevertheless, the double cable pattern (Fig. 2F) (from 7–10 cms. in overall width) decorates many mihrabs of the sixteenth century—in Kenya at Mnarani, Gedi (Plate X) and Takwa; in Tanganyika at Songo Mnara; in Pemba at Shengejuu. Later the quality declines further at eighteenth century Kua (Figs. 2G, 43) and later still at nearby Chole (Fig. 49), the cable is recessed between its plain borders, necessitating far less depth of carving, while in the seventeenth century Lamu group it is replaced by the herring-bone pattern (Fig. 2H), an extremely popular mihrab embellishment there. In this, small blocks of coral, only 5 cms. wide, receive a series of straight grooves in a chevron pattern. They have no border and they are not moulded as the strands of the cable were, though they are obviously derived from this motif; nor is there any attempt at mitring the corners—the blocks abut their neighbours without any continuation of the pattern. This is a clear example of "mass production" replacing the slower skills of a single craftsman, at the expense of quality. By the eighteenth century, as blocks in Songo Mnara Palace show, only rudimentary and irregular scratched chevrons remain. The south door of the small mosque of Dege (Fig. 41), probably late eighteenth century, has unique capitals which have a border of shallow, scratched, slanting grooving—not chevron, for there is only a single line. This probably marks the end of this moulding type. With this moulding again, one single pattern survives many centuries, yet slowly deteriorates as surface incisions replace a simple, bold and deep moulding.

Pilaster recesses

The pilasters of the rectangular architraves surrounding the mihrabs or monumental doorways frequently contain rectangular or arched recesses, made of dressed coral blocks, no doubt to contain a lamp (Plate V). These too are extremely homogeneous in their style. The earliest form is probably the simple rectangle, framed by a single recessed order 2 cms. wide (in fact, the familiar rebated arris moulding), such as occurs at Ras Mkumbuu or Tongoni (Figs. 4, 5), followed by those in which the frame is doubled and has two rebates—as in the later mosque of Kaole (Fig. 20) or those of Shengejuu or Chwaka (Fig. 22). The four carved blocks that form the recess are not mitred at the corners, instead the two side blocks rest on the base block and have rebates cut in their backs to fit over and mask those forming the base frame whose façade rebates continue to the outside edges. This variant of a "mason's mitre" is repeated at the top corners, and is the invariable technique used in forming such recesses on the coast.

The later arched recesses that decorate both architrave pilasters and mihrab apses are even more idiosyncratic in design. In their recessed orders to jambs and arches they resemble, on a miniature scale, the monumental mihrabs. The arched niches that line the mihrabs of Songo Mnara (Fig. 48) and a mosque at Kua (Fig. 47), the recesses in the pilasters of the monumental doorways of the Palace of Songo Mnara (Fig. 16, Plate V), recesses in the panelled façades of pillar tombs at Kaole in Tanganyika and Malindi in Kenya, fragments of numerous recesses found loose in a single room in the domestic buildings south of the Great Mosque at Kilwa—all can probably be dated to the late fifteenth and early sixteenth centuries and all exhibit a closely uniform and individual treatment. In essence each jamb consists of a single carved block. The outer shaft of the jamb turns inwards through a right angle to become the "capital", which is thus a flush continuation of it and of the same width. In the jamb of a single isolated recess this forms an inverted L, and in a jamb separating a series of recesses, a T. Below this, and recessed from it, a second order (2 cms. square) repeats this inverted L form and this may be followed by a third similar order. A final inner order is normally contained within the last inverted L to make the inner reveal of the arch jambs flush with the "capitals". These jamb blocks, in which the capital mouldings are substituted by inward turning continuations of the jamb shafts, are strangely coarse and disproportionate to our eyes. Unlike the normal large-scale mihrab or doorway capitals they have an unnecessary crudity that ignores the essential distinction between shaft and capital always observed in any sensitive design. The arches that cap them are formed of a single block, carved to imitate the normal arch with its recessed orders. This arch is framed by three blocks, two pilasters rising from the jamb capital and a lintol. A rebated arris moulding is always used to edge these blocks.

The moulded pilaster recesses in their final form—again arched (e.g. those of Ndumi, Fig. 51, Kitoka, Fig. 35, Msuka Mjini, Fig. 59 and Chole, Fig. 49)—have the entire recess formed by only two carved blocks. The mouldings of jambs and shafts are half the size of the earlier type and the earlier strange capital design is not repeated, except in a modified form at Msuka Mjini. These recesses are all more delicate and satisfactory than the earlier ones. At Kitoka in fact a complete niche of the second type rests on the jambs of the earlier type.

Unmoulded recesses occur in the architraves of some mihrabs of the Lamu group (Figs. 32, 33), but previous to them, the pilaster recess does not appear to have occurred in Kenya except in two cases. The only pre-seventeenth century mosques north of Tongoni to have it are the small mosque of Mnarani and the nearby Kitoka Jamia, both unusual also in being the only pre-seventeenth century mosques in Kenya to have octagonal columns. Both these mosques have strange little niches in the columns also (Figs. 19, 35). The pilaster recess always occurs in Pemba but not at Tumbatu, Zanzibar.

Arch decoration

Two decorative elaborations of a basic structural motif—the absence of a keystone—have already been discussed. These are the ogival or keel-shaped nick at the arch apex or the raised panel at the arch apex. The most emphatic and possibly the earliest example of the former is the early mihrab of Kaole (Fig. 3)—only here can one talk of an ogival arch. In time, there is no restriction or pattern to the presence of the nicked arch apex—it is present from first to last. It is found in arch fragments at Husuni, and in the thirteenth century arch at the entrance to the Tower of Mogadishu (Fig. 67). On Pemba it always occurs and is also found in the doors and mihrab of Tumbatu, Zanzibar. In the fifteenth century Kilwa group it occurs in the mihrab of the Great Mosque (Fig. 13), in the squinches of the Jangwani mosque (Fig. 17) and in all doors and niches of Songo Mnara Palace (Fig. 84, Plate V), but not in the Kilwa Small Domed Mosque. At Gedi it occurs only in the Mosque of the Sarcophagi (Fig. 10) but not in the neighbouring town mosques, though Kiburugeni nearby, and of the same date, has one. It does not occur at Ungwana or nearby sites nor is it frequent in the Lamu area—though it is found in one mosque in Siu (Fig. 33). In northern Tanganyika it is absent at Ndumi and Tongoni, but occurs further south in the mosques of Muhembo and Mnarani. The sites near Dar es Salaam all appear to have it—from the earliest to the latest pre-nineteenth century types (e.g. Kaole, Kunduchi, Mbweni, Bandarini, Dege, Kimbiji). It continues to be found in eighteenth century arches too—the trefoliate arch of Kizimkazi and all four centred arches (e.g. Malindi mosque and tomb at Kilwa, Mafui)—but it is not found in the Mafia area. There is therefore a certain broad regional distribution pattern—strongest in Pemba, Zanzibar and the mainland opposite and to the south of them but rarer, though by no means absent, in the northern area of Kenya. This distribution is probably of almost no significance—it was a minor element of decoration used or not used at will.

The raised archivolt (that is the raised outer arch order) continuing from the arch apex across the spandrel as a vertical panel formed of two separate blocks is a much less frequent feature. It occurs in one mosque mihrab at Gedi (the Small Mosque, Fig. 10), in a door at Gedi Jamia and several doors and frames to water cooler niches in the houses of that town. A door (which appears to predate the remainder of the eighteenth century mosque) at Siu has it, combined with the nicked apex; this combination of the raised archivolt and panel with a nick at the arch apex also occurs at the later Kaole mosque (Fig. 20) and at Shengejuu (Fig. 22). The raised archivolt is thus not common but has a wide distribution. It was probably not introduced before the late fifteenth century.

Bosses

The spandrels of mihrab arches are frequently decorated with inset carved coral bosses (Figs. 82, 83); less frequently door spandrels and tombs contain similar bosses. The mid-fifteenth century Jamia of Mnarani in Kenya has probably the finest collection of such bosses—five occur in the mihrab spandrels, the south door had two further examples, and the fifteenth century tombs behind the mosque contain similar ornate bosses. At the same time, bosses of similar intricacy occur on a dated tombstone of A.H. 866/A.D. 1476 from Mombasa, a tomb near the Palace of Gedi (which had a background painted in red ochre) and the Small Domed Mosque of Kilwa. The intricate, interlaced designs are illustrated in Fig. 83. Most of the bosses of the Mnarani tombs (mid and late fifteenth century) are broadly based on the interlace—but the bosses of the mosque itself at Mnarani (early fifteenth century) contain four or six palmettes pointing inwards from the circumference. Much smaller (8–10 cms.) bosses, from both the building behind the Great Mosque of Kilwa and from Ungwana, contain four similar palmettes but carved with considerably more naturalism. The more natural motifs would seem to be earlier than the later intricate geometric interlace designs, with the palmette motif possibly dying out in the early fifteenth century. Intricately carved bosses appear to be characteristic of the fifteenth century alone. Two further bosses, one from Siu and one from the Makutani Palace of Kilwa, may be of similar date and built into later structures. This is certainly true of the Palace example which is found on the side wall of a latrine duct, though less certain at Siu. The completely abstract nature of the latter design may possibly be contemporary with the early eighteenth century mihrab in which it appears.

A noteworthy theme occurs on the border of both the Gedi and Small Domed Mosque bosses—a repetitive pattern of "angular S-shaped" motifs. It obviously has the same ornamental basis as the cable pattern, and is broadly related to it. It appears, curiously, in a graffiti in the entrance hall of House 1 at Gedi in the precisely excised bow of a ship engraving. It is also the basis of a finely carved and unique moulding within the mihrab of Mnarani (Fig. 82). All these examples are fifteenth century.

After the fifteenth century, bosses have much simpler and less deeply incised carving requiring far less skill. The designs of bosses in the early sixteenth century Jamia of Ungwana are now obliterated, but in the small mosque of Mnarani, at Kunduchi and then in three mosques at Pate (Figs. 19, 46, 31), a series of up to four concentric circles, sometimes combined with straight lines radiating from the centre, decorate the boss. In the two latest of the Pate mosques (Fig. 32) these bosses are not carved but of plaster-work, imitating the bosses of the earlier Pate Mosque of Bwana Bakari (Fig. 31). In the very late eighteenth century, the south door of the mosque of Kilindini, Mombasa, has tiny bosses with the same design while the bosses of the late eighteenth century reconstruction of the mosque at Kizimkazi, Zanzibar, and the somewhat earlier Jamia of Chwaka (Fig. 22) on Pemba, have a scalloped edge to their designs of concentric circles. In every mosque of the Lamu group (Figs. 31–33), without exception, a spear-shaped boss or lance head is inserted above the mihrab arch apex, and often repeated as a tiny replica above the apex of the inner trefoliate mihrab arch. These are not found elsewhere in this typical form. It is tempting to relate this to the main honorary title of the Pate rulers which was Fumo—derived from the old Swahili word meaning a spear. The lance head motif is found in a less clear form in the outer spandrel of one of the entrance doors of the Jamia at Gedi (said to have been matched by a shield in the other spandrel) and possibly in one of the strange little boss types of the mihrab of Ndumi (Fig. 51). The bosses of Ndumi are of three shapes —plain circular, oval and lanceolate. The two former shapes are incised with straight lines forming a cross or other seemingly meaningless designs, while the lance head shape is plain. At Mgao Mwanya (Fig. 47) an irregular carved crescent decorates one mihrab spandrel. In pre-seventeenth century Somali the flat disc of the bosses of the rest of the coast is replaced by a very characteristic conical boss (Plate VIII, Fig. 65) carved with lines or flutes radiating from its apex. This is quite unlike the southern types, but is found in the strange mihrab of Mgangani, near Gedi.

Ceramic insets

It has already been seen how small, imported, Islamic bowls were inset into many fifteenth century vaults in the Kilwa area. In the mid-fifteenth century, after the introduction of blue and white Chinese porcelain imports to the coast, such decoration in the new porcelain spread to the spandrels and even apses of mihrabs. The number of bowls used multiplied as development proceeded. Mbweni has only two, the early sixteenth century Ungwana Jamia one, the small mosque at Ungwana five, the mid-sixteenth century Gedi Jamia thirteen (Plate X) and the eighteenth century mosque of Mafui seventeen. They spread from spandrels to pilasters and then to the upper part of the north wall until in the extraordinary nineteenth century mosque of Tundwa over fifty bowls cover the entire north wall (Fig. 61).

Rectangular decorative panels were also inset in spandrels or pilasters from the fifteenth century. These have how disappeared, but they were no doubt of glazed ceramic tiles. They occurred at Ungwana, at nearby Shaka and in the Small Domed Mosque of Kilwa.

Identical imported motifs

In the mihrab apse of the mosque of Fakhr ad Din in Mogadishu a marble plaque (Fig. 65) depicts, in relief, a vase or, more probably, lamp, with circular body and curved flared neck and matching foot, suspended at three points on its rim from a chain which hangs from the apex of the cinquefoil arch that surrounds it. Supported by this marble plaque is a glazed tile containing an inscription and the date A.H. 677/A.D. 1269. Two marble finials, now standing loose in the portico of this mosque, have their square shafts, with recessed corners, adorned with a series of carved diamonds within square recesses. The feature of both finials and plaque are repeated in identical form in the relief carved on a marble plaque found in the Sultansmausoleum[1] of Kilwa. Again a vessel with circular body, flared neck and foot is supported by a chain at 3 points on its rim and hangs from a cinquefoil arch which now springs from two square shafts, with recessed corners, decorated by a diaper of diamonds within squares identical to the finial shafts found at Fakhr ad Din. Turned finials cap the shafts and foliage and rosettes border the central design. This Kilwa plaque is a horizontal rectangle now broken at the centre and the arch motif was repeated on the absent half (now in the Berlin Museum für Völkerkunde). Both the Mogadishu and Kilwa plaques have religious verses round their edges. The striking identity of these marble carvings found at sites at the north and south extremities of the coast and in buildings which otherwise have very little in common is of great interest. They were no doubt imported (to judge by their rarity, quality and the use of marble—a material not found on the coast). Neither building is securely dated—though the fabric of Fakhr ad Din most probably dates from the mid-thirteenth century, the date of the inscription. There is little to compare with this mosque in design in Somaliland, though there are many points of similarity between it and the thirteenth century tower of the Jamia at Mogadishu, while the conical dome over the portico resembles those of thirteenth century Husuni Kubwa. The building of the Sultansmausoleum has doors of identical form to those of the thirteenth century part of the Great Mosque of Kilwa though similar door forms continue and are found in the fifteenth century Palace of Songo Mnara. An isolated correspondence of the degree of identity shown in these imports does suggest that there was a connection between widely separated regions having distinct architectural styles, a connection pinpointed by their use of such identical embellishments. All traces of these unexpected links have been lost, apart from this strange exception. The style of the foliate arches found in these plaques is not used architecturally for mosque mihrabs for almost another three centuries. Similarly, the mihrab arches and columns depicted in the thirteenth century glazed lustre tiles incorporated in the mihrabs of the mosques of Fakhr ad Din and Arba Rukn, are quite different in shape and character to those of any designs in the early coastal architecture. This is of great significance. The builders of the coast were clearly aware that design in a completely different style to that of the coast was practised abroad, in the countries from which the glazed tiles and marble plaques were imported. Yet they made no attempt to imitate this style, although they were technically competent to do so. Although the universal, square-sectioned mouldings of the coast are easily made and possibly most suitable to a material such as coral, there seems little reason why circular column shafts of a small size, suitable for mihrab jambs, could not have been carved from coral if desired. In Kizimkazi such shafts are indeed

[1] So named by early German investigators, though there is no evidence that the Sultans of Kilwa are buried there.

found (Fig. 49) and in thirteenth century Kilwa Great Mosque (Fig. 15) large octagonal coral monolithic columns were used. These are however unique. The style of the coastal architecture was sufficiently individual, developed and confident to be able to disregard the evidence of differing styles abroad. This evidence they clearly had —it is incorporated in these ceramic and marble plaques used to embellish the mihrabs of coastal mosques.

Doorways

The typical capital, in all arched openings, is a block whose height is approximately equal to the width of the orders of jamb or arch (normally about 8–10 cms.) with two or more rebates to its underside. These rebates may occur only on the reveal of the capital (Fig. 84C) thus breaking the profile of the opening with the face remaining a flush unbroken surface, but more often they continue round to give a moulded base to the capital on both reveal and face (Fig. 84D). In the Kilwa group of buildings, the capitals are all noticeably thicker than elsewhere—from 17–20 cms. in height including the rebated mouldings at their bases.

The series of doorways found in the Palace of Songo Mnara (Figs. 16, 84) best illustrates the variety of doorway types and shows that there is little chronological, or indeed regional, significance to the design of these openings. Most of the main types occur within the Palace and thus all are contemporary and of the fifteenth century.

Probably the earliest external opening form (and one not found at Songo Mnara) is a simple arch, its profile unbroken at the level of its springing, and the only relief being one (or possibly two) recessed orders, following the line of the arch. Such arches occur at Tumbatu, the Jamia of Mnarani (Kenya), and the early mosque of Kaole. This doorway type may well have ceased by very early in the fifteenth century. More common is the simple arch with unbroken profile surrounded by a rectangular recess. This type is found in the early mosque of Ras Mkumbuu (Fig. 84A), in the House of the Barrel Vault and the main mosque of Songo Mnara, at the Jamia of Gedi, at the later Kaole mosque and at Kunduchi (Fig. 84B). In a more complex version of this, the rectangular recess remains, but encloses an arch of one or more orders to jamb and arch separated by a typical capital which breaks both the face and the profile of the arch. Such arches occur in the subsidiary doors of the main Palace court of Songo Mnara (Fig. 84D), in the south part of the Great Mosque at Kilwa, in the fifteenth-century section of the Malindi mosque of Kilwa, and at Dege. The outer face of this capital is however, frequently flush with both spandrel and outer jamb (with only the recessed orders of arch and jamb set back from it) or, as at Songo Mnara, flush with the outer face of the surround. This, the opening with recessed orders in a rectangular recess, was probably the basic and commonest doorway type. Many doorways of which only the floor plan remains have rebates on their inner and outer faces, which would correspond to such doors (the early Jamia of Ungwana; Mnarani; Muhembo; the Small Domed Mosque, the Jangwani mosque and the fifteenth century part of the Malindi mosque at Kilwa; and many more). This is also the basic form of all mihrabs—though in these the rectangular frame is formed by a projecting architrave. Architraves also frame the main doors of the Palace at Songo Mnara (Fig. 16). In these doors the capitals only interrupt the profile or reveal of the two outer orders of the arch and not their faces, while the inner arch profile and arch face remain unbroken. This arch type with all the emphasis on the little rebates breaking the arch profile is unusual and these Palace doors are almost the only example of it on the coast. It is perhaps a treatment more suited to a facing for there is little depth to the mouldings or emphasis on the capital.

In the inner central door of the mosque of Fakhr ad Din (Fig. 65), the finest surviving doorway of the entire coast, this type of capital occurs. This doorway is entirely faced with marble slabs, 10 cms. thick and up to 50 × 110 cms. in area (Fig. 82A). The four orders of the door are recessed only 1 cm. from their neighbour so that these little "corbels" or mouldings are the only emphasis given to the springing. They are curvilinear in form based on a cavetto on two cyma reversa mouldings. The architrave is replaced by a diaper patterned surround above springing level, surmounted by a triple frieze. This arch had bosses inset in the spandrels and a nick at its apex. The shallow depth necessitated by using a marble facing is more than compensated by the richness and precision of surface decoration of the carving. This type of arch springing in coral occurs elsewhere in this mosque, and in the thirteenth century Mogadishu Jamia tower entrance (Fig. 67). Brackets at capital level supporting only an upper architrave to frame the opening, the broken profile of tiny corbels as the only emphasis of the springing, the projecting conical boss and the frieze above the architrave (to contain an inscription) may be considered characteristic features of the Somali architecture of the thirteenth century and are not found to the south.

At the Palace of Songo Mnara, the simplest door form (Fig. 84C) is that in which the capital again has rebates to the reveals alone and its face is flush with the wall face, with a rectangular recess only above it. In other words, there are no recessed jamb orders but the arch spandrels are recessed. The "recessed spandrel" type of arch framing also occurs typically in the doors of the thirteenth century inner lining wall of the northern part of the Great Mosque of Kilwa, and the doors of the Sultansmausoleum nearby (Fig. 18). The "recessed spandrel" is also characteristic of a group of simple mihrabs of the late sixteenth century and later.

The simplest opening type is a plain archway, without recessed orders, rectangular frame or capitals. It does not occur at Songo Mnara and it is probably most common after the mid-sixteenth century, at such sites as Tiwi, Diani, Kitoka, Jumba la Mtwana and the Jemadari mosque of Malindi, and characteristic of them. It was probably also found, however, at earlier sites—in the minor mosques of Gedi, at Tongoni, Ndumi and the outer doors of the earlier Kaole mosque side rooms—for the floor plans of these mosques show that the doorways had neither mouldings nor recesses at their base, though they are destroyed above the level of the capitals and may have had recessed spandrels or even been square headed.

On their inner faces many of these openings are contained within a rectangular recess, its head and foot lined in timber. These have already been described when their structural considerations were discussed in Chapter II. The square headed doorway with timber lintol is a much rarer form. It is universal after the eighteenth century, and frequent on Pemba a little earlier. But it occurs earlier at Husuni Kubwa, the Mosque of the Sarcophagi at Gedi, and early sixteenth century Ungwana. With these exceptions it is not found before the late eighteenth century.

Husuni Kubwa

As one would expect, many of the decorative elements found in the Palace of Husuni Kubwa are of unique design, and of a quality and variety unparalleled elsewhere on the East African coast. They are found particularly in the domestic quarters and the vaulted reception rooms of the Palace (the latter have been described in Chapter III while the layout of the Palace is described in detail in Chapter VIII, Figs. 68, 69). The self-contained "house" at the northern tip of the headland of Husuni Kubwa, commanding the sea approaches to the Palace, had a richer variety of applied decoration than any other part of the whole complex. These elements are all now fallen and in fragments, and their original positions cannot be established with certainty. It seems clear however that dadoes, door jambs, cornices and the gable ends of barrel vaulted rooms were all embellished with finely carved coral panels of varying design. Although these single storied rooms, with a standard domestic layout, were not the main living quarters of the owner (which are found further south in the central core of the Palace complex), they were not only more richly decorated than the main house, but were also vaulted in part. From them came the only three inscriptions found at Husuni. One invokes God's guidance on al Hasan ibn Sulaiman al Malik al Mansur, the second contains good wishes to the occupants of the building, while the third, a highly intricate and decorative work, with foliage interlacing the text, is as yet undeciphered.

Several openings were surrounded by fine, carved coral, cable pattern mouldings, in single or double strands, mitred or, more usually, continued round corners in a single block (Fig. 2E). Others had a frame of a plain faced, but equally precise, carved coral surround with chamfered sides (Fig. 72A). The angle brackets, between the ceiling rafters of the main domestic quarters, were particularly large and elaborate, with a concave curved face surrounding a plain, semicircular moulding (Fig. 72B). The use of such curved forms is extremely unusual on the coast and is only found outside Husuni in the almost contemporary thirteenth century capitals of the monolithic columns of early extensions of the Great Mosque of Kilwa (Fig. 15) and in the almost identical column capitals of the thirteenth-century portico of the Mosque of Fakhr ad Din, Mogadishu (Fig. 65).

At Husuni, carved coral friezes, probably at cornice or door head level, continue the curved motifs in a series of delicate, concave faced, semicircular headed mouldings, forming a small "blind arcade" (Fig. 72 D and E). The concave face may be either carved directly from the coral (Fig. 72E), or formed in plaster between tiny ribs of coral—an easier but less delicate technique (Fig. 72D). More elaborate still were the carved blocks which probably filled the gable ends of the barrel vaults of the rooms of the "house" at the northern end of the site (Fig. 72 F and G). Rooms in this "house" also had as a frieze, probably at cornice level, a series of square coral panels with a strange "dart" motif (Fig. 72K)—a unique design. Below them, a series of coarse triangular recesses, in, and of, the masonry of the wall, and plastered, form an emphatic string course. This is the only case, before the eighteenth century, of a moulding that is not entirely, or almost entirely, of carved coral. Both its size and depth prevented the use of the normal technique.

In the same area, there was a dado (Fig. 72I) of square coral panels or "tiles", laid diagonally. Each tile is decorated with a raised cross, the arms pointed and running from corner to corner. Once assembled, there is a regular eight pointed star shaped area between the raised arms of the adjoining crosses. Because this area now appears to have an unsightly and irregular surface between tiles, it has been supposed that it was intended that star shaped glazed tiles (a typical thirteenth century Near Eastern type) should fill the areas between the raised crosses. No trace of such glazed tiles has been found and, in fact, the irregularities of both the carving and the spacing of the coral tiles would have prevented the insertion of standardized glazed units between them.

Tiles carved with a raised cross with pointed ends have been found elsewhere only at Ungwana (Fig. 72J)—a site where the vaulted side room of the Ungwana Jamia is closely linked in design to the vaulted rooms of Husuni Kubwa. The tiles of Ungwana have two upright crosses set vertically, not diagonally, on each tile. The similarity between these and those of Husuni is, however, close and clear.

In the same Northern "house" of Husuni from which the "dart" shaped tiles, the "raised cross" tiles and the inscriptions came, two bosses were found also (Fig. 82B, C).

These large, finely carved, coral bosses are unlike any others of the coast, for though they do not have the naturalistic elements of early bosses (such as those of Mnarani), the large geometric decoration of "star" and "curved radii" are far better designed and carved, simpler, and more emphatic than the shallow, incised patterns of radii and concentric circles of bosses of the sixteenth century and later, which are not related to them.

Finally, a single large "fleur de lys" (Fig. 72H) carved in coral was found in the area of the vaulted rooms of Husuni. This, though simplified and slightly rigid in shape, is a typical motif of the Near East—and is closely paralleled, for instance, in a stucco dado in a room in the ninth century Palace of al Mutasim at Samarra.

The applied decoration of Husuni, like the complex plan and the vaulted roof forms, remains a unique flowering of a quality never subsequently paralleled. The carving was done locally and many of the "tiles" and "bosses" remained unfinished, still retaining the carver's guide lines. One "dart" tile was found, still incompletely carved, isolated on the floor of a room in the central domestic core of the Palace, well away from the site of the finished work. All the tiles exhibit slight irregularities in their carving, which is naturally most noticeable in the more complex designs.

CHAPTER V

ARCHAEOLOGICAL EVIDENCE

Archaeological excavation has, in the last fifteen years, played an increasing role in understanding the culture of the coast and dating some of the more notable remains. The sites that have been excavated and dated provide the most satisfactory "datum points", from which one can attempt to build a sequence of architectural development. All the published dating conclusions resulting from excavation, and a very brief description of the evidence on which these are based, will be given below.

Dating depends predominantly on finds of imported porcelain and glazed ware from the Islamic Near East and from the Far East. Locally made unglazed wares exist on every site but they vary greatly from area to area and cannot, in themselves, provide more than a relative date applicable only to a limited locality—they cannot give the absolute dating that the imports, common to all coastal sites, give with greater or lesser precision. Their value is great in amplifying the evidence of ceramic imports, and in clarifying detailed and local problems of date and relationship, and, even more, in giving a clear picture of the everyday life of the coast, but they can be largely ignored in this brief résumé.

The earliest imported pottery is Islamic "sgraffiato", a ware with a mottled glaze applied over a light slip, which has had hatched patterns incised in it. It is a characteristic Islamic ware, known from ninth and tenth century Samarra to the early sixteenth century, and spreading not only to East Africa, but to Bhambor in Scinde, where it occurs in eighth to twelfth century levels. The date of its occurrence in East Africa has been difficult to fix with precision. The sherds found in East Africa appear to resemble most closely those of Samarra. The dating of ninth- to tenth-century at this site, if correct, cannot in any way be reconciled with the East African evidence, nor with the evidence of the Far Eastern imports associated with the latter. In East Africa, sgraffiato is probably most characteristic of the thirteenth century. It probably also occurred somewhat earlier, for the earliest levels at Kizimkazi contain sgraffiato and they are probably contemporary with the early twelfth-century inscription. At Ungwana, sgraffiato continues into the fifteenth century. Early in the fourteenth century sgraffiato is largely replaced, especially in Kenya, by a poor quality glazed Islamic ware, in which black linear and geometric patterns occur on a yellow background—"black on yellow" ware. This ware continued into the early fifteenth century but then ceased. It is rare in the south and at Kilwa, and may well be absent from many sites. Chinese celadons were introduced in the mid-thirteenth century, increasing at the end of the century, when small quantities of porcelain, of the Yuan dynasty (1279–1368), appear. In the second half of the fourteenth century large quantities of Ming dynasty (1368–1644) celadon occur. Chinese blue and white porcelain occurs from the early fifteenth century and by the end of the century is dominant over the celadons, very rare examples even being found in the early part of the century. The development of blue and white porcelain provides good dating evidence from the fifteenth until the nineteenth century. In the second quarter of the fifteenth century, the black on yellow Islamic ware was replaced by the very common, lead glazed, monochromes, predominantly in blue and green, and by rarer figured bowls with a tin glaze on a sugary body. The latter were the wares so characteristically inset in the vaults of the fifteenth century buildings of the Kilwa group. Iberian majolica imitations of the Chinese blue and white porcelains appear in the sixteenth century, with the advent of the Portuguese.

Husuni Kubwa and early Kilwa

One of the many factors that make Husuni Kubwa (Figs. 68, 69) a key site of the coast is that it is an entirely homogeneous building of a single period, occupied for only a short time. Indeed, from the many examples of unfinished building work (such as the partially dressed and carved blocks [found in several areas of the site] and the frequent walls that were intended to have, but did not receive, their final plaster finishing coats) it may not have been completely finished before it was abandoned. The excavations conducted at Husuni[1] have yielded little imported ware—some Chinese celadon, porcelain and stoneware, and a fine Yuan dynasty flask. The latter has been dated to A.D. 1300, a date supported by the porcelain sherds. An intricate, interlaced inscription, as yet unread, has been compared to an inscription of A.D. 1240 in Cairo. A further inscription contains the name of a Sultan, al Hasan ibn Sulaiman al Malik al Mansur, while all four coins found in the fill of the small well in the domestic court are of a Sultan Sulaiman ibn al Hasan. These two sultans can be related to the Kilwa Chronicle sequence of the sultans Sulaiman ibn al Hasan, reigning in 1294–1308, and his son, Hasan, reigning in 1310–1333. The latter's reign was securely dated for he was the sultan visited by Ibn Battuta in 1331. All the evidence quoted thus points to Husuni being occupied and abandoned at the very beginning of the fourteenth century. More recent finds (to be published by H. N. Chittick) indicate that it was built somewhat earlier, but it is most unlikely to have been in use for any lengthy period.

In the vicinity of, but not within, the Great Mosque (Fig. 15) in the town of Kilwa itself, sherds of local Husuni wares are stratified in early levels yet above those containing sgraffiato wares. We have seen how the Chronicle tells that a great dome was used by al Hasan ibn Sulaiman for prayer. This can only be the great dome at the south-east corner of the Great Mosque, which is certainly contemporary with the earliest extensions of that building. These early extensions must also therefore belong at least to the very early fourteenth century, and, indeed, coins of a Hasan bin Sulaiman have been found in floor levels corresponding to these extensions in another section of the mosque. The original mosque and the reinforcing wall lining its inner face predate these extensions and must date back at least to the thirteenth century. The coursed masonry of the walls and finds of sgraffiato sherds beneath the earliest floors confirm that the original mosque and the inner reinforcing wall belong to the earliest surviving building period of the coast, predating Husuni Kubwa. It is reasonable to presume that the original mosque predates the early extensions of the mosque by a considerable period, to allow for the decay and consequent collapse of the first roof and the subsequent strengthening of the walls, by the addition of an inner lining, to take a new roof.

Ras Mkumbuu

The mosque of Ras Mkumbuu (Fig. 4) on Pemba island has been excavated.[2] The mosque is considered to be a homogeneous structure, with only minor subsequent alterations. Excavation shows that north wall, mihrab and columns are certainly

---

[1] H. N. Chittick: Journal of African History, IV. 2 (1963).
[2] J. S. Kirkman: T.N.R. 53, 1959.

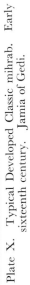

Plate X. Typical Developed Classic mihrab. Early sixteenth century. Jamia of Gedi.

Plate IX. Typical Early Classic mihrab. Fifteenth century. Tongoni Mosque.

contemporary. While there are three occupation levels or floors outside the mosque, there are certainly no earlier floors within it. The sherd pattern, not only from inside and outside the mosque, but also over the entire site is identical. It could not, therefore, have been occupied for more than two hundred years at the most, and such a completely stable sherd pattern is unlikely to span much more than one hundred years, with the building of the mosque taking place towards the end of this period. Not a single Chinese blue and white, Islamic monochrome or black on yellow sherd was found. The absence of the latter may not be significant, but the absence of the former types must mean that the site was abandoned by the mid-fifteenth century if not by the start of this century. The imported sherds consist of Chinese celadon, plain white porcelain and sgraffiato. The only bead was of blue wound glass, a typical early bead form. The majority of the porcelain compares with fourteenth century, or very early fifteenth century sherds from Gedi, though the earlier sherds are wares of the late thirteenth century. The sgraffiato sherds are also comparable to sherds from late thirteenth and fourteenth century levels at Gedi, Kilepwa and Ungwana. The evidence all indicates, therefore, an occupation basically of the fourteenth century, but probably stretching from the late thirteenth century to the early fifteenth century. The mosque was, therefore, probably built in the late fourteenth century.

Mnarani

The Jamia of Mnarani[1] (Fig. 28) has passed through three major stages of reconstruction.

The only sections of the original mosque that survive are the lowest portions of the external walls of the main hall and, apparently, the mihrab. The mosque had a western extension, probably only a sunken court. The levels corresponding to this period of the mosque yielded no dateable sherds at all.

In the second mosque, side rooms were added on the west and east (the latter divided into two to form an entrance lobby at its north end) and a verandah on the south, while rectangular piers (46 × 81 cms.) ran longitudinally north and south. The ablution arrangements of the south court date from this period. The characteristic sherds of this period are Islamic black on yellow wares. These are fourteenth century wares which die out in the early fifteenth century. The celadon sherds are fourteenth or fifteenth century types, and so are the local wares, though certain of these, on comparison with dated Gedi sherds, belong to the fifteenth century only. Because of the latter, the second mosque has been dated to the very early fifteenth century, rather than to the fourteenth century.

This mosque collapsed and the south and west walls and doors were rebuilt on the earlier foundations, as were the piers (now 46 cms. square); the doors of the south-east side room were blocked, except for that at the south-east corner of the mosque. Two of the west doors of the mosque were also blocked, while a large cistern was built in the south court. Alterations to the west side room and the south verandah also took place. Chinese blue and white porcelains of the late fifteenth century dominate the imported sherds, which included blue and green Islamic monochrome sherds and the fragments of an almost complete late sixteenth century blue and white porcelain dish. All were found, however, in unsealed levels above the second mosque floor. These alterations cannot, therefore, be securely related to sealed, stratified archaeological levels. The large cistern, however, was artificially filled with builder's rubble which included a late fifteenth century Chinese blue and white sherd. Surface finds indicate that the site was occupied until the late sixteenth century, but not after that. Traditionally,

[1] J. S. Kirkman: Ars Orientalis, III, 1959.

5

Mnarani was destroyed by the Galla in the early seventeenth century and archaeological evidence seems to confirm this.

The Small Mosque at Mnarani (Fig. 19) is best dated by a blue and white majolica dish set in the mosque cistern, a Portuguese imitation of a Chinese design. This can only have been acquired subsequent to the Portuguese incursions of the early sixteenth century. However, the mosque is built on the site of a smaller, earlier mosque, whose mihrab foundations are still visible beside the present mihrab and whose central axis lay 180 cms. east of the present mosque axis. It adjoined the large panel tomb, whose wall is now incorporated in the north wall of the mosque. The make-up of the floor of this earlier mosque yielded late fifteenth century sherds, so it had only a short life immediately previous to the existing mosque.

Kilwa

The dating of the early sections of the Great Mosque of Kilwa have already been briefly discussed. Finds from the excavations of the great southern vaulted extensions (Fig. 15) of this mosque will be published by H. N. Chittick and cannot therefore be described here. It is sufficient to say that all the evidence appears to confirm the report given in the Kilwa Chronicle of the rebuilding of these portions of the mosque in the reign of Muhammed ibn Sulaiman in 1421–1442. This date can be extended to cover the extremely uniform style of all the vaulted buildings within the Kilwa area, including the major part of the town of Songo Mnara. All archaeological evidence strongly supports dates within the fifteenth century for virtually all these buildings, though some of them, especially on Songo Mnara, may well be sixteenth century. Songo Mnara also contains minor building additions clearly of much later date, typical of the late eighteenth century.

Gedi

The Jamia of Gedi (Fig. 24) again has a complex history of building and rebuilding.[1] Little remains of the earliest mosque, though the plan of its main hall was followed in subsequent rebuildings. The site of Gedi was probably not occupied until the very late thirteenth century. The earliest levels contain Islamic sgraffiato, yellow on black wares and Chinese celadon sherds but, by the time of the building of the first Jamia, Islamic monochrome and Chinese blue and white sherds are already present. It cannot be earlier than the mid fifteenth century.

The mosque was rebuilt and it is this second mosque that forms the major part of the existing building. The floor of the main hall was raised 15 cms. and piers (54 cms. square) built. The east and west verandahs, the ablution arrangements, and the staircase to the roof outside the north-east corner of the mosque belong to this period. Mid fifteenth century blue and white porcelain occurs in the make-up of the floor.

In the third and final mosque, rectangular 54 × 88 cms. piers run across the mosque, built on the earlier stubs. The mihrab and south wall were rebuilt and pilasters added to the other walls. A single sherd of Iberian blue and white majolica found in the fill of the floor dates this mosque (like the Small Mosque of Mnarani) to the early sixteenth century at the earliest.

Finally the south ends of the mosque and the east verandah were divided off from the main mosque by solid walls, while the roof stair collapsed and was left unrepaired. In the early sixteenth century Gedi was sacked and abandoned, but then briefly re-occupied. Late sixteenth century Chinese blue and white wares were found in the occupation deposit on the mosque floor. By the end of the sixteenth century, building

[1] J. S. Kirkman: The Arab City of Gedi.

and town life had ceased, probably due to the Zimba raids of 1589 and the move by the Sheikh of Malindi to Mombasa in 1593. In the early seventeenth century the coming of the Galla probably brought about the final desertion of the town.

The houses, minor mosques and Palace of the town of Gedi (Fig. 76) date in the main from the fifteenth century, though one house goes back to the fourteenth century and the two latest houses were built during the final sixteenth century reoccupation.

Ungwana

Ungwana[1] (Fig. 23) was probably the town known to the Portuguese as Hoja, and sacked by them in 1505. Excavation confirms that certain structures were burnt at this date and that soon after there was a period of major rebuilding activity.

The town was founded at the end of the twelfth century. The first of the two adjoining Jamia was built in the early fifteenth century—prior to the introduction of blue and white or Islamic monochrome wares. Late varieties of sgraffiato (which apparently survived at Ungwana longer than elsewhere) and black on yellow wares comprise the imported wares. In the late fifteenth century the vaulted side room was built to the west and soon after the second Jamia was built to the east. During this period both Islamic monochrome and Chinese blue and white porcelain occur.

The second Jamia, in its early form, had three rows of columns across its width. In the great rebuilding of the early sixteenth century, this Jamia was rebuilt and the columns reduced to two rows. This period is marked by an increase in the amount of Chinese porcelain found, including certain sixteenth century types in small quantities. The small mosque with the domed mihrab (Fig. 30), built originally in the early fifteenth century, was also rebuilt in the sixteenth century at about the same time as the second Jamia, for the sherd patterns are identical. By the end of the century, like all the towns of the northern mainland, Ungwana was abandoned.

Takwa

The minor excavations of Takwa (Fig. 25)[2] unfortunately yielded little dateable material—the only cut in the main hall of the mosque itself gave no indication of date at all, though it showed that there were no earlier structures below the present floor. The main evidence only provided dates for the foundation and abandonment of the settlement itself. An examination of the fabric of the mosque shows that the main hall and mihrab and the enclosure walls to the south of it are the earliest structures. There is a possibility that the walls of the hall itself were rebuilt, particularly the south wall and the south-west corner. The east verandah and a room adjoining the south west corner of the mosque were then added. Finally, the west verandah was added with semicircular arched openings and a pitched thatched roof of light timbers, supported not on the wall top but on timber beams spanning between masonry stub pillars to leave a ventilation gap under the eaves. These features are normally very late in date and the eaves ventilation gap is found in many of the better Swahili houses today, while sloping thatched roofs are typical of present-day structures and never occur in the early architecture of the coast. A pitched roof also occurred on the south room.

Set in the cistern, added to the east outer wall of the south chamber, are three bowls—one an early variety of Islamic monochrome, the second a typical green glazed Islamic monochrome, and the third of Iberian blue and white majolica with a Maltese cross at its centre—a mid sixteenth century piece. The main hall of the mosque predates the cistern which would probably have been added at the same time as the east verandah.

---

[1] Excavated by J. S. Kirkman, unpublished.
[2] J. S. Kirkman: Ars Orientalis, II, 1957.

In a cut by the well, the lowest levels yielded sixteenth century, late Ming, blue and white wares and Near Eastern imitations of these wares of the same date. There were also two sherds of celadon, of a type commonest at Gedi in the late fifteenth century and early sixteenth century. Nothing older has been found at Takwa. The commonest of the later sherds was a glazed earthenware which at Gedi occurs in the very latest levels, of the late sixteenth century and early seventeenth century. A tomb at Takwa has the date A.H. 1094/A.D. 1682. The settlement appears then to date from the sixteenth century, to flourish in the seventeenth century and to have been abandoned soon after. The main hall and mihrab of the mosque probably belong at the start of this period. This is however, largely a conclusion drawn from negative evidence— the absence of earlier or later sherds—and therefore not completely reliable, though the abundance of eighteenth and nineteenth century porcelain at other sites in the Lamu group is certainly absent here.

Summary

The archaeology of these few sites provides the most reliable evidence of the date of the coastal buildings. The degree of precision that is obtainable is also apparent—little can be fixed more precisely than a quarter of a century. Written records and the broad indications of the early known history amplify the archaeology but are, in most cases, less completely reliable. Only the Kilwa Chronicle (used in conjunction with Ibn Battuta, and certain Portuguese records) and the inscriptions of Mogadishu give precise dates in terms of actual years to any coastal building.

The original Great Mosque of Kilwa and the inner wall built to reinforce it date from at least the thirteenth century and probably considerably earlier, for the earliest southern extensions to it (that is a court lined with an arcade supported on monolithic columns, and the Great Dome in the south-east corner) date from the very early fourteenth century. Husuni Kubwa was probably built in the thirteenth century, for it was abandoned in the early fourteenth century. Ras Mkumbuu is late fourteenth century, and the main part of the Jamia at Mnarani very early fifteenth century with late fifteenth century additions. The great vaulted extensions to the Great Mosque of Kilwa are mid fifteenth century, as are related vaulted buildings at both Kilwa and Songo Mnara. The houses and minor mosques of Gedi are also fifteenth century while the mihrabs and important surviving structures of the Jamia of Gedi and Ungwana and the small mosques of Mnarani and Ungwana are all early sixteenth century, as is the mihrab of the mosque at Takwa. The final alterations to the latter date from the late seventeenth century.

From these fixed points it will be attempted to build up a typological sequence for the architecture, based in the main on the design of the mihrabs of the mosques. This must fundamentally depend for its validity on the evidence given in this chapter—which in both quantity and precision is less than is desirable for any degree of certainty. As typological inferences are drawn, so the little certainty there is must be lessened, for it is already clear that the architecture of the coast is homogeneous and within it, for long periods, development was sparse and erratic. The prosperity of the independent towns varied greatly under such influences as the arrival of new immigrants, Portuguese or Omani interference or the Galla invasions. Towns isolated from external pressures continued to use the old and slowly declining style of the early architecture long after towns in other areas had adopted new and vigorous designs adopted from abroad.

CHAPTER VI

MIHRAB DESIGN

The most sensitive indicator of change and development in style and decoration is bound to be the mosque mihrab. It has no other purpose than to indicate the direction of Mecca towards which all worshippers face. There are therefore no limitations placed on its design by its function, beyond the fact that it should be easily visible and, indeed, the focal point of the mosque. As such, almost all internal decoration is spent on it. Through its religious associations, this decoration will be strongly disciplined in style by tradition. Decoration, especially surface carving, was also applied to the timberwork of rafters and cornices. But virtually none of this survives, by the very nature of its material, whereas the mihrab, protected by Islamic law against the re-use of its materials for anything but another religious building and by the inherent strength of its construction, is the likeliest element of any building to survive.

The basic mihrab form on the coast (Fig. 2) is a simple apse roofed by a semi-dome, within an arched opening, surrounded by a simple rectangular frame or architrave. By its size alone it dominates the mosque. It is however, frequently partly obscured by a central row of columns, and the rectangular, compartmented nature and unarticulated space of all mosque plans fails to centre attention on the mihrab or lead the eye towards it. This is compensated by the fact that it normally occupies at least a third of the surface of the north wall and the architrave usually approaches the ceiling cornice in height.

A clear and unbroken development of style and technique links the earliest surviving mihrabs to those of the eighteenth century. The mihrabs have however been divided into groups for convenience of analysis. The early, developed, and neo-classic styles are followed in the eighteenth century by either derivative developments of, or manner-ist departures from, the basic style.

Kaole

The earliest mihrab studied appears to be that of the early Kaole mosque (Fig. 3). The arch of this mihrab is made, not of close fitted blocks of dressed coral, but of un-dressed ragstone with a plastered finish. The arched entrances to the main hall are identical in design to the mihrab arch, and they also, like the shallow external pilasters which occur at each corner and in the centre of each side wall of the main hall, are of ragstone. Nothing of the original structure, besides the wall containing the mihrab, these pilasters and entrance arches (i.e. the wall of the main hall of the mosque) survives unaltered. The technique used in their construction certainly precedes that of fitting and dressing coral blocks, which is found in the mihrab apse itself, in the east side room, and in the fourteenth or fifteenth century panel tombs which abut the main hall to north and east. All these have been very clearly added to the main hall at a later date. The main hall, with dressed coral angle brackets between the rafters, has even been re-roofed at a later date. External pilasters occur at each corner and down the sides of only one other mosque—the original Great Mosque at Kilwa. There, the existing mihrab and doors are later additions and their original form is consequently unknown. The salient angles of the Kilwa pilasters are also un-dressed, while the masonry of the wall is coursed—a characteristic early form of walling, but one not found at Kaole. This part of the Great Mosque has been shown to be no later than the thirteenth century. The mosque of Sanje ya Kati, which has been visited, but not planned, by the author, also has walls of coursed masonry while its mihrab, like that of Kaole, has its mouldings formed in undressed masonry. At Sanje ya Kati the mihrab apse is entirely contained within the wall thickness, a feature unique on the coast, except for the tiny mihrab in the side room of the mosque of Tumbatu (Fig. 12). Before its alteration, the mihrab apse of Kaole may well have been similar in form to that of Sanje ya Kati, an archaic feature which was therefore necessarily altered when the Kaole mosque was enlarged. Excavations at Sanje ya Kati, with large quantities of sgraffiato ware as the sole import, confirm the very early date of the mosque and its characteristic coursed masonry walling.

At Kaole, the single wide, but shallow, recessed order of the mihrab arch without a capital or break at its springing; the ogival shape of the arch resulting from the partic-ularly large nick at its apex and the absence of an architrave surrounding the mihrab (which is placed instead in a shallow rectangular recess) are all unique. The tiny main hall had a central row of columns whose rafters spanned only 2·00 m., while an early side room on the east was only 1·80 m. wide. A room of similar dimensions probably also occurred on the west These small spans are also unique—and it is not surprising that these side rooms were later demolished and extended to their present dimensions. Excavation of the mosque showed that it is built on an artificial fill of sand, 1·20 m. deep, which rests on a thin but very profuse occupation deposit covering the original shore sand. A single sgraffiato sherd of an early type occurred in this basal deposit, which certainly does not represent a settlement but either rubbish thrown on the shore or, more probably, intensive but temporary camps. It is a deposit com-posed almost entirely of large broken sherds of coarse local cooking vessels containing the shells of edible shellfish and fishbones. The mosque was certainly the first building, either temporary or permanent, in this area of the site at least, but the fill which would date it contains not a single imported sherd. There is no reason archaeologically to suppose that this mosque is not middle or late thirteenth century—the date so strongly suggested by the architecture—but this is not, unfortunately, conclusively proven by excavation.

Kaole remains unique in its mihrab design and paralleled in other features only at thirteenth-century Kilwa and Sanje ya Kati.

The coursed rubble walls of Kilwa and Sanje ya Kati, the external pilasters of Kaole and Kilwa, the undressed ragstone mouldings of Kaole and Sanje ya Kati, and the mihrab apse contained within the thickness of the north wall of Sanje ya Kati (and possibly originally at Kaole), would all seem to be characteristic features of the very rare remnants of the earliest mosques of the coast.

Early classic mihrab

The true early classic mihrab (Plate IX, Fig. 2) is surrounded by a plain architrave (about 250 cms. wide and 280 cms. high), formed by pilasters and lintol (all about 42 cms. wide, and projecting 8 cms. from the north wall), their edges formed by rough blocks with only the faces dressed to give a precise corner. A rectangular recess may occur in the pilasters with its base at the level of the capital. This recess, no doubt de-signed to contain a lamp, is framed by a single rebate. Within the architrave, finely dressed, close fitting and dry jointed coral blocks form arch orders and jamb shafts 7–8 cms. wide, recessed a similar depth. There are two recessed orders to the simple pointed arch and one to the jambs.   The capital is a plain square block of coral about 10 cms. high, normally projecting from, but often flush with, the spandrel and outer jamb face. It has one or more rebates to its underside.   The semicircular mihrab apse and semi-dome are regular in shape and have a completely plain plastered finish, sometimes broken by a string course (which occurs at the level of the capitals, and continues them round the apse, and reflects their mouldings).

Pilaster recesses may be absent and a nick or a raised archivolt and raised vertical panel at the arch apex may or may not appear.

The early classic mihrab occurs at Ras Mkumbuu in Pemba (Fig. 4) dated to the end of the fourteenth century; at Tongoni (Fig. 5), and in the two nearby mosques of Muhembo (Fig. 6), in Tanganyika; in the Small Mosque at Gedi (Fig. 10) (with raised archivolt, and an additional recessed jamb order) and in the other minor Gedi mosques of the Sarcophagi, the Long Conduit and the Three Aisles—all dated to the fifteenth century (Fig. 10); and at nearby Kiburugeni (Fig. 7).

In the mosque of Tumbatu (Fig. 12), the early classic mihrab form is found in the tiny mihrab of the east side room, whose shallow apse is contained in the wall thickness. Tumbatu, off north-eastern Zanzibar, was an important settlement when visited by Yaqut in the thirteenth century when it was also a refuge for the inhabitants of Unguja, the main town of Zanzibar.   It is not mentioned by the Portuguese so may well have been of only minor importance in the sixteenth century.   In the particularly large mihrab of the main hall of Tumbatu mosque (which only survives to capital level) the only development on the early classic type is a refinement of the architrave by excising two rebated mouldings from its inner edge.

Kilwa group

The mihrabs of the mid fifteenth century Great Mosque (Figs. 13, 15) and Small Domed Mosque (Fig. 14) of Kilwa are more difficult to relate to the normal classic mihrab.   A mosque at Kisimani Mafia (Fig. 13) is obviously very closely related to the Great Mosque in mihrab form and it also will be considered here.   All the mihrabs have the tall capital typical of the Kilwa area (though that of the Small Domed Mosque is unique in its double form and is grooved, a feature probably added much later).   The Small Domed Mosque mihrab does not have an architrave—only because the function of a frame is performed by the adjacent pilasters and structural arches. The architrave of the Great Mosque mihrab has a projecting outer moulding and two rebates to its inner edge (like Tumbatu) and this architrave is repeated at Kisimani, while rebates also occur on the recess framing the Small Domed Mosque mihrab. All have chamfered pilasters, and the arch of Kisimani is stilted.   The Small Domed Mosque mihrab has carved spandrel bosses, with bowls and a plaque inset above it. All these are characteristic features of the developed classic mihrab discussed below. The arrises of the Great Mosque arch orders are rebated, and the apse has a fluted semi-dome and multiple string course.   The two latter features occur in the mihrab of the Mnarani Jamia, but otherwise do not normally occur before the seventeenth century, when they are associated with a fluted apse which at Kilwa is plain.   Because of their atypical nature these designs are difficult to place precisely in the typological sequence. They are however, clearly developments on the early classic mihrab, though they are not typical of the true developed classic mihrab group.

Developed classic mihrab

The severity and simplicity of the early classic mihrab, with only large simple mouldings and many plain undecorated surfaces, is refined and the largest plain surfaces of the architrave broken, in the succeeding developed classic mihrab (Plate X). The advances introduced in this mihrab enhanced rather than destroyed the earlier style, and its forms are only the logical successors to the early classic mihrab, with no new or basic changes visible. In particular, the apse remains completely plain. The first developments on the early classic mihrab, if the mosques of the Kilwa group are neglected, took place in the early sixteenth century and the type may well have continued into the seventeenth century, overlapping with the later neo-classic mihrab, which is largely a regional development in the Lamu area.

The desire to break up the large plain area of the architrave, already seen at Tumbatu and Kilwa, is seen also at the small mosque of Mnarani (Fig. 19) where, above the level of the pilaster recesses, a plain recessed field framed by a single rebated moulding runs round the top of the architrave. In the main Palace doors of Songo Mnara (Plate V) the architrave is elaborated in an identical way. At the later mosque of Kaole (Fig. 20) too, the field of the architrave is very slightly recessed, both above and below the pilaster recess. There, a similar shallow recessed field also occurs in the outer jamb shafts of the mihrab. In both mosques there is an additional recessed order to the jambs, so that they, like the arches, now have not one but two recessed orders. Necessarily the moulded areas of the architrave are now formed of fine fitted blocks rather than the earlier type which had only their surfaces dressed.

The transition between architrave and mihrab may be elaborated by a second frame—a plain rectangular moulding of the normal square profile—occuring within the rectangle framed by the architrave: as at Kaole and the doors of Songo Mnara, mentioned above, at Mbweni (Fig. 20) and at Shengejuu (Fig. 22). In the latter mihrab this inner frame is doubled, to comprise two mouldings. Frequently this inner frame occurs only above the capital as an inner "spandrel frame", as in the mosque at the entrance to Mida Creek (Fig. 22). The multiple inner architrave frames of alternate outer cable pattern and inner plain mouldings—a characteristic development of the later stages of the developed classic mihrab—are broken by the capital but continue below it. These occur at Gedi Jamia (Fig. 21) and Takwa (Fig. 21). At the even later Jamia of Chwaka (Fig. 22) this is again doubled to give four orders to the spandrel frame. The multiplication of orders is characteristic of the developed classic style. At Takwa there are only the two normal arch orders, but at Gedi there are four, plus a raised archivolt. At Shengejuu, there are five orders to jambs and arches, each jamb united to its arch order by individual flush capitals, within a double inner architrave framing. Five orders occur in the jambs of Chwaka, but there each order consists of two parts, an outer herringbone, and an inner plain moulding, except for the innermost, which is a chamfered pilaster. As a result of the increased orders and the consequent increase in depth, both above and below the capital, a single capital no longer suffices. The capitals are, therefore, usually broken to form an inner and outer capital. The result is that the innermost jamb shaft (now changed in form from the remainder to become a chamfered pilaster, projecting in from the mihrab apse) has its own capital supporting the innermost arch order. This is a feature that will subsequently become extremely important, for, by uniting innermost jamb, capital and arch to form a single unit, the way lies open for treating the inner mihrab arch in a completely different way from those that frame it. Already the jamb, by becoming a chamfered pilaster, is treated in an individual manner. This feature occurs in the developed classic mihrabs of Takwa, Mida Creek and Gedi Jamia. All have a total of five orders within the outer architrave, and chamfered (except at Mida Creek) pilaster, inner capital and inner arch order are united.

Consequent on the introduction of Chinese blue and white porcelain in the late fourteenth century, and its subsequent popularity, porcelain bowls are often inset in spandrels and architraves of developed classic mihrabs. The number varies from the two bowls in the spandrel of Mbweni to the twelve spandrel bowls (plus three coral bosses) of Chwaka Jamia. The Jamia of Gedi has five spandrel, two pilaster and six apse bowls. Coral bosses may also be inset in the spandrels (as at Chwaka) or even in the architrave (as at Ungwana Jamia, Fig. 21). In the mihrab of the later Jamia of Ungwana it is only these bosses, with the rectangular tiles inset in both spandrels and architrave and the two additional orders to the jambs, that set it apart from the early classic mihrab—but this mihrab was probably largely rebuilt of earlier components when a change in the columniation and move of the main axis of the Jamia necessitated its repositioning.

The stilted arch is introduced in the Jamia of Gedi and occurs in an extreme form in the mosque at the entrance to Mida Creek.

Minor features, first found in the developed classic mihrab, are a raised floor to the mihrab apse and bases to the jamb shafts or chamfered pilasters. Only Ungwana and Mnarani would seem certainly to lack them.

It is difficult to date precisely the individual mihrabs within the developed classic mihrab group. The simple early types of Ungwana and the small mosque of Mnarani are early sixteenth century, with virtually only their boss or bowl insets to distinguish them from the early classic mihrab. No doubt the mosques of Kaole and Mbweni, where only the mouldings of the inner frame within the architrave are added, were built at the same time or soon after. By mid century, cable pattern mouldings, multiple arch and jamb orders, chamfered inner pilasters and broken capitals have been added. At Gedi the slightly stilted arch has also appeared—to be followed by the extreme form of stilting in the mihrab of the mosque of Mida Creek. This is not found in the Pemba mosques, but there the multiplicity of mouldings at both Chwaka and Shengejuu may well indicate a late sixteenth century or seventeenth century date—especially as there are no neo-classic mosques on the island. Chwaka especially, with its multiple herring-bone ornament, is likely to be late.

Mnarani

The mihrab of the Jamia of Mnarani (Fig. 27) has a slightly stilted arch with five orders of plain mouldings (without the rebated arris) plus a raised archivolt containing an inscription. The innermost arch order springs from a separate capital surmounting a chamfered pilaster. Cable pattern mouldings occur in the decoration, and the architraves appear to have had a recessed field, with a spandrel frame added within it. The spandrels are embellished with five carved coral bosses, the naturalistic palmette motif of the one remaining (Fig. 82H) being typical of the earlier boss styles. But for the latter detail, all these features are typical of the later developed classic mihrab.

The apse however, is completely different. A skirting lines its base in which a carved inscription (repeating the word "Allah" in monumental Naskhi script) is surmounted by a cable pattern moulding with a moulding unique to Mnarani, carved with an "angular S" pattern, above it (Fig. 82F). The apse itself has a delicate plaster vertical fluting, the flutes triangular in section, and at 5·5 cms. centres. These rise to a cornice which repeats the three parts of the skirting in reverse order (the inscription here is a verse from the Koran). The semi-dome is more coarsely fluted—the flutes measuring 15 cms. across their base, and again triangular in section.

The jamb shafts of the mihrab are replaced by a single panelled block—the outer face of which contains a rectangular panel surrounded by a cable pattern moulding framing a now heavily weathered inscription. The inner part of the jamb block, supporting the arch orders, was heavily restored in 1939, and it is not certain that there was not a series of the normal jamb shafts; but as restored, it again has a panel (with alternate cable pattern and "angular S" mouldings), running vertically, to decorate the inner edge of its reveal.

Apse and mihrab jambs therefore are quite unlike anything found in the developed classic mihrab, and are in fact typical of neo-classic mihrabs, while the remaining features of the design are those of late developed classic mihrabs. However, this mihrab is part of the second Jamia built in the very early fifteenth century. Only minor alterations to the Jamia took place in the late fifteenth century, and late sixteenth century sherds occur only in the topsoil and in no stratified mosque deposit. This seems an extraordinarily early date for a design such as this; typologically, only the bosses might suggest such a date. The style of the Jamia mihrab itself suggests a late sixteenth century date, at the end of the developed classic sequence and foreshadowing the neo-classic mihrab. The mihrab of the small mosque nearby (Fig. 19) belongs to an early phase of the developed classic style, and is dated archaeologically to the early sixteenth century, like several other mihrabs of this type. Yet this is a century later in date than the stylistically far more advanced Jamia mihrab. This anomaly between archaeology and architecture can probably only be explained by further excavation or study. It is possible that the mihrab alone was reconstructed in the Jamia to accord with a new style, in the same way that the mihrab of the Great Mosque of Kilwa certainly was— and this may well leave virtually no trace in the archaeological record if the floor level is left unaltered. Alternatively, at Mnarani a new design was introduced, to remain unique and without influence, even in the town itself, for over one hundred years.

Neo-classic mihrab

The small mosque of Ungwana was rebuilt after the Portuguese had sacked the town in the early sixteenth century. The mihrab of the Jamia of Ungwana is a simple version of the developed classic type, but the mihrab of the small mosque (Fig. 29) marks a major advance and initiates the neo-classic mihrab style. This mihrab is of great importance for it shows that this new style grew naturally from the old—occurring within the same town and during a period of major rebuilding affecting the whole town and, from the archaeological evidence, virtually contemporary with a mihrab rebuilt in the older style.

It retains many features of the developed classic mihrab—the architrave, the three orders of the inner spandrel frame, the inset bowls in the spandrels and the two orders of the slightly stilted, simple pointed arch. The chamfered pilaster is temporarily discarded. The arrises of the two inner arch orders now have the characteristic rebated moulding to their edge, while the innermost arch has a single semicircle cut from its apex—the first precursor of the trefoliate inner arch. The arches spring not from the normal shafts and capitals, but from a single "jamb block", panelled on its face and reveal, and whose wide top replaces the capitals. This, the panelled jamb block, is an important feature of neo-classic mihrabs, replacing the jamb shafts. The mouldings of the panels and within the upper part of the architrave are triangular in section. The strange domed mihrab apse, with its coarse, triangular fluting (covering only part of the apse) and its triangular plan, is unique. (The triangular apse did occur in the earlier Jamia but nowhere else.) Sensibly, the dome form was never repeated, for the complications of the apse dome are invisible from, and have no visual effect on, the mosque interior, while externally, the dome looks incongruous against the plain bulk of the mosque itself. It does, however, indicate that the whole design of this mihrab was at a pioneering and experimental stage, when such extravagances might be tried once and then discarded; and further, that this experimentation was taking place locally.

In the much larger mosque, the Jamia of Shaka (Fig. 27), a few miles to the north, the same new features—the rebated arris on the spandrel frame, and the panelled jamb blocks with a triangular moulding—are combined with the same wide, slightly stilted arch orders. Here the apse and innermost arch (supported on chamfered pilasters) have unfortunately been destroyed.

The mihrab of the little Jemadari mosque at Malindi (Fig. 29) was almost certainly built before the Sheikh of Malindi moved to Mombasa in 1593, and before Malindi faded quickly with the consequent economic decline, while under the menace of the Galla. Here the mihrab arches are extremely stilted and rise from panelled jamb blocks. The inner arch, supported on chamfered pilasters was certainly trefoliate—probably in no exaggerated form, though the cusps are unfortunately lost. The apse is fluted and has only a single cornice, while the semi-dome is more coarsely fluted—the flutes radiating from the arch apex (as at Kilwa and Mnarani). The architraves are completely plain and, indeed, the whole design has little surplus decoration—little more than vertical cable pattern mouldings to spandrel frame and jamb blocks. This is probably because it must, after all, have been only a minor mosque in sixteenth century Malindi, though it is the only one to survive. Nevertheless, its inner arch and apse forms approach still closer to the true neo-classic types which follow, soon after, in the Lamu area. Malindi is an early southern outlier to them.

At Manda (Fig. 31, Plate VI) the typical neo-classic mihrab, developed from the precursors of Mnarani, Ungwana, Shaka and Malindi, occurs full fledged for the first time. From the developed classic mihrab it retains the rectangular architrave or frame, the inner spandrel frames, coral bosses or bowl insets, the multiple orders of the (now very stilted) simple pointed arch, the chamfered pilaster to support the inner arch and (not at Manda itself, but elsewhere) the cable pattern moulding, though this has now deteriorated to the simpler herring-bone moulding. It is used particularly to frame and to break up into panels the recessed field of the architrave (in a manner very reminiscent of the north-western door of the thirteenth century mosque of Fakhr ad Din, Mogadishu, Plate VIII). New developments include the vertical fluting of apse, capped by multiple cornices corbelling inwards, frequently (as at Manda), having up to eleven separate moulding elements. These support a small and irregular semi-dome whose flutes radiate not from the arch apex but from a central spine of herring-bone moulding. New moulding forms, very characteristic of the neo-classic style, are the rebated arris and the multiple V-grooving to the moulding face. The panelled jamb block invariably replaces the earlier jamb shafts and capitals. It has already been seen how the innermost arch was, in the developed classic mihrab, already being treated as a separate unit of the design—a development carried a stage further at Ungwana, where a single semicircle or foil is cut from its apex—to become trefoliate at Malindi. This growth prepares the way for the climax: the almost rococo exaggerations and flared, double cusping of the complete trefoil of the neo-classic mihrab.

The mid seventeenth century, in which the neo-classic mihrab flowers, is also the period in which the first effect of Omani interest in the coast was felt, and this new influence on the culture may well have contributed a new but extremely characteristic feature—the exaggerated cusps of the trefoil arch—to the neo-classic mihrab. Much later, in the nineteenth century, when Omani influence was paramount, trefoliate mihrab arches are a characteristic feature, occurring universally, in many distorted forms, wherever, and whenever, the older culture had been submerged. Here, in the seventeenth century, when Omani influence had started but was by no means strong, and in the areas where Pate, representing the indigenous culture, was not only strong but growing in prosperity and power (as both the rival towns of the mainland and Portuguese interference declined)—a single strong new design element is incorporated in the otherwise slowly changing body of the neo-classic mihrab. Most importantly, the neo-classic mihrab is a development of the classic mihrab and not a departure from it. It can be seen arising at Ungwana, and many of its forms were present before that, at Mnarani. It is an organic growth of style, with minor elements from outside grafted on to it, but there is no abandonment of the early forms or replacement by something completely new. In its true form, the neo-classic mihrab is entirely restricted to northern Kenya; even its remote precursor exists no further south than Mnarani, and the immediate forerunners of Malindi and Ungwana are even nearer.

The neo-classic mihrab does represent a certain decline in the classic standards of design and workmanship. Complex surface decoration, represented by the incised mouldings, covers and elaborates the face of every moulding, obscuring and detracting from the simplicity of the previous forms. The intricacy and detail of this surface carving is such that it outruns the technical capabilities of both material and carver and irregularities abound. Moulding joints are rarely mitred, and the small herring-bone blocks, which replace the carefully joined earlier lengths of cable pattern, are particularly carelessly formed. Arches, and especially apse semi-domes, are irregularly made. The small size of the latter, further spoiled by the central spine and the multiple cornices, is a great decline from the large, simple forms of the earlier plain or simply fluted semi-dome. The lance-head boss above the arch has already been seen to be characteristic of mihrabs in the Pate area, and it occurs in all such neo-classic mihrabs.

The mihrab of Manda is typical of the early neo-classic style. So also are those of the small mosque (Fig. 31) and the mosque of Bwana Bakari (Fig. 31) in Pate (the latter uniquely retaining jamb shafts rather than the usual panelled jamb block). The Jamia of Siu (Fig. 33) and the Mosque with the Mnara at Siu (Fig. 33) have fine, and probably early, neo-classic mihrabs. As the style develops, the exaggerated flared double cusps of the trefoils may be replaced by a simple pointed cusp. This occurs in the two Siu examples and in the very plain mihrabs of Bwana Tamu, Pate (Fig. 32) (Bwana Tamu, after whom this mosque is named, and with whom it is almost certainly contemporary, greatly extended the power of Pate in the early eighteenth century), and the south-east (Fig. 32) and south-west (Fig. 32) mosques of Pate. The two latter are certainly late imitations of the earlier, purer style for plasterwork largely replaces dressed coral for the bosses and the outer arches, and the mihrab apses are plain. The mouldings of the neo-classic mosques of Faza (Plate XI, Fig. 33) and the Fort of Siu (Fig. 33) are entirely in plasterwork, and semicircular arches replace the simple pointed arch, though the earlier, flared double cusps of the trefoil are retained.

The neo-classic mihrab, foreshadowed at Mnarani, and introduced at Ungwana and Malindi, flourished and developed from the seventeenth century. The last example illustrated, from Siu, stands in an Omani fort of the very early nineteenth century. The neo-classic mihrab continues, in a coarse and simple form, to be built in the Lamu islands today, though all the subtleties of craftsmanship and design are lost and they are only crude imitations of the true neo-classic mihrab.

The towns on the islands of the Lamu group to which the neo-classic mihrab is restricted, were (particularly Pate) the last powerful and independent cities of the coast, flourishing anew and capable of extending their power outside their boundaries in the seventeenth century, in conjunction with their rising Omani allies or, frequently, rivals. This situation is reflected closely by the architecture. A vigorous and exuberant development based firmly on the earlier basic styles accepts minor, but very distinctive, features of its design from outside. It flourishes only in a restricted area, while elsewhere slowly declining and coarsened early design types persist.

Simplified classic mihrab

The neo-classic mihrab is restricted to northern Kenya. It is replaced in southern Kenya by a simplified classic mihrab and in Tanganyika by a mihrab whose design is a close imitation of the classic mihrab.

The simplified classic mihrab is, in its mouldings and construction, a typical classic structure. It has the plain apse, and simple pointed arch of this type. It is distinguished from it by the absence of an architrave, the only frame to the mihrab arch normally being a rectangular recess framing the arch spandrels. The jambs are plain, as is the arch itself, though the latter may have one recessed order. The origin of the simplified classic mihrab can be seen in the Jamia of Kitoka (Fig. 35). The simple mihrab of the Jamia has two orders to jamb and shafts. The capital is flush with the wall face but above it a recessed rectangle frames the arch spandrels. The pilasters of the architrave, in order to line up with the two rows of structural columns, are set so far to each side of the mihrab itself as almost to cease to act as a frame for it and, but for these pilasters, this would be a simplified classic mihrab. The octagonal columns, with brackets and niches to take lamps or incense burners, are identical to those of the early sixteenth century small mosque of Mnarani, six miles away, and are found nowhere else. The mosques must be close in time, therefore. Kitoka, like Mnarani, would have been abandoned under Galla pressure in the early seventeenth century. At the small mosque of Kitoka (Fig. 35), a short distance away, the simplified classic mihrab is present in a typical form (though the recessed rectangle framing it here extends to the floor). Simplified classic mihrabs (Fig. 35) occur at Diani, Mtwapa, Tiwi (an extreme form in which the mihrab has no frame or mouldings at all), and Jumba la Mtwana (Fig. 37). Outside the area it is also found in the domed mosque of Chwaka on Pemba (Fig. 35) (whose mihrab is completely plain like that of Tiwi) at Mtitimira near Kilwa (Fig. 42) and Kua off Mafia (Fig. 43). The mosque of Mgao Mwanya (Fig. 47) in the far south of Tanganyika is related to this group and would be identical to it, but for its coarse and simple inner trefoil arch. Possibly the little mosque of Mnarani, Tanganyika (Fig. 45), also belongs in this group. Its simple pointed arch, constructed in dressed coral blocks, had a single shallow recessed order but no further decoration; it is difficult to relate this mosque to any other group.

The plans of Diani (Fig. 36) and Tiwi (Fig. 38) are closely related to that of the Jemadari mosque of Malindi (Fig. 30) which, with its early neo-classic mihrab, probably dates from the late sixteenth century. It seems likely therefore that the simplified classic mihrab arose in the late sixteenth century and, no doubt, continued in the seventeenth century. The plans of the mosques of Kua and Mtitimira indicate that outside Kenya it probably dated from the mid eighteenth century. It is notable that the only post classic vaulted mosques, those of Tiwi, Chwaka and Jumba la Mtwana, though very different in their plans and vaulting, all have the simplified classic mihrabs of this group.

Derived classic mihrab

A series of mihrabs found in Tanganyika, particularly just south of Dar es Salaam, are closely modelled on those of the classic style. The quality of the workmanship is far inferior, however; dressed blocks are still used but they tend to be irregular in shape.

Mouldings are reduced in size and covered by a coarse plaster finish unlike the earlier fine white skim coat. The mihrabs also tend to be small in size (about 200 cms. wide, 220–250 cms. in height) and simplified in design.

Kimbiji (Fig. 40, Plate XII) is the most complex of the mihrabs of this group. It has two spandrel frame mouldings, five orders to the jamb and four to the arch, but the arch shape is extremely irregular, more triangular than a simple pointed arch. The orders vary as much as 10 cms. from true and these irregularities are taken up by their splayed, rather than right-angled, returns. The capital is also splayed and bent to enable it to remain a single unit of the design, instead of using the more normal two capitals to each side. The apse is not roofed by a semi-dome but by four massive and irregular corbelled cornices supporting a flat roof block.

Bandarini and Dege (Fig. 41), close together and close to Kimbiji, are typical of this group. Sala and Kutani (Fig. 46) nearby, whose mihrabs have been destroyed may, from the little evidence left, well fall within it. The mosque of Jibondo (Fig. 42), an island off Mafia, certainly does. The elaborate south door of Dege has incised capitals related to the neo-classic herring-bone mouldings.

In this group the designs remain static, imitating the classic mihrab; there is no development on this or departure from it. One may therefore well presume that this part of the coast, like that of southern Kenya, felt none of the influences from abroad that were stimulating the architecture of the north of Kenya. Here, design is static and standards of workmanship show a clear decline. These mosques are certainly no older than the seventeenth century, and more probably date from the mid eighteenth century, preceding the many mannerist designs of the late eighteenth and nineteenth centuries.

The foliate arch in Tanganyika

The inner trefoliate arch, so characteristic of the neo-classic mihrab, occurs at three sites in Tanganyika—Ndumi, Mgao Mwanya and Songo Mnara. These mihrabs, however, are not neo-classic in style but have a much firmer basis in the preceding developed classic mihrab.

Ndumi (Fig. 51) has a recessed field to its upper architrave, a moulding framing the spandrel, a plain apse and three orders of jamb shafts (rather than panelled jamb block) typical of the developed classic mihrab. But this only forms the basis for further developments. Architrave, spandrel frame and arch mouldings all have rebated arrises, typical of the neo-classic style, while the arch orders have a double moulding incised in their face, very similar to the typical neo-classic incised mouldings. Similar, but smaller, incised embellishments decorate the unique series of small bosses (which include a small lanceolate boss reminiscent of Pate lance-head bosses). The chamfered inner pilasters support an inner trefoil arch whose gentle curves would seem to be a precursor of the flamboyant neo-classic trefoils, in the same way that the inner arches of Ungwana and Malindi precede this form. The fine mouldings of the pilaster niches are also a typical late development on the developed classic mihrab forms. Every element of the design of Ndumi would thus seem to indicate that this is a southern outlier of the typical seventeenth century neo-classic mihrab form—and probably earlier than it, for Ndumi has closer affinities with developed classic forms.

The mihrab of Mgao Mwanya (Fig. 47), in southern Tanganyika, has already been mentioned as a simplified classic design, like those of the early seventeenth century in southern Kenya, with only a recessed spandrel frame to its arch. But it has in addition an inner trefoil arch springing from chamfered pilasters. The cusps of the trefoil are quite unlike the two flared lobes of the true neo-classic mihrab for they are square ended, and the normal rebated arris moulding to their edge is rather deeply and coarsely cut.

Songo Mnara

A single block found loose in the main mosque of Songo Mnara (Fig. 48) indicates that here too the inner mihrab arch was trefoliate and closely similar in form to that of Mgao Mwanya. The outer orders of this mihrab arch have completely disappeared. This single fallen block cannot, however, have come from any other position.

This mihrab has six recessed orders to its jambs, alternate orders being of herring-bone, with the innermost order a chamfered pilaster. The architraves are plain. In the apse a series of square pilasters form a blind arcade with semicircular arched heads supporting an upper row of arched niches. This apse decoration is entirely formed of fine dressed and carved coral blocks, and the niche forms have already been described as being of identical technique and design to those of the Palace doors of Songo Mnara (Fig. 16, Plate V), the south-east building of Kilwa, and a mosque at Kua (Fig. 47). The apse semi-dome is fluted with regular, triangular flutes radiating from the arch apex (c.f. Mnarani, Malindi and Kilwa Great Mosque). The main body of the mosque is crossed by transverse arches set in a rectangular frame supporting a flat roof. It has already been inferred that this arcade may well be an indigenous development from the arcade forms of vaulted mosques containing transverse barrel vaults.

The jamb shafts with their herring-bone mouldings (late developed classic style), the mihrab apse niches (typical of the fifteenth or early sixteenth centuries particularly in the Kilwa area), the semi-dome form (which certainly precedes the neo-classic mihrab dome in style), and the transverse arcade of the main hall (at the end of the development of the fifteenth century Kilwa vaulted buildings)—when considered together, suggest a date late in the development sequence of the classic mihrab, and late in the development of the vaulted Kilwa buildings, but certainly within both these sequences. Typologically, these features combine to imply a mid sixteenth century date, probably at the very end of the main building and occupation of the town of Songo Mnara.

A small mosque at Kua (Fig. 47), on Juani island off Mafia, has an "arcaded apse" whose recesses are made in the same fine carved coral technique used in Songo Mnara, whose arched upper niches are identical in form. The lower part is not however, a blind arcade but two superimposed rows of square recesses, the central ones originally containing inset porcelain bowls. It also has, like Songo Mnara, the plain architrave and three jamb orders, rather than a neo-classic jamb block. This mosque is certainly very close to that of Songo Mnara in every element of design and technique. It too may well have had a trefoliate inner mihrab arch.

The three mihrabs with inner trefoil arches in Tanganyika—Ndumi, Mgao Mwanya and Songo Mnara—would all appear to belong to the mid sixteenth century, representing early indigenous southern precursors to the neo-classic mihrabs of the north. They therefore precede known Omani influence on the coast and, like Ungwana, they are firmly based on varieties of the classic mihrab style. This does not, therefore, disprove that the vigorous style and flamboyant trefoils of the area round Lamu are due to external influence from Oman, instead of being a purely indigenous development. The strong and assured forms of the neo-classic mihrab, flowering completely, and comparatively suddenly, in a restricted area seems most likely to be due to an infusion of new purpose—and to a lesser extent, perhaps new ideas—from abroad. Parallel with this, it must be remembered that in the Lamu area and, in fact, everywhere along the coast the old culture and style continued its slow progress, perhaps not strongly, and often uncertainly. It was never completely halted or stultified.

Arcaded apse

The blind "arcaded apse" in the mihrabs of the main mosque of Songo Mnara and the Kua mosque marks a type which not only continued into the nineteenth century, but had its roots far back in the architecture of the coast. It is restricted to Zanzibar, Mafia and Tanganyika. Evidence for the date of the mosque of Kisimani Mafia, excavated in 1957,[1] where arcade pilaster stubs were found encircling the mihrab apse floor, is mainly based on stratified coins of the Kilwa sultans. In the light of the recent excavations at Kilwa itself these dates may well need revision. From the pottery evidence, however, the early levels of this mosque are mid thirteenth century. They contain sgraffiato ware, the only import associated with these floors, and the walls are of coursed rubble masonry. Imported celadons, porcelains or Islamic wares only occur above the last floor of the mosque and postdate the entire building. It is certain that the arcaded mihrab here, though dating from towards the end of the building period, is pre fifteenth century, and probably thirteenth century.

The mihrab of Kizimkazi, Zanzibar (Fig. 49), has an arcaded apse. The lower arcade supports a cornice containing the celebrated twelfth century Kufic inscription. The niches of the upper order are of fine coral, showing an extraordinary dexterity in carving. They are separated by vertical mouldings of fine cable pattern, very like those of Husuni Kubwa. The arch spandrels of the small niches are cut from single panels of coral, only 2 cms. thick. Tiny trefoils are cut from each spandrel and the arch itself is trefoliate. The fineness of this carving would seem to indicate that these niches are part of the twelfth century work and like the inscription were reused in the eighteenth century reconstruction. These delicate little coral panels with foliate arches, carved at a time long before the foliate arch was known in buildings of the coast, may be compared with the marble reliefs in the mosque of Fakhr ad Din, Mogadishu and the Sultansmausoleum, Kilwa. They may well have occurred in a position similar to the one they occupy today, though, like the inscription, they are not curved to the apse curve.

The mihrab arch has two simple pointed, stilted, outer orders and a regular trefoil, with square cusps of the Songo Mnara or Mgao Mwanya type. These, with the panelled jambs, the plain rectangular architrave, the two inner orders of the spandrel frame (with rebated arris mouldings) and the fluted semi-dome all form part of the reconstruction of A.H. 1184/A.D. 1773. This mihrab shows, therefore, that the trefoil arch form (found in the apse niches) and arcaded apse may well date from the early twelfth century—an extraordinary span of time, for they do not occur again until the mid sixteenth century. Further, the design of the mihrab, admittedly an extremely conservative design for the late eighteenth century, is closely similar to mid sixteenth century mihrab forms. This extreme conservatism is no doubt due, in part, to conscious imitation of former mihrabs of Kizimkazi, if not of its original mihrab: an imitation fostered by the value obviously laid on the early carved inscriptions and mouldings incorporated in the existing mihrab.

A large mihrab apse (Fig. 49) is the only surviving trace of one mosque at Kisimani Mafia. The mosque has been entirely destroyed. This apse is lined with a tall, blind, semicircular headed arcade made in dressed coral. This supports a small frieze whose mouldings are of plaster. They consist of a series of circles, each supported by two shafts. This strange frieze can only be compared to the late eighteenth century plaster arcade on the north wall of Kizimkazi, formed by a series of interlocking trefoils (Fig. 49). The eastern arcade of Kizimkazi shows clearly that the basis of this pattern is the overlapping trefoil. The overlap of the trefoils is much greater in the western

[1] H. N. Chittick: Occ. Paper Antiquities Division of Tanganyika, No. 1 (with plan illustrated there).

Plate XII. Derived Classic mihrab. Probably mid eighteenth century. Kimbiji mosque.

Plate XI. Typical late Neo Classic mihrab. Eighteenth century. Shala Fatani mosque, Faza. Note the absence of dressed coral in most mouldings.

arcade, resulting in the overlap of the lower foils forming a complete circle. If the foil of the heads is omitted the resultant pattern is that of Kisimani. This frieze may therefore be safely dated, with the Kizimkazi arcade, to the late eighteenth century. The technique of using dressed coral in some mouldings, and forming others in plaster-work alone, is also common to both sites.

Chole, off Mafia, has a mihrab (Fig. 49) very closely related to that of Kizimkazi in every respect. The inner arch is cinquefoil and had the pointed cusps and gentle curve of the Ndumi arch. It probably, therefore, like Kizimkazi, dates from the late eighteenth century. It is entirely built of undressed masonry with its mouldings formed in plaster. This is the main mark of late eighteenth century mosques. The declining standards of workmanship of the eighteenth and nineteenth centuries, particularly in carving and dressing coral, differentiate features of this period, which, in design, closely follow earlier types.

The mihrab of the Jamia at Kua (Fig. 43) has a blind arcade to the apse. The pilasters of this arcade have single and double cable pattern mouldings of very degenerate workmanship—the cable recessed within its plain borders, to lessen the depth of carving (Fig. 2). The flutes of the semi-dome are very irregular and, unlike any earlier examples, radiate from the rear of the apse. The shape of the innermost arch is not recoverable, but it was possibly also trefoliate.

The typical arcaded apse is found also in nineteenth-century mannerist mosques of the Shirazi confederacies at, for example, Mboamaji (Fig. 52), Kipumbwe (Fig. 53), and Kisikimto (Fig. 54), in a typical regular form, often with delicate and regular mouldings, now entirely in plaster work. Some have the single blind arcade alone but, more often, an upper row of niches surmounts it. Toten Island has a mosque with a mihrab of this type but with the same lower rectangular recesses as the early Kua mosque. In mosques built very recently the apse may well contain a variety of irregular niches and recesses, such as are illustrated at Bweni (Fig. 55).

Late eighteenth century mannerist forms

From the late eighteenth century, many new factors in plan, design and, especially, workmanship result in entirely new forms. These are the mannerist mosques, in which the discipline and unity of the early designs give way, not to the flamboyance of the neo-classic; nor to the tired imitations of the forms simplified, or derived, from the early classic mosques; but to a series of individual and exaggerated distortions of basic forms, containing some new elements, but more often a pointless and undisciplined deformity of forms already in existence. Still, many of these mosques retain, in their arcaded apses, a form which goes back very clearly, and with almost no variation, to mid sixteenth century Songo Mnara, a mosque itself clearly based in classic mihrab traditions. The arcaded apse may even, if it was the original twelfth century form at Kizimkazi, have been a component of the design of the earliest mosque of the coast. Continuity of detail can hardly be carried further.

Among the characteristic features of the latter half of the eighteenth century and the nineteenth century, are the almost square mosque plans resulting from the use of transverse masonry and timber beams and, later, transverse arched arcades. These are supported on wide octagonal columns, with engaged columns at the side walls. Undressed poles replace the former dressed rectangular timber rafters and square headed doors, with similar poles acting as lintols, replace the earlier arched masonry openings. The spans of both beams and rafters tend to be reduced and the thickness of walls and columns increased. The unit of measurement may possibly be a "cubit" of 52 cms., in place of the earlier 44 or 48 cms. cubit. The technique of dressed coral dies

6

out and is only rarely found. It is replaced by incised and moulded plasterwork, thicker or coarser in texture than the earlier plasters, and by mouldings with curved profiles; in particular, the "half keyhole" moulding (Fig. 2D) is introduced. Many complete wall surfaces are decorated in plasterwork, but with little depth to the mouldings. All of these features have already been discussed in Chapters II and IV. The ablution arrangements, now normally within the mosque at its southern end, will be described in the next chapter, and only the mihrab forms will be discussed here. All these features of the eighteenth century occur only in the south, with very rare exceptions on the northern mainland. Kilwa revived in prosperity in the late eighteenth century, and Kua, on Juani Island, has already been seen to have been a large town at the same time. The mainland opposite Zanzibar and Pemba had many small towns— the so called Shirazi confederacies—which flourished in the late eighteenth and nineteenth centuries. In Kenya, mosques of this period are found only at Kilindini on Mombasa Island, and Tundwa on Pate Island. The settlements of the northern mainland had been largely abandoned, while the neo-classic style remained vigorous on the Lamu islands. On the mainland, only a strange mosque, Mgangani, near Gedi, belongs to this period. It has very close affinities with Somalia. In Somalia too, the late eighteenth and nineteenth centuries were a period of rebuilding. The mihrabs of all the mosques of Mogadishu, Merca and Brava belong to the late eighteenth century or later—even the mihrabs of the Jamia and the mosque of Fakhr ad Din at Mogadishu were rebuilt at this time.

Among the new arch forms introduced in the eighteenth century are the irregular and stilted four centred arch, the stepped arch and the parabolic or semicircular arch.

The four centred arch

The irregular, four centred arch always has a pronounced nick to its apex. It occurs in a tomb in a cemetery at Kilwa, on the shore to the east of the original town adjoining the Malindi mosque (Fig. 56). A gravestone, now in the Museum für Völkerkunde, Berlin, came from this tomb and is dated A.H. 1124/A.D. 1712. Constructed in rough masonry with incised plaster decoration, this tomb is a tiny imitation of the fifteenth century Small Domed Mosque of Kilwa. It has two shallow domes with fluted interiors and, on the roof between them, an octagonal pillar imitates the twelve sided pillar that surmounts the central dome of the Small Domed Mosque. Thus, this is a structure consciously seeking to imitate the past, yet the arch takes a very different form from its model and is clearly four centred, and not a simple pointed arch. The Malindi Mosque itself (Fig. 57) was extensively altered at this period, with the typical impoverished techniques of the eighteenth century, though it retains a fifteenth-century core and a fifteenth-century south door. A new mihrab and an inner skin were added to the north wall. This mihrab has a four centred arch, surmounted by a rectangular recess with rebated arris and an inner moulding. The capital is a flush projection of this moulding. Far to the north, at Mafui (Fig. 58), a four centred mihrab arch occurs, surrounded in the same way by a rectangular moulding, with which the capital is flush. This mihrab however, has an architrave similar to that framing classic mihrabs with a recessed field to its upper half. Further, the architrave and outer jamb shafts and capitals are of dressed coral, and the rafters of the roof are dressed and rectangular. Thus earlier influences and technical standards remained stronger here than in the Kilwa mosque. The stilted four centred and stepped arches of the transverse arcade and the moulded plasterwork of the south wall at Mafui are however, very typical of the late eighteenth century. The vertically fluted apse is unique in this context.

Semicircular arch

The elliptical, or semicircular, arch was rightly chosen by Pearce, in 1920, as a characteristic feature of the mosques of the late period, when he described the ruins of Pemba.[1] This arch form is also typified by the small size and simplicity of its plaster mouldings and by the fact that the outer face of the capital is always a flush continuation of the wall surface of the mosque. The apse is normally plain, broken only by a string course. This mihrab type is found at Tundwa (Fig. 61); at Kilindini, Mombasa (Fig. 59); in the Makutani mosque within the late eighteenth century Palace enclosure of Kilwa (Fig. 59) and in a mihrab within the Great Mosque added at the same time (Fig. 15); on Pemba at Msuka Mjini (Fig. 59); and in two mosques of Kua (the Jamia, whose mihrab has an arcaded apse, and the mihrab of Kua 3, Fig. 43). It is also, now, the mihrab form of the mosque of Fakhr ad Din, Mogadishu (Fig. 65). (In Msuka Mjini and Fakhr ad Din, the mihrab apse is for the first time rectangular in plan.) Semicircular arches also occur to the outer orders of the later neo-classic mihrabs (e.g. Faza and Siu Fort; Fig. 33, Plate XI).

It is interesting that loose coral blocks of absolutely identical form containing mouldings with incised grooving forming four recessed triangles and a rebated arris, so popular in neo-classic mihrabs, have been found at both Msuka Mjini and Makutani (Fig. 2C). These confirm the contemporaneity of these mihrabs in the late eighteenth century. A similar single recessed triangle moulding embellishes the south door of the Kilindini mosque, which also has an irregular parabolic arch. This mosque probably dates from A.H. 1232/A.D. 1808 for Guillain in 1840 records an inscription giving this date over the entrance. It was certainly built after 1634 when Rezende states that this area of Mombasa was deserted and before 1836 when Kilindini was destroyed by Sayyid Said. The very curious mosque of Tundwa (Fig. 61) has eighteen recessed orders (each 2 cms. wide and deep), and over fifty bowls decorated its north wall—the only surviving bowl is late eighteenth century. It has jamb blocks, not shafts, and a fluted apse—features not found elsewhere, and no doubt adopted from the neo-classic mosques of the area. Only it, Msuka Mjini and Kilindini have architraves framing the mihrabs. Kilindini retains the use of dressed coral in the salient angles of its architrave and in the panelled frieze above it and in the inner jamb shaft. But the curved profile of the outer order of jamb shafts is formed in plaster. Dressed coral blocks are also used at Msuka Mjini—notably in the capitals and carved pilaster niches. But these are, most probably, the last examples of this technique.

The crudely built, thatch roofed verandah added to the west side of the mosque of Takwa, probably as early as the late seventeenth century (Fig. 25), has an arcade of semicircular headed arches, while the stepped arch is used in two little northern windows to this verandah. One of the houses within the late eighteenth century Palace enclosure of Kilwa (Fig. 79) has its main room lined with a series of crude, arched niches, of different forms, which include the semicircular, the stilted four centred and the stepped arch. This is further confirmation of the date and contemporaneity of these forms. The workmanship at both Takwa and Kilwa is notably crude and irregular, without any dressed stonework.

The mihrab which is all that survives of the mosque of Mgangani, on the shore of Mida Creek, is unique outside Somalia (Fig. 62). The proportions alone of this strange mihrab set it apart. The semicircular arch is broken by ribs which radiate irregularly from the rear of the apse, a characteristic mihrab form in eighteenth or nineteenth century Somalia; such ribs occur in the rebuilt trefoliate mihrab of the Mogadishu Jamia (Fig. 63), but ribs to a semicircular arch are particularly common in

[1] Zanzibar, p. 351.

Merca.   The plain frieze above the architrave, no doubt designed to take an inscription, and the projecting conical bosses, set in a square panel containing excised diamond patterns, are all Somali features, found in the main doorways of Fakhr ad Din (Fig. 65), and also in many late eighteenth or nineteenth century mosques.   The mihrab of Mgangani is considered to be eighteenth century because of the quality of its workmanship, particularly in the irregularities of the fluted semi-dome; because the diamond patterns and surface decoration are formed in moulded plasterwork, characteristic of eighteenth century tombs (not the excised coral of Fakhr ad Din); and because the ribbed semicircular arch is a feature of late eighteenth and nineteenth century Somalia. The reason for a single isolated example of such a mosque on the Kenya coast (and very close to the important, but by this time deserted, town of Gedi) is unknown, but it is a problem clearly posed by the architecture, for its affinities are beyond doubt.

Distorted foliate arches

The simple, regular, symmetrical foliate arches of late eighteenth century Kizimkazi and Chole, with their basis clearly in earlier traditions, give way, in the nineteenth century, to distorted mannerist derivations from this arch, particularly on the mainland opposite Zanzibar (the Shirazi confederacies) and further south.   The simple pointed arches that surrounded the inner trefoil disappear, to leave the inner arch standing alone to dominate the design.   This arch is still supported on coarse, thick chamfered pilasters.   The pilaster capital now, normally, has the new "half keyhole" moulding immediately below it (as at Kipumbwe (Fig. 53), Bweni (Fig. 55) and Mkwaja (Fig. 56)).   The inner arch foils, in particular, are distorted or multiplied —Kisikimto (Fig. 54) is an extreme example of distortion.   The seven foils of Bweni and Mkwaja, and the nine of Mboamaji (Fig. 52) are more regular, but the trefoil of Kipumbwe has particularly unhappily distorted proportions.   Later examples, many of the very late nineteenth century, have their cusps so elongated and deformed that it is only comparison with typologically earlier designs that declares their origin.

The architrave, like the outer arches of the mihrab, is absent in these mihrabs— though echoes of it occur at such a mosque as Bweni.   These design elements are replaced by coarse, irregular, shallow mouldings in plaster, often with curved profiles, framing panels.   With mihrabs such as these, one is virtually within the field of the architecture of the mosques built today.

In Somalia, as has been said already, every surviving mihrab seen by the author in Mogadishu, Merca and Brava is of a typical late eighteenth- or nineteenth-century form.   The irregular mass of shallow plasterwork mouldings that confuse the entire mihrab of the Jamia of Mogadishu (Fig. 63) are very typical of the degeneration of design of this period.

Recessed minbars

A feature of the late eighteenth century congregational mosques is the minbar recess in the north wall.   The minbar, or pulpit, is a feature only of the congregational or Friday mosque and is not found in mosques other than this.   This feature and its introduction have been studied in detail by J. Schacht.[1]   It occurs sporadically very early in eighth century Islam in the Near East, but then only in a very limited area of north-west Africa from the ninth century to today.   It cannot be an indigenous development of East Africa, nor is there a direct link in East Africa back to such an early period, for it is never found in an East African mosque before the eighteenth century; nor is there any other link between the coastal architecture of East Africa and

[1] Ars Orientalis, II, 1957.

north-west Africa. The clear similarities in plan represent either a tantalizing relationship between widely separated and otherwise unrelated areas, or a revival, several centuries later, of a primitive plan form. It is certainly most unlikely to be an indigenous parallel design evolved in East Africa, though it may have survived in isolated areas of the Near East (e.g. Oman) to be brought from there to East Africa in the late eighteenth century.

In the late eighteenth century Jamia of Kua (Fig. 43), the minbar is placed in a small, rectangular recess with a semicircular arch, in the north wall of the mosque, immediately to the right of the mihrab but separate from it. The minbar here is also of normal form—a straight flight of four steps. At early nineteenth century Mboamaji (Fig. 52, Plate XIII), the next typological stage is found, in which the minbar is still a recess in the north wall separate from the mihrab; but in which an entrance in the north wall leads into a raised "pulpit", expressed as a timber faced "balcony" behind which the preacher stood. At Mkwaja (Fig. 56) and Kipumbwe (Fig. 53) such a pulpit is entered from an opening in the mihrab apse itself, which gives onto a short flight of steps. The arched, timber fronted opening in the north wall, well above floor level, framed the preacher and replaces the former minbar. In the final stage of the sequence, illustrated at Bweni (Fig. 55), the decoration of this minbar arch is incorporated within the plastered mihrab surround to form a single design entity. The mihrabs that provide for access to the minbar from within the apse can, from a practical point of view, no longer be apsidal in plan and consequently cannot retain the fluted semi-dome roofing them. Nevertheless, a square mihrab plan such as that of Kipumbwe manages to retain the characteristic, arcaded apse decoration. Although, typologically, there does appear to be a developing sequence of recessed minbar designs, it must be repeated that this is most unlikely to represent a sequence of designs evolved in East Africa, particularly in view of the similarities with other areas, the short time span covered, and the limited distribution.

The neo-classic mosques of the Lamu group never have a recessed minbar. Instead, fine carved timber minbars, consisting of a single straight flight of steps, project into the mosque from the north wall. This is, of course, the normal Islamic minbar. It is found in all congregational mosques of the Lamu area today. But on the rest of the coast today, the arched minbar opening in the north wall, entered from the mihrab, remains the normal minbar form.

In Somalia, the minbar recess occurs in many of the nineteenth century mihrab reconstructions—though it is not found in the Jamia of Mogadishu, which retains the normal projecting carved timber minbar. The Jamia of Merca has a separate arched recess to the right of the mihrab containing a normal timber minbar. This resembles the arrangement in the Jamia of Kua. Brava Jamia, on the other hand, has an arched minbar opening entered from the mihrab.

CHAPTER VII

MOSQUE PLANNING

The buildings of the coast show little evidence of overall planning concepts, but rather comprise the repetition and aggradation of small easily conceived and constructed units with no adaptation or response to broad visual or functional requirements. This has already been taken as a clear indication that foresight in detail and conventional plans were not considered necessary—any more than the architect needed to produce these was available or found desirable. He was replaced by a competent technician, and the problems that arose in construction and planning were solved as they occurred, although within the strict unified traditions of the artisan. Within the strict geometry of the units that comprise each building, dimensional irregularities abound and these were adjusted as they arose. These irregularities naturally make the discernment of the measuring unit employed extremely difficult. Nevertheless, it is obvious that measurements must have been taken and, as the buildings were laid out on the ground and construction progressed, some means of mensuration must have been employed. The normal module, or unit of measurement, or cubit, is likely to have approximated to 50 cms.—or the distance from a man's elbow to the end of the middle finger. This has been a means of measuring used in many countries and many periods. The Meccan cubit at the time of Muhammed was 50 cms., in late eighth century Abbasid Raqqa it was 52 cms.,[1] while in fourteenth century Persia it appears to have varied between 45–52 cms., with no clear preference visible. Therefore, it has been considered very likely that the cubit was determined for each construction by the master builder, with no universal standard.[2]

On the East African coast the same conclusions seem to apply and no clear dimensional preferences emerge from a study of the dimensions of the plans illustrated. The problem is obscured by the many minor irregularities in dimensions, by the renewing of plaster finishes, by the ruinous condition and resultant movement of walls and columns, and by the weathering of so many walls. The excavator of Gedi believes the cubit in use there to have been 44 cms.[3] It does seem clear that, over the whole coast, the cubit varied from 44 to 52 cms. At Kilwa, the fifteenth century Small Domed Mosque and domed extension to the Great Mosque appear to have used a cubit of just under 48 cms. —in these buildings there is a clear preference for 192 or 238 cms. (4 or 5 cubits) room or bay widths and walls of 48 cms. (1 cubit). The column capitals are 16 cms. high ($\frac{1}{3}$ cubit) in both mosques, but the columns of the Small Domed Mosque are 54·5 cms. square and those of the Great Mosque 57·5 cms. square, while the arches above the capitals are 32 and 38 cms. in width respectively. Several walls in these two mosques are 51–52 cms. wide. These important dimensions appear to have no clear relationship to the supposed cubit. Vertical dimensions particularly appear to have little relationship to the cubit. Column heights are 146 cms. and 138 cms., and heights from capital to cornice are 182 cms. and 147 cms., in the Great Mosque and Small Domed

[1] K. A. C. Creswell: Early Muslim Architecture, p. 1 and 184.
[2] D. N. Wilber: Architecture of Islamic Iran, p. 44.
[3] J. S. Kirkman: The Arab City of Gedi, p. 10.

Mosque respectively. Moreover, as the bays do appear to be multiples of a cubit, it means that in laying out the plans, a convenient column size would have been first determined from the point of view of structural requirements, ignoring the cubit; and then the bay dimensions laid out between columns, using the cubit unit. This seems a clumsy and impractical method of laying out a plan, yet the dimensions show that the more normal method of laying out a regular cubital grid and then building columns of the required thickness at the intersections of the grid lines was not followed. It is interesting to note that measurements in the perimeter bays were in fact taken to outside walls, ignoring the projecting engaged half columns that carry the perimeter arches. This means that the perimeter bays are slightly smaller than the remainder—a clear indication that the detailed dimensions of the larger units of constructions were considered of little consequence. The Great Mosque vaulted extension, six bays long and five wide has, of necessity (as the overall size of the extension was determined by already existing walls), a discrepancy of 50 cms. in 20 m. between its two sides. This has been quite easily adjusted in the bay lengths, but means that the longitudinal column spacing varies by as much as 20 cms. Naturally a large modular unit such as the cubit was not usable in this instance. The vaulted mosques of Kilwa have been used as a test case in this analysis of the method of mensuration, as one would expect maximum accuracy in dimensions in large vaulted structures, and moreover, the fine preservation of the buildings and the precision of the workmanship enable accurate measurements to be taken.

The overall dimensions of all mosques will be tabulated below in three broad groupings, according to the cubit considered to have been used. This will give a clearer idea of the broad pattern of plan sizes, proportions and preferred dimensions than any verbal description. The pattern is however blurred and discernible only when a large body of buildings is considered together. For this purpose, the group into which a building falls has been largely determined by its wall thickness. The groups using 44 cms. and 48 cms. cubits form more homogeneous stylistic groupings than the third (52–56 cms. cubit) group. It would seem that the 44 cms. cubit is earliest in date, the 48 cms. cubit next, while the last group is not earlier than the seventeenth century. But there are too many exceptions for this to be of any real significance, and little absolute reliability can be placed on given cubit sizes.

The main halls of most mosques commonly have a single central row of columns. Two rows of columns, though aesthetically and structurally sounder, occur less frequently, while only the large congregational mosques have three column rows. The vaulted extensions of the Great Mosque of Kilwa, with four column rows, is the only plan to exceed this. It seems a universal law that the main structural beams tend to determine the dominant axis of the mosque. Where they are longitudinal the mosque tends to be long and narrow. Where they are transverse, as in the early Jamias of Gedi and Ras Mkumbuu, but more particularly in the eighteenth or nineteenth century neo-classic and other mosques (where the transverse beam or arched arcade is very characteristic), the mosque tends to be square in plan.

Plan dimensions

Mosques with 44 cms. cubit or wall thickness, 2·20 m. maximum width of side rooms (if any). Mihrabs in early classic style, unless noted.

	Overall Internal Dimensions in centimetres	Column spacings	
Gedi: Sarcophagi	335 × –	1 × 2	
Gedi: South Wall	338 × 596	1 × 2	
Gedi: Long Conduit	336 × 630	1 × 2	
Gedi: Small	363 × 498	1 × 2	
Gedi: Between Walls	367 × 525	1 × 2	
Dege	351 × 905 (orig. 667)	1 × 3	derived classic
Jibondo	343 × 688	1 × 2	
Tongoni	450 × 1230	1 × 4	
Muhembo 1	487 × 773	1 × 3	
Kiburugeni	507 × –	1 × –	
Ndumi	560 × 1071	1 × 4	trefoliate
Chwaka	415 × 835	1 × 3	simplified classic
Jumba la Mtwana	486 × 600	1 × 2	
Tiwi	500 × 960	1 × 3	
Gedi: Three Aisles	549 × –	2 × –	
Muhembo 2	568 × 925	2 × 3	
Mbweni	570 × 1020	2 × 3	
Ukutani	565 × 991	2 × 3	
Mnarani Jamia (Kenya)	737 × 1545	2 × 5	
Tumbatu	940 × 1319	3 × 3	
Mkumbuu Jamia	1265 × 1445	3 × 3	
Gedi Jamia	1142 × 1916	3 × 6	
Manda Jamia	1126 × 1560	3 × 5	early neo-classic
Kisimani Mafia	560 × 820	1 × –	
Kilwa: Small Domed Mosque	728 × 658	2 × 2	
Jangwani Mosque	730 × 794	2 × 2	early classic vaulted mosques
Songo Mnara: Main Mosque	755 × 782	2 × 2	
Kilwa: N. Great Mosque	693 × 1181	3 × 3	
Sanje Majoma	400 × 600	1 × 2	
Kilwa: Barrel Vaulted Mosque	305 × 676		
Songo Mnara: Barrel Vaulted Mosque	278 × 827		
Mwana	586 × 924	2 × 3	

Mosques with 48 cm. cubit or wall thickness, 240 cm. minimum width of side rooms (if any).   Developed classic mihrab or derivations from it.

	Internal Dim. in cm.	Column spacings
Mnarani (Tang.)	405 × 640	1 × 2
Kua 1	421 × 685	1 × 2
Chwaka	430 × 1235	0 × 4
Diani	453 × 840	1 × 3
Jemadari, Malindi	456 × 915	1 × 3
Kitoka	498 × 800	1 × 3
Kutani	478 × 820	1 × 3
Sala	520 × 721	1 × 2
Bandarini	535 × 731	1 × 2
Takwa	535 × 1230	1 × 3
Ungwana: Small	555 × 1030	1 × 3
Mida Creek	569 × –	1 × –
Mnarani: Small	672 × 590	2 × 2
Kaole 2	600 × 805	2 × 3
Mtwapa	640 × 1700	2 × 5
Shengejuu	857 × 802	2 × 2
Kitoka Jamia	880 × 1046	2 × 3
Kunduchi	780 × 1330	2 × 4
Shaka	775 × 1650	2 × 5
Ungwana: Jamia 1	750 × 1554	2 × 5
Ungwana: Jamia 2	840 × 1607	2 × 5

Mosques with 52–56 cm. wall thickness, square plans with transverse beams.   Neo-classic or later styles.

	Internal Dim. in cm.	Column spacings
Pate: Bwana Bakari	1185 × 1340	3 × 4
Pate: South-West	937 × 921	3 × 2
Faza: Shala Fatani	913 × 839	2 × 3
Siu Castle	642 × 646	1 × –
Kizimkazi	590 × 859	1 × 3
Chole	704 × 821	2 × 2
Kilwa: Makutani	490 × 745	1 × 2
Kimbiji	681 × 1185	2 × 5
Kua 3	694 × 734	2 × 2
Kua 4	720 × 708	2 × 2
Kua 5	700 × 707	2 × 2
Kua Jamia	880 × 1070	2 × 3
Msuka Mjini	740 × 1270	2 × –
Tundwa	750 × 713	2 × 2
Kilindini	780 × 1323	2 × 3
Mafui	580 × 581	1 × 1
Mkwaja	597 × 574	1 × –
Mboamaji	654 × 403	1 × 2
Utondwe	655 × 880	2 × 2
Kisikimto	688 × 700	2 × 2
Kipumbwe	680 × 690	2 × 2

Ablutions

Immediately before entering a mosque, the worshipper will normally perform the ritual ablutions of hands and feet required in Islam.   These can be performed elsewhere, but provision of a well, supplying water for a tank, and a washing area, often with permanent footscrapers built into its floor, is normal in all but the most minor mosque.

In major mosques, a latrine is also provided besides the tank, footscrapers and well. The well is very frequently also used to supply water for domestic use to the whole village or settlement, and so access to it is frequently possible without entering the precincts of the mosque—a desirable feature, especially as the womenfolk normally draw the water.   The ablution arrangements of the coastal mosques are not standardized.   Their placing is often governed to a large extent by the position of the mosque in relation to the plan of the main buildings or alleys or roads of the town or village. The position of the well may also largely be determined by other outside factors and its position will naturally govern the position of the ablution arrangements.   Nevertheless, the arrangements for ablutions do fall broadly into two groups—wells and tanks to the east of the mosque are most frequent in classic designs, while in eighteenth and nineteenth century mosques, the ablution tanks and the well are normally placed in a small enclosed court or room at the south end of the mosque, which is virtually, if not actually, part of the mosque itself—in rare cases they are within the mosque.   The thin, unroofed ablution court walls and the subsidiary nature of all ablution courts (resulting in poor construction and, frequently, stone robbing after abandonment) often results in little trace of these surviving even in mosques otherwise reasonably complete.

In all the fifteenth century mosques of Gedi, and in the sixteenth century Jamia of Gedi, the ablution arrangements are almost completely standardized (Figs. 7–9, 24). A circular stone-lined well, from 150 to 400 cms. in diameter, gives onto a low conduit at about knee height whose channelled top is formed of dressed coral blocks.   This leads to a low rectangular tank, 100–150 cms. wide and 250–300 cms. long.   Very characteristic of every such tank on the coast are the masonry quadrants, with a radius of about 15 cms., built in each corner to render these weak points of the tank waterproof.   At Gedi the low tops of the tank walls are surfaced in square, close fitting, coral tiles.   The wells of Gedi were normally divided into two by a cross wall spanning across their tops, one half opening into the mosque court from which water could be drawn, to run along the conduit to fill the tank; while the other half of the well was available to the townsfolk for domestic use.   These dividing walls only extend about 1 m. below the top of the well kerb.   This arrangement is rare elsewhere at this time, but it occurs in the early nineteenth century mosque of Kilindini, Mombasa (Fig. 60), and is frequently found in the mosques of Somali towns today.

In the larger congregational mosques of classic style, footscrapers, consisting of three or four large, natural and uncut bosses of rough coral (or at Kilwa where sandstone is available, of sandstone) are set in a section of plastered pavement, beside the tank and lowered below the normal pavement level (to prevent waste water spreading).   Alternatively the footscrapers are surrounded by a low plastered kerb to form a shallow tank. These scrapers are found in the Jamia of Gedi, Ras Mkumbuu, Ungwana, Takwa, Kilwa (in both north and south ablution courts) and the early mosque of Kaole.

Latrines within the ablution court occur at the Jamia of Gedi, and at Kilwa, in the Great Mosque (in both ablution courts), the Small Domed Mosque, and the fifteenth century ablution court of the Malindi mosque.   These latrines are enclosed in a small rectangular compartment abutting the main walls of the court, added to and projecting from them.

While the majority of classic mosques have their ablution arrangements to the east of the mosque, several have them to the south.   At Kaole (Fig. 3), the square well at the south end of the mosque adjoins the tank, which here is vaulted with a small barrel vault.   The vault is, in this case, freestanding, supported on an arched arcade.   This is unique, but small barrel vaults roof small tanks and wells in the early parts of the Great Mosque at Kilwa (Fig. 15).   A similar tiny barrel vault occurs over a small room in the southern ablution court of the thirteenth century mosque of Fakhr ad Din, Mogadishu (Fig. 66). This may, therefore, well be a feature of the thirteenth century but only these few examples remain of it. The wells in all these cases are square and this well shape (found also at Husuni Kubwa) appears to be more characteristic of the earlier classic and pre-classic periods than later (though this is by no means always true). Having the ablution facilities to the south of the mosque may well have been the preferred arrangement of this early period, for it is found not only at Kilwa, Kaole and Fakhr ad Din, but also in the original fifteenth century parts of the Kilwa Malindi mosque (Fig. 57) and at early fifteenth century Mnarani (Fig. 28). But this is too little evidence on which to base a rule governing what was always a flexible arrangement (e.g. southern ablutions also occur in the developed classic mosque of Kaole (Fig. 26), probably early sixteenth century). Traces of tanks show that east ablution courts were present at Jumba la Mtwana, Mtwapa, Kilindini, Kua Jamia, Chole (actually within a side room), Chwaka Domed Mosque and Ungwana Jamia. Only the two latter are certainly earlier than the eighteenth century, but all tend typologically to precede the mosques with south ablutions described below.

From the time of the neo-classic mihrab and mosque, on into the nineteenth century, tanks are normally found in a room immediately at the rear of the mosque or even within it, against the rear wall (as at Shaka, Manda and Shala Fatani, Faza), fed by a conduit leading from a well immediately outside. At Manda (Fig. 34) the well is within the mosque itself, and this strange feature occurs in the early classic mosque of Ras Mkumbuu (Fig. 4) as well. At Ras Mkumbuu, it is difficult to believe that this well and the conduit it feeds (which lines the south wall and leads to the cistern outside the south-west corner), are part of the original late fourteenth century structure, though all the archaeological evidence from this site indicates that this is the case.

Examples of this arrangement, with the ablutions in a narrow, roofed southern room formed by extending the side walls of the mosque by little more than one bay width to the south are found in every neo-classic mosque, and all the nineteenth century mannerist mosques of the Shirazi confederacies of Tanganyika (though in the latter they tend to be in a small unroofed court). They are also found at Mwana Kiwambi on Songo Mnara, the eighteenth century Makutani mosque at Kilwa, Msuka Mjini, Chwaka Jamia, Kizimkazi, Tundwa and Sala. All of these are probably late eighteenth or even nineteenth century.

One has thus a very generalized sequence for ablution arrangements—first, an early type with an open south court, up to the early fifteenth century; second, an open eastern court typified by all Gedi mosques and continuing on into the late eighteenth century; and third, a roofed south room containing the tank, found in the neo-classic mosques (from their initiation to the nineteenth century) and in the later mannerist mosques.

Ablution arrangements occur at the north-west corner of the early northern mosque of Kilwa (thirteenth century), the small mosque at Mnarani (early sixteenth century) and the small mosque at Ungwana (early sixteenth century). This arrangement was probably enforced by extraneous considerations and was not a desired feature. In the pre-fifteenth century Great Mosque of Kilwa (Fig. 15) there was a great open court to the south of the mosque (to be vaulted in the fifteenth century). This was no doubt only used for congregations of worshippers at the Friday prayers, when the southern ablutions immediately to the rear of this court would be used. Normally, individual worshippers would make use of the smaller north west ablution facilities and from them enter the mosque direct. These were, thus, a convenient subsidiary to the larger southern ablutions, and their position was determined by the barrier, to the south of the mosque proper, of the great open court. At Mnarani (Fig. 19) a small ablution tank abuts a large panelled tomb at the north-west corner of the mosque.   The position of this tomb ensured that the west side of the mosque gave onto an open space, while the south and east sides may well have been restricted by the roads and buildings of the town.   In this mosque access is provided to the tank from the mosque itself, through an arched opening in the north-west corner.

Arrangements were made for some cisterns to be filled by rain water led from the mosque roofs.   In sites that lacked a well, such as the small Mvinje mosque at the north-east tip of Kilwa island (not illus.), two tanks abut its south wall and were filled in this way.   An isolated house on the east shore of Songo Mnara (Fig. 79) obtained its water from a similar arrangement.   Excavation reports show that the tanks of the small mosque at Ungwana (Fig. 30) and Ras Mkumbuu (Fig. 4) had similar arrangements—though the former obtained most of its water from an adjoining well, and the latter seems to have been supplied from the well within the mosque.   No doubt, wherever feasible, tanks were fed with rain water from the roof—if only to lessen the labour of drawing water, but Mvinje is the only mosque forced to rely completely on this method. With the collapse of almost all roofs, it is only rarely possible to state certainly that rain water was thus conserved.   It is however, an obvious and convenient thing to do.

Side rooms

Prior to the seventeenth century, almost every mosque was provided with side rooms or verandahs—often they have been added to the main hall.   This may be suggested by differing doorway treatments or wall thicknesses.   In some cases the unbonded junctions, plastered on the earlier face, prove conclusively that these rooms are additions. In several cases more than one addition had taken place—as in the early Kaole mosque (Fig. 3), which has an east side room added, to replace a still earlier very narrow east side room, and followed by an east verandah.   A similar arrangement occurs at Ungwana Jamia (Fig. 23).   At Tongoni (Fig. 5), whose main hall and two original side rooms appear to have a 44 cms. cubit, a second west side room of larger dimensions and with coarsely constructed windows, probably using a 48 cms. cubit, is a further example of a secondary addition.   All these side rooms were probably intended simply to provide further space for worshippers, as the population of the settlements grew. The narrow widths—which never exceed a single rafter span—and the disproportionate length necessary for these rooms to line up with the ends of the main hall (which they always do) give room shapes of particularly awkward proportions.   It seems unlikely that rooms of such proportions would be specifically intended for any purpose (such as the Koran school for example) other than overflow of worshippers.   Though they may well have been used for such other purposes, these would seem to have been a subsidiary consideration in their function.   They would however also have been used as a place for people to talk and rest, without interfering with worshippers in the main hall of the mosque; and, no doubt, were in part built to fulfil this purpose.   They are connected to the mosque proper by an arched arcade of two, three, or more doors; the number depending entirely on the length of the mosque.   This indicates that an intimate connection with the mosque was considered desirable and that the side rooms are a subsidiary annexe to the main hall rather than independent entities.   Frequently, the easiest access if not the only access, to the main hall was through the side rooms.   This lack of isolation shows that they were certainly not intended for the use of the women. In East Africa, only the early classic mosque of Tumbatu (Fig. 12) has a second mihrab in the side room, though this feature is found in the much later Jamia of Mogadishu (Fig. 64) and Merca, and in a further mosque at Merca.

When one considers the very small and restricted floor space of most mosques, it is not surprising that such additional side rooms were necessary. They provide an emphatic illustration of the broken up, compartmented nature of mosque planning, with narrow rectangle added to narrow rectangle, and with neither ordered spatial planning nor visual focus nor indeed any consideration of the final aesthetic results.

Only at the Shala Fatani mosque, Faza (Fig. 34), where the added east room does not extend the length of the mosque, and only communicates with it via a single door; and at the Jamia of Mnarani (Fig. 28), where the east additions are divided into a north-east entrance lobby and a south-east room, do the side rooms appear to have been intended for a purpose other than an extension of the main hall. In both cases they were probably used as Koran schools.

Naturally when side rooms occur they tend to be symmetrically placed on each side. If, however, only one is found, it is almost invariably on the east—as in the one containing a mihrab at Tumbatu, and in the Small Domed Mosque and Jangwani mosque of Kilwa.

Because of the propensity for ablution arrangements on the eastern sides of the classic mosque, it is frequent to find that these mosques have an east verandah. This would have served as an amenity to people using the ablution court, a place to leave one's footwear and to congregate before entering, or after leaving, the mosque. Such verandahs are found in the Jamia and in most of the minor mosques at Gedi, at Ung-wana and at Takwa adjacent to the ablution arrangements, and also on the west side of the small Ungwana mosque, adjacent to its north-west ablution tank. Mwana, Chwaka Jamia, Chwaka Domed Mosque, Mtwapa and Jumba la Mtwana, all with their ablution arrangements to the east, seem all also to have had such a verandah. Southern verandahs or side rooms are rarer and like the first type of southern ablution arrange-ments, almost always early in date. They are found at the early Kaole mosque and at the Jamia of Mnarani, both of which had their ablution arrangements to the south, and also in the early classic mosque of Tongoni. The fine south portico of Fakhr ad Din is a further example. A strangely isolated later example of such a south portico occurs in the main mosque of Songo Mnara, unconnected with any ablution arrangements. Before the end of the sixteenth century, only the later Kaole mosque, Mbweni, Ras Mkumbuu and the smaller vaulted mosques of the Kilwa area lack side rooms. But, after the classic period, side rooms are virtually absent. The mosque of Shala Fatani has a side room proper and its nature has already been shown to differ from that of the earlier types. The whole plan of the eighteenth century, neo-classic, south-east mosque of Pate (Fig. 34) is a typical early form and it has side rooms to both east and west—the reason for this anomalous plan is unexplained.

A very individual plan is found in the mosques (probably late sixteenth century) of Tiwi (Fig. 38), Diani (Fig. 36) and the Jemadari mosque at Malindi (Fig. 30). The two former have mihrabs of the simplified classic type and the latter an atypical neo-classic mihrab. As can be seen in the complete mosque of Tiwi, these not only had side rooms to the east and west, but a room to the rear of the main hall, of the same width as the main hall but considerably shorter. This room had its own ancillary side rooms, and was undoubtedly designed for the use of the women. Only a small window con-nects it to the main hall. In these three cases the side and rear rooms are not additions to the main hall but an integral part of the original plan. This may well indicate that the side room, previously always an addition, was by this time accepted as an essential and, consequently, universal feature of every mosque plan. These mosques are the only ones to make any provision for women worshippers; though, only just earlier in the sixteenth century, the southern half of the main hall and the side verandah of the Jamia of Gedi were walled off to provide a separate area for women. The small mosque of Kitoka (Fig. 36), also with simplified classic mihrab, possibly had a similar plan.

Minarets

The minaret never occurs in East Africa before the late nineteenth century. In Somalia, at the south-east corner of the Jamia at Mogadishu (Fig. 67), the thirteenth century tower served the purpose of the minaret. A similar tower is the sole remaining structure of the Abd al Aziz mosque, Mogadishu. An identical tower to that of the Jamia occurs in the south-east corner of the Jamia of Merca, and like the Mogadishu example, is surrounded by a later mosque. The only parallel to these in East Africa is found in the late fourteenth century early classic mosque of Ras Mkumbuu (Fig. 4). Here, a small door in the north wall to the left of the mihrab gives on to a short flight of steps entering a circular structure, 3 m. in diameter, projecting from the face of the north wall. This probably never extended to any great height, for its walls are thin, and it has not got the circular masonry core and steps of the Somali towers. It may well have been more in the nature of an external pulpit, though from it a ladder may have given on to the roof. Short flights of two or three steps leading to a square platform are found externally, in the angle formed by the north wall and one side of the mihrab projection, in several Pemba mosques (e.g. the Jamia of Chwaka and Shengejuu, Fig. 26). These platforms were also, no doubt, pulpits or places from which to give the call to prayer. Doors in the north walls of mosques, very rare outside Pemba, are found there at Ras Mkumbuu, Shengejuu, the side room of Chwaka Jamia and at Msuka Mjini. These gave access to the external stairs. This "external pulpit" therefore appears a minor variation in design restricted to Pemba, and descending from the earliest example, that of Mkumbuu, which is also the most elaborate.

Occasionally, a rough, straight flight of masonry steps leads to the roof of the mosque, from which the call to prayer would be sounded. Such stairs adjoin the early ablution arrangements at Kaole (Fig. 3), and occur in the north and south courts of the Great Mosque at Kilwa (Fig. 15) (two mosques linked already by many other features); and in the fifteenth century ablution court of the Malindi mosque at Kilwa (Fig. 57). A similar stair is found in the later Kaole mosque—one is led to believe that this mosque must, in many aspects of its plan, have been imitating its predecessor. At the Jamia of Gedi, a stair leads to the roof from the north end of the east verandah. Tongoni also had a stair in a similar position.

Doors, windows, niches

The classic mosques, with side rooms attached, normally have two or three doors on each side, leading to these side rooms, and a central southern door. The side rooms normally have one less external door than the main hall. However, at Muhembo I, there are two doors, both externally and leading to the main hall. In the Small Domed and Jangwani mosques at Kilwa (Fig. 17), the position is reversed and there are two external doors in the east side rooms and one door to the main hall. It is another of the strange crudities of the coastal architecture that the doors of the main halls never follow the bay spacing, but have a completely separate and unrelated spacing of their own, so that two separate and completely disconnected rhythms are established. This occurs even in a mosque of the length of Mtwapa (Fig. 39) which has six bays yet seven openings to its side walls. Only in mosques with engaged columns or pilasters to the side walls, and thus where the external openings are forced to comply with the bay rhythms, does this position alter. On the other hand a regular alternation of door openings and windows or internal niches does occur, to give a rudimentary formal pattern to the side walls—as at Mtwapa, Gedi Jamia and the southern extensions of the Great Mosque at Kilwa (though in the two latter both rhythm and patterning are strongly helped by the engaged columns). Many mosques have two doors and a central niche between them—

(e.g. Diani, the small mosque at Kitoka, the Jemadari mosque at Malindi, and Kisimani Mafia).

The fact that multiple side doors are only found in mosques with side rooms to which they lead, and the fact that these doors are never alterations to the original fabric, would seem to contradict the fact observed at some sites that most side rooms are additions. Windows are never found between main hall and side room, though they do occur opening on to verandahs (e.g. Mtwapa). This anomaly is possibly explained by the supposition that temporary structures may well have preceded the permanent stone-built side rooms, or that for some reason the original side rooms may have been replaced, as has been shown to have been the case at Kaole. This indication that side rooms were frequently part of the original intention of the plan does not alter the purpose envisaged for them—that of transition between mosque and the external world, where one could shelter, talk or rest, and which would take any overflow of worshippers from the main hall.

Because side rooms are found so frequently in the early mosques, windows are not often found in the main halls—though where openings on to the exterior or on to a verandah are possible, they frequently occur. It is, however, difficult to reconstruct window layouts, because the side walls of so many mosques have collapsed above threshold level. The windows and the large wall recesses (intended for storage, not for lamps) of all mosques are simple rectangles, with a timber lintol, flush with their inner wall face, to support the wall above. They rarely have dressed coral to the corners, nor are they ever relieved by any mouldings (with one exception: in a house at Kua). Smaller square windows or arched "portholes" are frequently formed in rough, undressed masonry alone. These openings thus form a stark contrast to the mihrabs and arched doorways.

Arched windows, framed internally by a rectangular recess, occur for a brief period in the late eighteenth century at, for example, Kua (Fig. 43) and Dege (Fig. 41). The arch forms normally take one of the many mannerist forms. The rectangular window does, however, persist, and indeed returns to the exclusion of other forms in the latest mannerist mosques of the nineteenth century.

A curious form of window is found in the mosques of Takwa (Fig. 25) and Shaka (Fig. 27). These are vertical slits edged in dressed coral (single at Shaka and in pairs at Takwa) placed high in the northern wall on either side of the mihrab. They ensure ventilation and some light while preventing glare from the direction that all worshippers face. Similar windows occurred at Ndumi (Fig. 51) and the Malindi mosque, Kilwa (Fig. 57) at capital level, but they were later blocked. At Ndumi, they were replaced by splayed slit windows, typical of the late eighteenth century, at a higher level. Small windows are found at normal height in the north walls of the later Kaole mosque, and in the small mosque at Ungwana, while pairs of small windows frequently light the north ends of side rooms.

Lamp niches are found in the pilasters of the Jamia of Gedi (Fig. 24), their edges of dressed coral, and similar small niches, though more coarsely made, occur near the doors of the mosques of Muhembo 1 and Ukutani at least. The decorated pilaster recesses on each side of the mihrabs of many mosques have already been described, and were also intended primarily for lamps.

Minbars

Within the mosque the normal minbar is a straight flight of three completely plain masonry steps, beside or in front of the eastern mihrab pilaster (Figs. 21, 49).

Only the minbar of the Jamia at Ungwana (Fig. 21), with its eight steps and masonry sides (which took a timber handrail), a masonry imitation of the normal timber minbar found elsewhere in Islam (and today in the modern mosques of the Lamu Islands), departs from the typical minbar form. A timber minbar was built into and supported by the east pilaster at Takwa, as the slots cut in this pilaster show (Fig. 21). The small masonry minbar at Mtitimira (Fig. 42) has a solid masonry balustrade to its east side, but is otherwise normal.

Tombs

Abutting the north wall of almost every mosque and then extending northwards, there are frequently a series of decorated tombs, which may be of very various designs and dates, often much later than the apparent date of the mosque. Only at the early Kaole, where incomplete early plain panelled tombs (probably of the fourteenth century) abut the north wall of the mosque, and at the Jamia of Mnarani, where decorated panel tombs of the fifteenth century do the same, are tombs of any assistance in dating the mosque and, in neither case, do they do more than confirm other evidence. Tombs with dated inscriptions are, in any case, unfortunately rare on the coast. Tombs may lie near the mosque on every side if for some reason it is inconvenient to build them to the north. The mosque of Mbweni is sited with a cliff edge at its north end and there the very large tomb group consequently extends to the west, while in the Malindi mosque at Kilwa and the vaulted mosque at Songo Mnara (both on similar sites to that of Mbweni) tombs are found on the east side. Walled cemeteries are not common, but the tombs, or rather plain graves, of the vaulted mosque of Songo Mnara, just mentioned, are within a rectangular low walled enclosure. Similar walls enclose a small cemetery extending north of the main mosque of Songo Mnara and there is a small walled cemetery near the south-east corner of the central Songo Mnara mosque. Later, at the Jamia of Manda, Utondwe and Kua, high walls, with a weathered coping to their tops, enclose small cemeteries to the south, west and south-east of the mosques respectively. At Kua, this cemetery has a mihrab in the centre of its north wall, a feature not paralleled elsewhere. This mihrab is now completely ruinous, but appears to have been very plain in design and poorly built. It was probably somewhat similar to the mihrabs of the minor eighteenth century Kua mosques.

CHAPTER VIII

DOMESTIC BUILDINGS

The architecture of the houses of the East African coast is not basically different from the religious architecture. The techniques used in construction are the same—plastered walls of coral ragstone support flat concrete roofs with rough coral tile ceilings, supported by squared timber rafters. No room is wider than a single rafter span so columns or piers are never necessary. The planning system of adding narrow rectangle to narrow rectangle in a monotonous geometry is found in the domestic buildings to an even greater degree than in mosques. Decoration and mouldings are used more sparingly than in religious buildings, but where they occur—in important doorways (particularly the main entrance doorways) and in niches and in ceiling angle brackets—they are identical in form and technique to those already described. This very sparseness of decoration makes the dating of the houses much more difficult than that of the mosques. Certain minor features do occur in the domestic architecture that have not been found previously. Important rooms were decorated with wall hangings (or timber plaques or carvings), as the double rows (about 50 cms. apart) of fixing holes (at 30 cms. centres) at eye level remain to testify. The open niches (Fig. 84), recessed in the walls of these rooms, tend also to be larger and more elaborately decorated than those niches in the mosque walls, and the majority contained timber shelves dividing the unit into compartments (each some 30 cms. square). These niches remained as the major surviving focus of decoration, and continued to appear after the eighteenth century, when entire walls may be faced with banks of up to 100 separate recesses. The latter are particularly characteristic of the domestic buildings of the Lamu area, contemporary with the later neo-classic mosques. There can be little doubt that they were used to display collections of imported porcelain. A much quoted early nineteenth century Swahili poem mourns the loss of former greatness in Pate thus: "Where once the porcelain stood in the wall niches, Now wild birds nestle their offspring". Beyond their main doorways, and the niches and wall hangings restricted to the one or two main rooms, the houses of the coast have little decoration. At Gedi, internal pilasters break up the surfaces of some of the longer walls, and there also, there are arched recesses at the end of the main rooms in which large, porous, earthenware water coolers stood in shallow, circular depressions, which collected and drained away surface water.

In the centre of the floors of the largest rooms there were soakaways, which have already been described on p. 20. These drained away the water used in sluicing these rooms down. They occur only very rarely at Gedi. Every house contains at least one latrine. Deep stone-lined pits (at Gedi some 6 m. deep and, from all appearances, little less at Songo Mnara, though at Kilwa they were smaller) are corbelled inwards and sealed at floor level, leaving a 15 cm. square opening formed of carefully fitted coral blocks, with a small runnel at its front for use as a urinal. Separated from the latrine by a small screen wall 1 m. high, was a washplace where two large footblocks, separated by a gap, formed a primitive bidet. Behind or beside this at a higher level was a stand for the necessary water containers. This washroom normally drains, via an enclosed channel, into the latrine pit. The building of latrines on the upper floor offered no plumbing difficulties. Large, quadrant shaped, masonry ducts (1 m. in external diameter with 30 cms. walls) in the corner of the rooms lead down to normal pits below. In the eighteenth century Palace of Kilwa, latrines from both upper and lower floors connect to a single such duct (Fig. 78). Where space was restricted, a square duct, 50 cms. square externally, was used, its inner face lined with square, rough dressed, coral tiles, similar to those of the normal ceiling. At Songo Mnara Palace such ducts are even contained in the wall thickness, and in some cases lead from the upper floor past what appear to be large, sealed, internal water tanks to the latrine pits below. The standards of sanitation were reasonably high and the amenities they provided were designed and constructed with care. Despite early Arab and Portuguese descriptions of coastal towns, particularly Kilwa, having two or three storied stone-built houses, such houses were by no means general. Before the eighteenth century, the typical houses of the coast, as exemplified at Gedi and Songo Mnara, are single storied and flat roofed.

Only in the two, probably fifteenth-century, buildings behind the Great Mosque at Kilwa (Fig. 75) have upper stories been found before the eighteenth century. In both these buildings the upper stories are late additions to the ground floors. The ground floor plans are typical of the normal single storey house of the coast, but the addition of an upper floor has necessitated considerable alteration and improvisation, including the doubling of wall thicknesses and the dividing of unroofed areas into spaces suitable for a rafter to span. The upper floors appear to have been separate units with their own external entrances. They have entirely collapsed and no plan is recoverable.

The roof of the typical house does not seem to have been used for outdoor living; at least no masonry steps ever lead to it, though timber ladders may have existed. The house plans are all extremely compact—a series of interleading rooms with no connecting passages necessary. Privacy, important in Islam and essential for the seclusion of the women folk, is provided by the high blank screen wall that, with the house and its wings, encloses the courtyard found at the front of every house. The height of these walls would, with the house, provide shade at most times of the day. The courtyards have raised walkways round the three house sides but not on the blank side of the screen wall. The centre of the court is sunk some 50 cms. so that the walkways also provide comfortable seating. If the depth of the court is greater than this (as in the houses south of the Great Mosque at Kilwa, at Songo Mnara Palace and at Husuni Kubwa Palace), the steps are frequently continuous over at least one side of the court, so that they may also be used as seats. All such houses, with deep courts and seating steps, probably belonged to important authorities. They could accommodate a large group of people and lent grandeur to the buildings flanking them.

All windows, in every house, open on to the courtyard and no window occurs in an external wall. This means that the inner rooms were dark and airless. This was, in a way, unimportant, for all normal daily life would be conducted in the courtyard—including cooking (many houses have a second domestic court at the rear for this) and receiving guests, who would rarely if ever penetrate beyond the first room or rooms of the house. The dark innermost rooms were used only at night, or for storage. Every important daytime activity took place in the open. The large windows and doorways in many cases may not have contained timber doors. They thus remained permanently open. This applies in particular to the internal doorways. The strong African light would penetrate from the rooms fronting the court far to the interior of the house and be softened to give a pleasant, subdued contrast to the external glare. A great disadvantage of the absence of external windows and the presence of high external courtyard walls is that there is absolutely no cross ventilation—virtually no breeze can penetrate court or house.   On the coast, with its high humidity, this is a very serious drawback—if there is no movement of air, discomfort is immediate at all times of the year.   It is strange that so fundamental a consideration was ignored by a people otherwise clearly conscious of their comforts and amenities.

The great majority of houses on the coast are orientated with surprising rigidity and exactness to the north, with their courtyard and main entrance on this side.   If this orientation is impossible, they are then orientated to the east.   In a town of largely individual and detached houses (such as Songo Mnara), houses facing east naturally occur less frequently than in compact town plans (such as Gedi or Mtwapa), where the orientation is to a much greater extent determined by the layout of streets.   Nevertheless, even in such town plans, no house faces in any direction other than north or east. In every town, a few of the most important, and largest, houses have a domestic court at their rear, in addition to the normal front court.   The rooms flanking the rear court are a close reflection of those at the front of the house.   Such houses (with only one exception: Gedi, House 2, Fig. 76) are invariably orientated northwards, so that their rear rooms face south.   Only two complete houses in the entire coast face westwards and both are subsidiary units within large palace complexes (Gedi Palace House V, Fig. 76; and the "Chamberlain's House" at Husuni Kubwa, Fig. 68).   This deep concern with orientation is a further illustration of the desire for comfort, so clear in the buildings of the early coastal towns.   Westward facing houses would suffer greatly from the heat of the afternoon with the setting sun penetrating deep into the house. The morning sun from the east is far less unpleasant.   There is little to choose between north and south orientated houses in East African towns, which lie so close to the equator.   As all the towns lie just south of the equator, houses facing north receive slightly more sunlight during the southern winter months, from July to September, than they do during the rest of the year.   This is a point of only marginal importance in reality, but possibly makes north facing houses slightly preferable.   Northern and eastern facing houses are, however, those most likely to capture the prevailing winds on the coast throughout the year. These strong preferences for orientation made the planning of towns difficult, for no house will have entrances to any street bordering its western or southern sides.   Blocks of building surrounded by streets are therefore scarcely practical, and street plans are as a result irregular or, more correctly, non-existent.   It is much easier to build a series of isolated houses, as at Songo Mnara.   However, as no town had more than 50 or so stone-built houses, and even that number is attained only extremely rarely, the problems of town planning do not figure large.

One of the most interesting features of the town buildings is the communal approach to, and cooperation in, planning.   All adjoining houses invariably share a single common party wall (there is a single exception in Songo Mnara).   Moreover, in almost every case, where houses adjoin, the plans interlock rather than simply abut one another, making for compactness and economy of building.   This is evidence of a far greater degree of cooperation in planning and construction than that which would be found if just one owner allowed his neighbour to build against the irregular line of his outside wall.   It entailed complete cooperation and joint planning from the start, followed by simultaneous building.   The construction of entire blocks of up to three or four houses must have taken place simultaneously.   Courts too, particularly domestic courts, frequently interlead, so that one well, in such a court, may serve three separate houses, and access to courts and wells is via one's neighbour's courts.   This whole concept is clearly illustrated in the Songo Mnara houses 19–22 (Fig. 74).

In several cases parts of an original house are, after alteration and addition, taken over and incorporated in an adjoining house—a clear example is found at Gedi (Fig. 76), where House 5 has thus annexed part of House 4. A similar situation probably occurred at Songo Mnara, between houses 26 and 27. These annexations quite certainly took place when both houses were occupied, and not after one had been abandoned.

This degree of cooperation between owners of separate, self-contained, buildings is, of course, entirely alien to the western property owner; nor, to the author's knowledge, is it found in African society today, nor was it in the past. It could be due to two causes. All ownership of land and organisation of building may have been vested in a single powerful authority—the Sheikh or Sultan—whose agents could thus determine in detail how a complex of buildings should be planned and used. This was, no doubt, the case in the Palace of Songo Mnara (Fig. 73), which will be shown (see Appendix I) to be not, as has always been assumed, a palace at all, in the normal sense of the word. It is rather a complex of fifteen separate, though standard, houses which adjoin, and even interlock with, each other. These fifteen houses have subsequently been unified by building a monumental vaulted arcade in the court at the central core of the palace, together with a unified façade to east, south and west sides of the court, each façade containing identical richly decorated doorways. Beyond this feature, the houses largely remained individual units. Such an imposition of unity on a complex of disparate units could only have been done by a single authority—the Sultan or Sheikh.

But it is most unlikely that such an authority extended to the details of the buildings over the whole site. The individual idiosyncrasies of planning and detail, found in every building, could not stem from a single authority. The obvious cooperation can, therefore, only stem from an identity of interests between the individual house owners, so complete that it must have sprung from a close degree of kinship, or very firm family or tribal ties. This is an unexpected, but apparently irrefutable, conclusion revealed by a study of the domestic buildings, and applicable to the whole coast, up to the eighteenth century at least. It does not necessarily mean that a single group or family built the entire towns of Gedi or Songo Mnara. But it does mean that such a single group controlled blocks of four or five separate houses which were then planned and built together. This group or family also had very strong ties with, and so collaborated closely with, the remaining builders in the broader layout and construction of the town.

In all coastal towns, outside the sphere of the stone-built houses, there were the temporary timber and earth dwellings of the bulk of the population. About them, the extent of their architecture, and their relationship to the imposing stone buildings, nothing can be said, for nothing now remains of them. If their presence is forgotten, however, a false emphasis is given to a study such as this, which, of necessity, concentrates on the architecture of the permanent stone buildings.

A detailed study of pre-eighteenth century domestic buildings has only been made at Songo Mnara and Husuni Kubwa, and to a lesser extent at Gedi and Mtwapa. Only these sites will be described in detail. But the degree of identity between them shows that the homogeneity of the domestic architecture at all times, and in all regions, was even greater than the close unity of style, already so apparent in the pre eighteenth century religious buildings of the coast. As a result, individual exigencies of site and owner appear largely to outweigh broad developments of, or regional variants in, style. Therefore, it seems unlikely that a wider study would reveal anything further of major importance. Further, the accidents of preservation, aggravated by the lighter construction of the houses and the lack of any religious prohibition against their destruction, mean that it is more difficult to recover the complete plan of a house than that of a mosque. Incomplete house plans have little value, as the basic homogeneity of the architecture is such that only the details of a plan are of diagnostic significance. The town of Songo Mnara will be described first and in greater detail than the others, for it is there that the bases of domestic planning were first distinguished, and are most clearly visible and typical. Husuni Kubwa is described last, though it is, of course, the earliest domestic building of the coast and predates the other sites by some two centuries at least.

Songo Mnara

The town of Songo Mnara (Fig. 74) is built on the north-west tip of the island of that name, which lies off the mainland, just south of Kilwa island. To the west is an anchorage facing the mainland and sheltered by the island itself from the open sea. This anchorage is entered by the narrow channel that separates Songo Mnara from Kilwa. Three miles south of the town and anchorage, there is the small subsidiary and contemporary settlement of Sanje Majoma. The south end of the island is separated from the mainland by a series of narrow and barely navigable channels. The town has seen only two main periods of occupation, neither very long lived. All the main buildings belong to the fifteenth century, probably the latter half of that century, with a few buildings, notably the largest mosque, probably dating from the early, or even mid sixteenth century. In the late eighteenth century the Palace and adjacent houses, if not other buildings, were reoccupied and extended. The latter period, in which only minor building work took place, will not be touched on at this stage.

Along the west shore opposite the town are four mosques—the strange barrel vaulted mosque (Fig. 18, described in Chapter III) with a cemetery adjoining it at the south; two small, plain, poorly constructed and now largely ruinous mosques, possibly of the late eighteenth century and not worthy of description; and at the north, a small fifteenth century mosque (Fig. 18) built on a stout platform of four wide sandstone paved steps. This mosque is about 15 m. offshore, below high water mark, and is now surrounded by mangroves. It is the tower or "*mnara*" that gives the island its name. The town itself consists of forty-eight separate houses, fifteen of which form the close knit complex, known as the Palace (Fig. 73), at the south-west extremity of the town. The remainder are, in the main, large, isolated houses. They extend east from the Palace, curve north and finally west in an irregular crescent, enclosing a central area which has many tombs and a small walled cemetery adjoining a mosque. (The latter is very ruinous, and now lacks a mihrab. It is, to all appearances, typical of the fifteenth century; it never had side rooms.) The largest mosque (Fig. 48, already described in detail in Chapters III and VI) is at the north-east end of the site. The town is not truly enclosed by a wall, but the rear of the houses, plus lengths of connecting wall form a semi-continuous protection to the south and east while a poorly constructed town wall was built along the North shore. Like all the town walls of the coast, it could never have offered a serious obstacle to an enemy.

The earliest description of Songo Mnara is that of Lieut. Prior R.N. who in 1811 described the Palace thus:[1] "Two or three hundred yards from this spot[2] lie the ruins of a stone building, larger than any at present possessed by the Quiloans, except the residence of the Sultan. Its apartments have been numerous, some large, others smaller, and a third class, with still minuter divisions, separated by thick walls, but opening at one end into a passage common to all. The walls, at least the present remains, are broad, though not so firmly built as those of the smaller edifice, and judging, from the quantity of rubbish, their height must have been considerable.

[1] G. S. P. Freeman-Grenville: The East African Coast, p. 208.
[2] The barrel vaulted mosque.

Several thick trees, of a spongy texture, issue not only from among the fallen ruins, but from the substance of the walls which seem held together merely by clay. These form various convolutions, and, by a kind of heterogeneous union, living wood seems inseparably combined and coexistent with stone. Captain B. thought he could distinguish the remains of Saxon arches; but this resemblance is probably accidental.'' The town was, therefore, certainly in ruins at the start of the nineteenth century and the ruins, with the many baobab trees growing amid them, have changed little in appearance in the intervening 150 years. Prior, in describing the classes of divisions, seems to have grasped the basis of the Palace plan probably better than any subsequent commentator.

Standard house plan

The typical standard house of Songo Mnara (Fig. 74. Houses No. 16, 17, 18 are particularly good examples) is entered from a monumental decorated doorway, at the head of a flight of five or six steps, flanked by raised seats. This door leads to a square entrance hall (E), from which a door in its west wall leads to the sunken forecourt of the house. This court has a blank north wall and raised walkways on the remaining three sides. It may vary in size and shape but is usually about 8 m. square. The main apartments are on the south side of the court, with subsidiary wings on its east and west sides. Adjoining the entrance hall to the south is a single isolated room (C), opening on to the courtyard only. This contains a "bed" (b., called a "bed" from its structure, and the room types in which it is found, which will be described later). From its small size, furnishing and isolated position, commanding the court and entrance hall, this room appears to be that of a caretaker, doorkeeper or senior servant of the house. Frequently there is a further room, and a washroom latrine, *en suite* with the caretaker's room.

The house proper is entered by a wide central door on the south side of the court. This leads into the main room (M) of the house. This room is normally just under 8 m. long and 2·35 m. wide. (The normal room width at Songo Mnara varies little from this figure, although the length may be from 7–9 m.) This room was usually decorated with wall hangings and sometimes niches. Guests would be received and entertained here.

At the east end of the main room a door leads to the smaller main private room (MP), 4 m. × 2·35 m. This has its axis at right angles to the main room, so that it projects north into the courtyard sufficiently to enable it to be lit by a single window at its north-west corner opening on to the court. This is always the most richly decorated room of the house, often with ornate niches to more than one of its walls, almost invariably with wall hangings, and in the case of one otherwise quite standard house (No. 17) barrel vaulted, with 121 small imported ceramic bowls inset in the vault in a grid of 11 bowls running in each direction, to give the richest ceiling on the coast. This usually well lit room probably represents the main room used by the owner of the house throughout the day for business and for receiving close friends or those worthy of special esteem—his study in fact. It was possibly also used as a retiring room. From the main private room a door at the rear leads to the latrine and washroom (W).

At the rear of the main room two doors lead to two identical rooms (B1, B2) set side by side, together equalling the length of the main room. These rooms are each, therefore, about 3·50 m. long and neither has any decoration. However, at one end, and away from the door, six or seven rough cylindrical timber poles span across each room from side to side, about 1 m. above floor level and extending 1 m. or more in width from the side wall. These obviously formed a wide timber shelf (b). It seems that this can only have been a built-in bed, however high and uncomfortable it appears at first sight. On plan these rooms are the only feasible bedrooms of the house, occurring in the obvious position for bedrooms, i.e. off the main room. At Gedi such "beds" are not found, but the rooms that correspond on plan to the Songo Mnara "bedrooms", had been labelled as such by the excavator of Gedi independently of, and prior to, the author's work at Songo Mnara. Two such rooms (Gedi, Houses 13 and 14, Fig. 76) have raised, plastered masonry platforms (of similar height and width to the Songo Mnara beds), which the excavator of Gedi considers to have been beds. There can be little doubt therefore that these strange, high, crude, timber shelves were beds. Even if they do not represent the standard of comfort and workmanship one would expect, the rooms in which they are found are the only rooms, beside the main private room, that could have been used as bedrooms. Nevertheless, there is a slight possibility that the rooms were only storage rooms and these "beds" were therefore only storage shelves. In this case, the position of two large rooms used for storage at the core of the house is a quite extraordinary planning feature. In one case, (in the eighteenth century house, No. 12) a very small third bedroom has a bed only 140 cms. long. This could, of course, have been a child's bed but, in this case alone, it seems probable that this structure was intended as a storage shelf. Such beds are also invariably found in the caretaker's room opening on to the courtyard. This ends the description of the essential constituent rooms of a standard house. But most houses have further rooms in addition. The west wing of the house, forming the west side of the courtyard, appears frequently to have consisted of a single long room of light construction. This was probably a verandah, providing shelter for many household tasks, including the cooking.

At the opposite end of the main room to the main private room, a second similar room is often found (MP 2). This is rarely as ornate as the main private room, nor does it project into the court, but it normally also has a washroom/latrine at its rear. It thus duplicates the main private room and must have been used for similar purposes, though it is not an essential element of the plan. Finally, there is very frequently a large ante-room (A) of the same dimensions as the main room placed between it and the court. In such cases, the functions of the main room are divided between it and the ante-room, and together they form the main public reception, or living, rooms of the house. The ante-room, like the main room, was decorated with wall hangings and niches. Where an ante-room occurs, the main private rooms often open off it, and not off the main room. If an ante-room exists, on occasion the main room itself contains a "bed" across its narrow end wall (Houses 16, 21, 37). This incidentally would seem to confirm that these structures are beds, for it is difficult to conceive of bulk storage taking place in a room decorated with niches and wall hangings, whereas, with the added privacy achieved by the ante-room, the main room may well have been used subsidiarily for sleeping.

Plan variants

There are two variations on the standard house plan. One is a considerable enlargement of it (Fig. 74. Houses, 21, 34, 45), consisting virtually of two standard houses back to back—one facing north to the normal forecourt and one facing south to a domestic court, where the domestic activities of the house (cooking, washing, etc.) took place. The domestic nature of the rear court is not particularly clear at Songo Mnara (except in house 21 where it contains a well), but at Gedi and Husuni Kubwa is much more obvious. It lacks the entrance walkways or benches of the northern forecourt. In these houses, communication between the two standard house units is achieved by converting one of the two bedrooms to a lobby (BL) which thus connects the north and south main rooms (the bedroom range is not doubled and therefore only one bedroom remains in houses of this type). The southern unit repeats exactly the features of the northern unit—main room, ante-room (always present in these houses), main private rooms, washroom/latrines and even a caretaker's room or suite opening off the Southern court. This house type will, for convenience, be called a "double house".

A much reduced version of the standard house, to be called the "minor house", (Fig. 74. Houses 1–6, 24, 28, 29) consists basically of only three rooms—a main room some 6 m. long, with a single bedroom (built in beds are not, however, found in these bedrooms) and a washroom/latrine, of similar size to the bedroom, opening off its rear long wall. These minor houses are never enclosed by a courtyard nor do they have side wings. Ante-rooms are rare, but may be replaced by a much more lightly constructed verandah (AV).

The standard house, with its two bedrooms in addition to the main private room, almost certainly represents the normal accommodation for an Islamic household of husband and two wives. The double houses are a more lavish means of accommodating the same household—here the front half of the plan was used by the menfolk, while the rear half provided almost duplicate accommodation for the women. Because of the different nature of the two courts—reception forecourt and domestic rearcourt—it is difficult to visualize the two halves of these houses being divided between two wives. The division by sexes seems more likely. It is more difficult to be certain about the typical household of the minor houses. These occur mainly in the Palace complex and it is possible that they belonged to single officials of the court. There is certainly no provision in them for the seclusion of women and they have only a single bedroom, so the owner certainly did not live with more than one wife at a time.

Naturally, there are many minor variations on the typical house plans. Besides the washrooms, minor rooms ("B") opening off the main private room are particularly frequent. These may well have been bedrooms—in two cases (in house 21) they do contain built-in beds. Frequently isolated minor houses are duplicated with two halves back to back in the same way as the standard house (Houses 32, 44 are good examples of this).

Many of the smaller isolated houses of the town do not have any trace of courtyards remaining. This is quite possibly because the original court walls were a simple timber palisade or of mud and wattle. This would be a more economical and practical structure in a house that lacks east or west side wings.

It is notable that at Songo Mnara there are no stone built commercial buildings, market places or servants' quarters. Some of the rooms round house 7 and the completely ruinous structure (marked as houses 25 and 35) fronting the central mosque were possibly small booths or shops. At the south end of the court of house 33 and the northeast corner of the court of house 47 there are ranges of three rooms whose purpose is unknown. They may well have housed stores or slaves. As all commentators have remarked, Songo Mnara, with its spacious planning and large isolated houses, has an air of relaxed leisure—it was, quite probably, more a residential retreat from Kilwa than a commercial centre.

Gedi

Gedi (Fig. 76), a large town lying inland from the coast and two miles from the shores of Mida Creek, is a more typical compact and close-knit town than Songo Mnara and the houses are, therefore, much more liable to variation. It is broadly contemporary with Songo Mnara, both dating, in the main, from the prosperous years immediately preceding the disruption caused by the Portuguese. Gedi has one fourteenth century house and several of the sixteenth century but most buildings belong to the fifteenth century. Gedi has been the subject of two monographs and several articles by its excavator, J. S. Kirkman; it is therefore dealt with here only as far as it confirms and amplifies evidence of general application to the coastal architecture as a whole.

There are many minor differences between Gedi and Songo Mnara. The houses at Gedi normally lack the projecting east and west wings of the Songo Mnara houses, and the courtyards are smaller. They also lack the richly decorated main private rooms, and as a result the latrine/washrooms are entered from one end of the main room, often via a small lobby. Finely carved niches and fixings for wall hangings are found less frequently, though they are still often present. On the other hand, the finely made recessed niches at the end of many main rooms, to contain water jars, are not found at Songo Mnara. No house at Gedi has built-in timber beds, but rare cases do occur of masonry platforms, replacing them, in the bedrooms. Most houses at Gedi have a small store, about 150 cms. wide, in the bedroom range. These stores have no doors at floor level and they appear to have been entered from trapdoors high in the wall, reached by a portable ladder. The excavator believes they may have been used to store the cowrie currency of that part of the coast. The store was thus, possibly, unnecessary at Kilwa and Songo Mnara where copper coinage was used.

The house plans of Gedi almost always ensure that the doors of outer rooms are never placed directly opposite the doors leading on to the inner rooms. Thus if both ante-room and main room occur, the ante-room will have two doors, and the main room a single central door at the front. At the rear of the main room, the bedrooms will, of course, again each have a door (e.g. house No. 1). If there is no ante-room, the main house will be entered from the court by a single central door, (houses 2, 5), unless there is only a single bedroom with a central door, in which case the main room has two doors (house 6). This neat design ensures privacy (for it is possible that there were never timber doors in these houses) but, to some extent, it sacrifices both light and ventilation. Such staggered doorways are a feature also of Husuni Kubwa.

These many minor differences between the houses of Gedi and Songo Mnara should not be allowed to mask their essential similarity in design. Gedi is more compact, and the houses smaller, simpler and more liable to variation, but its basic similarities to Songo Mnara still far outweigh the differences. Because of the many idiosyncrasies of the Gedi house plans, several houses will be described individually. From them, the overall unity in design will become apparent. House 1 has a narrow sunken courtyard, 7 m. × 2·50 m., with raised walks to east, west and south and an entrance hall (a rare feature at Gedi) at its north-west corner. It has an ante-room, with a small lobby and washroom off it, a main room, two "bedrooms" (one of which was clearly used as a kitchen) and a store. House 3 is the same, house 8 even simpler with only a main room and single large bedroom. House 6 also has only a main room with a single bedroom at the rear, but it also has a main private room and washroom, opening off the east side of the main room, separated by a lobby leading to a second main private room, with a washroom *en suite*. These houses (except for house 3) with their single bedrooms and long narrow courtyards are among the earlier Gedi buildings; for, in the sixteenth century, the courtyards became larger and square in plan, domestic courts often occur at the rear, and the bedrooms are doubled, so that each front bedroom becomes a lobby leading to a further true bedroom at the rear. This feature is not found in houses with an ante-room, so it can be described in a different, and perhaps more correct, way by saying that the ante-room leads to a main room, divided down its centre into two separate rooms, off each of which a normal bedroom leads. Indeed, in the Palace, this is precisely what did happen; a wall was added to divide the main room. House 7 is a typical example of this type. Consequent on the introduction of the domestic court, the double house plan becomes possible—it is found in house 2 (which is one of the few having a west domestic court) in which main room leads to bedroom and bedroom lobby, which in turn leads to a second bedroom lobby (an unusual feature) flanked by a second bedroom, and leading to the rear main room and out to the domestic court. House 4 is basically a similar double house; so is house 5, though here only the south bedroom suite connects with a south domestic court. These two houses were considerably altered, as house 5 took over part of house 4, and the original plan is difficult to distinguish. House 18 is a further typical double house, facing east and west, with main private rooms opening off both west and east main rooms, and with ante-room/verandahs.

The Palace of Gedi,[1] as it stands today, dates in the main from the late fifteenth century. It has, though, seen four periods of building from the early fifteenth century to early sixteenth century.

Originally the Palace core consisted of a typical standard house (I) facing a north forecourt, and consisting of a richly decorated ante-room, a main room, and a bedroom and bedroom/lobby (separated by a store) leading from the main room. On the east are a lobby, washroom/latrine and two main private rooms. This layout was very similar to that of house 6. The bedroom lobby leads to a south domestic court. Subsequently the main room was divided by a central wall, thus forming part of two "bedroom suites" and a range of rooms ancillary to the domestic court was added behind the bedrooms, with further ranges adjoining it. This complex formed the Palace core. To the west, in the early stages there was a smaller but still typical house (II). It consisted also of a small north court, main room and single bedroom, with a large main private room leading from the main room to form a west wing to the court. Much later this main private room was divided to form a latrine en suite with the main room (a typical Gedi plan form). This western house, the excavator considers, formed the women's quarters; it certainly connected with the Palace core. In the later stages further accommodation was added to the south end, forming a west wing to the main domestic court of the Palace, and a similar wing was added to the east side of this court. These two wings were, very probably, each typical minor house units, (III, IV) consisting of main room, a single bedroom and a latrine: very like the five or six minor house units that encircle the south side of the Songo Mnara Palace and which were probably used by court officials. Further such minor houses are found north of the Palace in the houses 15, 16 and 17 (part of the excavator's "Palace Annexe"). Such a minor house (V) was certainly added to form an east wing of the main northern Palace forecourt. This house commands this forecourt or audience court and the entrance to it from the entrance court (added at the same time). It also commands, and has access to, the domestic court with the Palace well (also added at this period). The official who occupied this house was certainly a person of many responsibilities. At Husuni Kubwa (Fig. 68) a house of similar size, and in a similar commanding position and without direct communication with the Palace, has been named the Chamberlain's House. The unit within the Gedi Palace seems, from its siting, to have belonged to the Chamberlain of the Gedi court. This view differs from that of the excavator of Gedi who considers it was a suite to which the Sultan retired while audiences were taking place in the main forecourt, but from which he was available for consultation and decision. Its plan, which is that of a typical minor house; its isolation from the Palace itself; its commanding position and access to the entrance,

[1] J. S. Kirkman: Gedi–The Palace.

domestic and well courts; and its similarities to the Husuni Kubwa Chamberlain's house—all lead the present author to see it, almost certainly, as the quarters of a senior official concerned with the running of both the domestic arrangements of the Palace and audiences with the Sultan, i.e. the Court Chamberlain. The Sultan may well have retired from audiences in the forecourt to his main private room in the Palace core, which has access to the forecourt via a small lobby off which an ornate washroom/latrine opens. This, the excavator himself considers to have formed the Sultan's retiring room prior to the building of House V. There is no reason why it should not have continued to do so.

At the south-east corner of the Palace a court, with ranges of three small rooms at east and west sides, reminds one of the range of three small rooms at the far ends of courtyards in houses 47 and 33 at Songo Mnara and, like them, may well have been used as stores or even small trading booths or shops.

Mtwapa

The town of Mtwapa, now thickly overgrown, may well exceed any other on the coast of similar date, in the area covered and completeness of its buildings. Much of it may belong to the late eighteenth, or even nineteenth century, but the small part of it planned by the author (Fig. 77), shows that a very standardized series of single storied houses are virtually identical in plan, construction and decoration to those of the early periods. These plans are more compact, regular and close knit than any others, and the houses appear, at first glance, to be grouped in regular blocks. They consist of a small forecourt, ante-room, main room and two bedrooms. A washroom/latrine projects into, and opens off the forecourt, adjacent to the main entrance. Both ante-rooms and main rooms were decorated with wall hangings, and most have their walls divided decoratively into panels by pilasters, in a similar way to many Gedi houses. Main private rooms (with one exception), store rooms, domestic courts, bedroom suites, niches for water coolers and the double or minor house plan variants are all absent. Unlike Gedi, but like Songo Mnara, the doorways to both ante-rooms and main rooms lie opposite one another, and consist of single central doors. Frequently the two bedrooms were not separated by a central masonry cross wall, though they still each retained a separate entrance door. It is probable, therefore, that they were divided by a simple timber partition or only by fabric hangings or curtains. In one case traces of a stout dressed timber rod, dividing the main room centrally at door head height, remain. Curtains may well have been hung from it. This, therefore, seems to confirm the theory.

The cooperative nature of both the planning and building of the houses at Mtwapa is particularly well illustrated, and houses within a block are clearly dependent on one another and were planned and erected together. This is carried even further in certain houses (e.g. houses 5 and 6, 10 and 11) which have small low doors connecting the bedrooms of separate houses. The reasons behind this are clearly open to flights of fancy—but it must indicate that such houses belonged to a single family.

Mtwapa deserves a much more comprehensive plan and description than is possible with the author's limited knowledge of only a small part of the site. The date of the houses described is unknown, but typologically it seems most unlikely that it differs greatly from that of Gedi or Songo Mnara.

Husuni Kubwa

From the knowledge of typical house plans gained from the towns of Gedi, Songo Mnara and Mtwapa it is now proposed to turn back some two centuries or more to the great complex of the Palace of Husuni Kubwa (Figs. 68, 69, Plates XIV, XV). This is the thirteenth-century local fountain head of all the pre-eighteenth-century architecture on the coast, barring the very rare mosques that precede it in date. The complexity, luxury, variety and sensitivity of its design were never matched again. Husuni is built on a flat topped, sandstone headland looking north across the entrance of the harbour of Kilwa. From it, the town and anchorage can be seen far down to the west, and the reef and harbour entrance are visible to the north, lying off the north-east tip of Kilwa island. The commanding height, the views and the constant cooling breezes from the sea give Husuni a sense of delight that is unique in East Africa. This was clearly appreciated and exploited by the owner. On the headland itself lies a large, single storied, domestic building, which is in all essentials typical of the standard house of the coast—to the north is a sunken forecourt, flanked by raised walkways on all sides (the Palace Court) and to the south, a Domestic Court, linked with servants' quarters and a well. One of the most interesting features of Husuni is the fashion in which this domestic core very closely resembles later domestic work. At Husuni the plan of a typical domestic housing unit is already complete and typical—all later domestic work must therefore derive from it. Extending south of the headland is the great South Court, surrounded by storage rooms, while many ancillary units flank the east and west of the domestic core.

From the beach, at the foot of the northern tip of the headland, a wide monumental stairway rises, in two flights, to the top of the headland. These stairs, and a large part of the south wall flanking them, are cut from the living cliff. As a result, each step is unusually large and somewhat irregular, with the tread of each sloping upwards to the next step—this, and their size, makes them noticeably uncomfortable to use. Large squared timber nosings were inset in the edge of each step to provide a crisp finish and prevent wear on the sandstone. Built on the edge of the shore, and flanking and facing the bottom of the stairway, there is a small building, whose northern end has been demolished by the sea. Its southern end has a single door, flanked by two small, square, low walled, water tanks. This little structure, a single room, only 2 m. wide, does not line up with the stair entrance, but is set at a splay to it, and as a result faces more truly northwards. It is an earlier structure than the wall immediately abutting it, at least: one of the very few instances of non-contemporaneity in the structure of Husuni. It may well predate the stairway and even the entire Palace. The only similar building to it anywhere is a small isolated mosque, set on a headland overlooking the sea at the north eastern tip of Kilwa island—the Mvinje mosque (not illus.). This small mosque is also only 2·40 m. wide, and its Southern entrance door is flanked by two similar tanks. It may well be of similar date to Husuni. It has been seen in Chapter I that small mosques very close to the sea on headlands (e.g. Mida Creek) or even built in the sea off the edge of the shore (e.g. the "Mnara" mosque at Songo Mnara) are a characteristic feature of the coast architecture. They were probably intended to be clearly visible to, and attract the attention of, the crews of passing vessels: mosques to which the prayers of seafarers were drawn. It is suggested that this small structure at the foot of the stair at Husuni was a mosque. The orientation, the tanks, the similarity to the Mvinje mosque, the awkwardness of its siting in relation to the stair foot, its possible antecedent date, and the precedent for such siting: all combine to suggest this. There is no mosque at Husuni Kubwa—a notable omission—and, while this mosque could not have served more than the owner of the Palace and his immediate retinue, it may well have been used by them for daily prayers, with the main congregational mosque either in the town of Kilwa or at Husuni Ndogo (a strange fortress-like enclosure 75 m. east of Husuni Kubwa, to be discussed later).

Possibly, however, this little structure is no more than an entrance hall, with the tanks used for washing one's feet—a useful amenity for someone who had just waded ashore from a boat beached or anchored offshore, and who was about to mount the stair and enter the Palace. Three points militate against this theory—the more convenient anchorage is under the shelter of the headland to the west, the stair was probably not a public access but led only to the owner's private quarters, and the little building is strangely and awkwardly sited, in detail, in its relationship to the stair.

On reaching the cliff top, the stair either led directly into the Palace court, centre of the domestic quarters of the Palace, or possibly a path bypassed this Palace court and led along the cliff top to a main entrance hall further south. This point can be more easily decided after the domestic quarters have been described. The Palace Court is an absolutely symmetrical rectangular court, entered by four shallow steps to north and south and flanked by raised walks to east and west, with long narrow arcaded rooms extending along both these sides. It is one of the most pleasantly proportioned, reticent and simple, yet well considered, pieces of design on the whole coast. Identical in nature with the normal domestic forecourt of Gedi or Songo Mnara, it rises far above them in the pleasant spaciousness of its atmosphere. There are no high blank walls. At each corner of the court, on the major visual axes, there is an isolated square chamber, entered by a step up from the court and accessible only from it. They are completely open to the court. They can have had little functional purpose other than to add to the visual effect of the court. In the centre of each room is a drainage hole and soakaway, otherwise almost never found outside the main rooms and ante-rooms of houses. This special provision for drainage in such small and public rooms may well suggest that they contained ornamental flowering plants or shrubs. Their positioning on the visual axes of the court makes them ideal for such a purpose. On the east and west sides of the court, long arcaded rooms, each with minor chambers opening off each end, provided shaded living areas for use during the day. Both appear to have had access to water tanks in one of their end chambers. A similar suite will be found flanking the entire south side of the Audience Court.

At the south end of the Palace Court there are the main domestic quarters of the owner of the Palace, in a double house unit very similar to those found at Songo Mnara and Gedi. This core consists of two interlocking standard house units, one facing north to the Palace Court, and one south to the Domestic Court. Thus from north to south, one has north ante-room, north main room, two north "bedrooms" inter-digitated with two south bedrooms, south main room, south ante-room, and so south to the domestic court. Both main rooms were decorated with both niches and wall hangings. The north ante-room and main room are unusually long (17 m.), but of the normal width—(the ubiquitous rafter module of 2·80 m.). This great length is necessary to accommodate the central range of four bedrooms, plus a lobby on their west (connecting north and south main rooms to each other and to a central corridor). This enables the four, 2·20 m. square, "bedrooms" to remain isolated from each other, and none is sacrificed to form a lobby, as at Gedi or Songo Mnara. It must be realized that the term "bedroom" is to some extent only a shorthand designation in order to give the rooms some name, and that their use as such is not completely certain. At Husuni, these "bedrooms" do not have the built in beds of Songo Mnara. Instead a 60 cms. wide shelf, supported by two small squared timbers, spans the rear wall of each room, at 1 m. above floor level, while there is a further shelf on one side wall, 1·80 m. above the floor. There is also evidence of wall hangings. It is notable that, in the domestic quarters at Husuni, main private rooms and latrines are absent, although the southern ante and main rooms do have square side chambers off them. The absence of latrines is accounted for by the difficulty of excavating the necessary pits in the sandstone, and further, the convenient proximity of gully, cliff and sea, over, or into, which latrines could discharge. Instead of these private suites, at the east end of the north ante-room, one enters a lobby with a triangular stand for a water jar and benches flanking a tank. It is quite probable that the latrines were situated in the now ruinous suite immediately to the north of this washroom/lobby. They would then have discharged into the eastern gully. From this lobby, a long, narrow room runs towards the south, and off it, to the east, open four separate rooms, two of which certainly contained built in beds of typical Songo Mnara type. This suite is domestic in nature, and formed the living quarters of the more senior and personal retinue of the owner of the Palace.

At the north end of the Palace Court there is a second typical house unit, though not, in this case, of the double type. It, like its southern counterpart, is entered from a main door on the main axis of the Palace Court, but due to lack of foresight in laying out the Palace before construction commenced, the axis of the main body of this unit behind the main door is moved 1 m. east of the Court axis. It consists of ante-room, with central door and flanking windows, leading, via two doors, to the main room (the staggered doorway system, present also in the southern units and already seen at Gedi, which ensures privacy even if doors are open or lacking) and thence to two bedrooms with shelves similar to those of the bedrooms in the southern unit. A lobby led to a single range of rooms behind the bedrooms: now completely destroyed but which, commanding the tip of the headland, may well have been an ante-room/verandah to take advantage of the magnificent views in complete privacy. It cannot be overlooked, nor is it visible from the stairway below. This unit was one of the most richly decorated areas of the whole palace; the bedroom range was probably vaulted: massive fragments of curved vaulting, thicker than the walls of the unit, have fallen nearby. Most of the carved tiles and motifs, described in Chapter IV, and fragments of carved inscription came from this unit.

The northern and southern house units and the Palace Court formed the private living quarters of the owner. The Palace Court is the only area of the Palace that provides sufficient privacy for womenfolk and it was clearly intended for secluded, shaded, comfortable, outdoor life. The main entrance to the Court is from the central door of the main southern ante-room which itself connects with the central corridor of the Palace. The Court probably also connected, via the small square chamber at its north-western corner, with the head of the stairway leading to the beach. It is impossible for this to have formed the main entrance to the whole complex of Husuni Kubwa. It is a contradiction of the complete symmetrical planning of the Domestic Court to suppose that one of four identical small chambers, offset in one corner, could provide the main access to this court, yet alone to the entire Palace. If this were true, all the visual impact of the court, so apparent when it is entered on its axis, would have been lost. Further, if this were the entrance to the Palace, it would completely destroy the privacy of the Palace Court: the only part of the whole complex sufficiently secluded for the use of women. Therefore, the stair either led to a main entrance hall elsewhere or, more probably, the stair was a private one and only used by the Sultan and his immediate retinue to get to the small mosque at the stair foot and to the shore, while the main public access to the Palace was elsewhere.

As has been said, a path at the cliff edge (all trace of which has vanished with the collapse of the cliff) may have led from the head of the stair, past the outside of the west of the Palace Court to a main entrance hall at the north end of the central corridor of the Palace. (The room marked "Hall" on the plan, Fig. 68.) This hall is lined with finely plastered benches for seating, which also contain recesses to hold the bases of four large water jars, filled from a storage tank just outside the hall. The hall connects with the central corridor of the Palace.   This central corridor is on the main axis of the Palace and, with the Pavilion, forms the true spine of the entire complex of Husuni, with every important element distributed about it.   It leads directly to the ante-room of the main Domestic quarters to the east, to the Pool to the west, and to the Pavilion, Audience Court and Domestic Court to the South.   From the hall also, one may descend a steep narrow stair to the west leading to the servants' quarters on a level below.   It would seem therefore extremely probable that this was the main entrance hall of the Palace.   One small but crucial point disproves it.   As has been shown in Chapter II, rebated doorways contain doors on their inner, or more private, sides with the masonry nib or projection of the door jamb on the outer or more public side—in order that the door may, as always, open inwards.   This is, of course, a universal practice followed in all buildings today, as well as at Husuni and elsewhere on the coast in the past.   In this case, an examination of the rebated doorway between the hall and corridor shows that the hall was not the more public, but the more private, part of the two—it could not therefore have been the main entrance hall of Husuni, for the connecting door would have then opened outwards—an occurrence as unlikely as the front door of any house today opening outwards.   The rebate of a ruined doorway on the west side of the hall confirms the evidence of the doorway between hall and corridor.   This hall must, instead, have served as a service lobby—a central area where the servants could await orders and where water and water containers were available for use or for transport elsewhere.   This would seem to confirm finally that the main entrance to the palace was neither at the north-west corner of the Palace Court, nor into this hall but in another area of the building altogether, which has been entirely destroyed.

The central corridor remains, however, as a major communicating link of the Palace. It gives, via a central door flanked by windows, onto the 13 m. square open area containing the decorative pool.   This pool is a fine and unique feature of Husuni.   The corners of the square are filled by four large, triangular seats, each bordered by a step up to it.   The pool itself is an octagon, 8 m. across, while inset in each side of the octagon are semicircular apses (the three western sides are partly missing but may safely be presumed identical to those remaining).   Each apse begins one step above the bottom step, bordering the bottom of the pool, and each contains a further step up to the kerb.   The plastered kerb of the pool is 60 cm. above the surrounding walkway, while the maximum depth of the pool is 2 m.   A drain leads out from the west and can be followed to its outlet at a lower level at the cliff edge.   The pool shape is the most elaborate example of decorative geometry on the coast, but there is possibly no need to presuppose that this particular form must be a direct copy of outside examples.[1]   The octagon is a common decorative form at Husuni, and given this geometric basis it is no great step to add a semicircle or apse to each face.   Indeed, the whole plan of the Palace shows delight in geometry for its own sake at the expense of any varied architectural expression.   The pool was probably flanked on north and south, if not completely enclosed, by long arcaded rooms, now quite destroyed.

Immediately south of the pool, the central corridor leads into a small lobby with a seat, and then, via a second, but open, lobby, again with a seat, opens onto the Domestic Court on the east and the Audience Court on the west, while the element of the spine continues south, in the form of a central Pavilion separating the two courts.   This Pavilion provides the more public core of the Palace plan and is the focal point of every vista from north, west and east.   Central doors, both flanked by large windows, fill both its east and west walls, while a wide dais, no doubt used for reclining, fills the narrow

[1] This opinion has been revised.   See p. 114.

north end, shielded from public view. It has niches above it, matched by similar niches at the south end.

The view from this Pavilion is particularly outstanding overlooking, as it does, the much lower Audience Court and buildings to the west, right across to the anchorage opposite the town of Kilwa far down to westward. Today it is a place of coolness with a constant breeze playing through the two courts, channelled by their flanking buildings and passing undisturbed through the pavilion, which certainly had no doors. There can be little doubt that here the owner of Husuni conducted his public business and spent much of the day. That this business was imposing in procedure and important is proved by the long flight of nine steps which descend from the walkway, immediately to the west of the Pavilion, into the Audience Court, whose floor is 3 m. below that of the Pavilion. These steps line, and form, the entire west face of the Audience Court. At the north corner of their foot is a small tank or footbath, no doubt used by the public before ascending the steps to the Pavilion and more private part of the Palace. The Audience Court is flanked to north and south by raised walkways. On the south side the raised walk is flanked by a long arcaded chamber with a small room at each end, closely similar to the flanking arcades of the Palace Court. This was certainly for the use of people of importance, as is indicated by the fine plaster finish and one surviving decorative niche, and was possibly used by staff attached to the owner, while he used the Pavilion. The walkways continue, as a walk along the roof of the large rooms enclosing the west side of the Audience Court, to link with the northern walkway and provide an imposing promenade round the entire perimeter of the Audience Court, looking down into it from all directions. The flank walls of the Court contain three rows of small, square niches (20 cms. by 30 cms. by 25 cms. deep, in a regular pattern, at 50 cms. centres), giving a total of some forty niches to each wall. There has been speculation as to their use, but it seems safe to assume that they are primarily decorative. The use of a series of fine dressed square recesses as decorative friezes, is a feature of the early "panel tombs" elsewhere along the coast, and although these differ considerably in detail from the Husuni niches, their aesthetic basis and appeal is similar. At night, these niches were probably also used to hold lamps. The use of this Court and the necessity for the wide flight of steps need explanation. The 15 m. by 13 m. Court itself is too small to contain any elaborate procedures necessitating a large number of participants, but its layout, with the view, restricted sides, and imposing Pavilion at the head of the rising tiers of eastern steps, is particularly theatrical in nature. There can be little doubt that the steps of the eastern side were used as seats, at least occasionally, their dimensions being more suited to this than to a staircase. Nevertheless, the main function of this stair is to give a dominating and majestic base or plinth to the Pavilion and an imposing approach to it. In fact, the court is designed to set off to the best advantage the crucial importance of the Pavilion at its head. Here the importance of Husuni and its owner, the occupant of the Pavilion, reach their maximum emphasis. The Pavilion, being on the eastern side of the Audience Court, occupies the same position as that which Kirkman assumes the Sultans took at the Palace of Gedi, and so follows the same principles as there—petitioners in the lower court would be looking into the sun above the Pavilion (which would be shaded and difficult to see in detail) at any function taking place during the morning—thus being put to certain discomfort and disadvantage.

There are several large rooms at Husuni treated in an identical way. Of normal width, they are exceptionally long (from 14 m. to 20 m.). At one end, they have rounded timbers, spanning across their width, at a height of 70 cms. above the floor——these, however, do not form a shelf the width of a bed, but are considerably wider.

Plate XIII. Mannerist mihrab, with distorted foliate arch, arcaded apse, and recessed minbar. Nineteenth century. Mboamaji Mosque.

Plate XIV. Reconstruction of the thirteenth century Palace of Husuni Kubwa, viewed from the west.

Otherwise, they are of identical construction to the "beds" of Husuni and Songo Mnara. The rooms themselves are entered by a door, or doors, at the opposite end to these large "beds". Characteristically, the rooms have a particularly coarse, thick, impure wall plaster, applied liberally and noticeably liquid, without ever being finished further, so that the strokes of the application are still clearly apparent (Plate II). This is completely unlike the thin coats of fine white plaster found in the house units of the Palace court, and is clearly an intentional differentiation of finish. The ceilings of these rooms are supported in most cases (not in those on the west side of the Audience Court) by un-dressed timbers—an ugly and crude yet more economical roofing method than the normal dressed squared timbers found elsewhere. It is most probable that these large, narrow rooms are the servants' rooms of the Palace. The well lit entrance end would be used during the day, while the large, communal beds provided uncomfortable sleeping accommodation, which was, however, no doubt adequate for servants.

From the northern hall, or service lobby, as has already been said, a steep, narrow stair leads off and down immediately, to the west, to the lower floor level (the level of the Audience Court) and enters the first of the servants' rooms. This has a note-worthy feature of two narrow slit windows, set in the particularly massive 2 m. thick north wall. These windows slope down to sight directly onto the edge of the beach below the cliff of Husuni to the north. This servants' room leads, at its western end, into a narrow passage running south, off which four narrow doors give westward. They lead, in the two surviving cases, to compartments each with a large cistern and a stand for a water jar. These are on the western cliff edge and the com-partments are now almost entirely destroyed, but they were no doubt the washing and latrine facilities for the servants. That there are two surviving, and probably a further two, identical tanks and rooms reinforces the argument that the adjacent rooms housed a considerable number of servants. The passage finally, at its southern end, leads to the two large rooms (each 20 m. long), the easternmost of which closes the whole western side of the Audience Court at low level. These two rooms contain virtually the only evidence of building alterations at Husuni. Originally they formed a single room, 5 m. wide, with a central dividing arcade of six square piers giving a particularly large communal living area. This was later divided by a screen wall down the line of the piers to separate the two rooms, leaving three large doorways to connect them. At their southern ends are the normal communal beds. These rooms were probably used not by servants, but by the general mass of petitioners etc. waiting to take part in the daily happenings of the Audience Court. Beneath the rooms, two drains finely made of dressed coral lead over the western cliff, draining the floor of the Audience Court. The easternmost of these large rooms gives onto the Audience Court, and adjoining this room, on the north and south flanks of the court, are two small covered verandahs with seats at each end. Here, possibly, minor petitions could be heard by court officials. Both have further rooms leading off them, and that to the south then leads on to a large lobby containing seat, tank and washing facilities. The roofs of these verandahs, with the roof of the large rooms, form the western continuation of the raised walks on the north and south sides of the Court.

Immediately east of the Pavilion is the Domestic Court, flanked on the north by the southern ante-room of the Palace house-unit, and on the south by two of the typical large servants' rooms. On the east of the court there is a standard house-unit, with ante-room with central door and flanking windows; main room with several wall niches, wall hangings and raised seating dais; and two "bedrooms", the northern of which contains a built-in bed. There is a north door in the ante-room, leading to the domestic suite previously described, and considered to house the senior retinue of the

Palace. It is reasonable to suppose that this housing unit belonged to the Palace Chamberlain in the same way that House V of the Palace at Gedi (Fig. 76) has been surmised to do. This isolated, well furnished, self contained unit has the same easy access to many salient parts of the Palace. Its access to the wing of the retinue and, via this, to the Palace housing and court, has just been described. It governs the Domestic Court and, from it, the adjacent service facilities and entrance to the south-east are easily supervised.

From the south-east corner of the Domestic Court, a passage runs past the eastern-most servants' room and, opposite this room, a covered verandah furnished with seats (very similar to the two little verandah alcoves in the Audience Court), to the deep masonry lined main well of the Palace. This is fronted by a large sump, sunk into the floor to take the well spill and overflow, and draining under the floor to the natural gulley outside the east wall. To the east of the well, and separated from it by a wall, is a cistern which was filled from the well, via a small conduit through the separating wall. This cistern served as the permanent source of water for the domestic requirements for the Palace. Two semicircular stands supported the containers while they were being filled from the cistern, while in the small area or court, in which the cistern stands, are a recessed water jar stand and the head of a spout to take waste and slops, which discharged into the east gully. A minor domestic entrance to the Palace from the outside most probably gave onto this area. This has been lost, with the disappearance of the area's eastern wall, if it existed.

This completes the description of the Palace proper. The great South Court is a separate entity, largely isolated from the Palace, and only entered from it via a door immediately south of the Pavilion and on the axial spine of the Palace. This door leads, via two lobbies, one flanked by side chambers, to the central staircase and lobby of the north range of the South Court. The South Court is an irregular square, 46 m. × 46 m. It is, therefore, more than nine times the area of any of the other courts; indeed, in size, construction, layout and function it is completely different to anything so far examined at Husuni. It no longer sits on the sandstone of the headland, and its boundaries are not restricted by cliff or gulley. Each side of the court consists of a double range of rooms—the north range backing onto the southern range of buildings of the Palace proper—and all are closely and intentionally similar. From the centre of the north and west ranges, a door leads into long staircase lobbies from which staircases rise to a first floor level. Both lobbies are identical in size and detail. Flanking the central lobbies are two remarkably long rooms (from 19 to 23 m. long), each with a central door, with small, square, high windows flanking it and in their turn flanked by narrow windows whose much lower sills enabled them to form subsidiary doors. It is remarkable how this layout is repeated in every detail on all four sides of the court—the only difference being that the south and east ranges lack the staircase or central lobby. From each of the long flanking rooms three doors lead to three isolated rear chambers (Rooms 1–3, 4–6; from 4·50 to 5 m. long and 2·50 m. wide), while in the centre of each long chamber a door leads to a rear chamber with two side chambers opening from it (Rooms 7, 8.) Thus, the rear range of rooms in each wing consists of nine chambers, giving a total of thirty-three. (The north range lacks the three central rooms as it connects instead to the Palace.) At the south end of the west wing, the south end of the east wing, and the east end of the north wing there are further suites of two similarly sized chambers (rooms 9, 10) entered from the end of their respective long flanking chambers. There is thus a grand total of thirty-nine chambers. There can be little doubt that these chambers were used as store rooms. Their walls are the thickest yet found—averaging 96 cms.—and were never plastered. Each is entered by a single door and, in the case of those in the north and east wings at least, their floor level was some 1·50 m. below that of the long flanking chambers, with no evidence of an access stair—no doubt a portable ladder was used instead. They all lack windows, and are therefore unlit, but for a series of, normally, eight roughly square "portholes" (40 × 40 cms.) with rough, irregular edges, set two to a wall, approximately opposite to one another. These closely resemble the irregularly square "portholes" found in the higher parts of several mosque walls, which are the remains of scaffold holes which were never made good. This is a satisfactory explanation for the Husuni "portholes"—the more so as they are so arranged that large scaffold poles could have been inserted at any time to form the frame-work of large, temporary storage shelves.

A further minor detail of planning that bears out that these were indeed storage rooms, is the fact that the entrance to each room is, wherever possible, directly opposite one of the main or subsidiary doors of the flanking chambers. This would make the entrance of goods for storage much easier. In contrast, in all the residential rooms of the Palace proper, wherever practical, the doors are staggered and no door of an inner room is directly opposite that of the outer room, but faces instead a blank wall. This is a neat and practical contrast in design.

Here in the South Court, with its vast area of uniform storage rooms, we have the economic foundation that enabled the great Palace of Husuni to be built and flourish in all its elaboration of planning and decoration. The subdivision of each range into identical suites of rooms, repeated four or eight times, must have been of functional significance, but this cannot be recreated today. Whether these storage rooms represent the means of levying taxes on the whole island's trade—the "bonded ware-houses" of Kilwa—or, less likely, due to their sheer volume, whether they represent the quantity of the owner's own trade—there is certainly nothing comparable on the rest of the east coast. Indeed, one would have to search widely to find such a bulk of trade buildings anywhere in the mediaeval period.

Finally, there is a suite of buildings outside, but adjacent to, the south-west corner of the South Court. A wide flight of nine steps rises eastwards to a paved terrace, while below and behind this are a suite of rooms, unlike any other unit in the complex and of no great size, but with finely dressed coral door jambs and some few carved decorative elements (found loose in excavation). The flight of steps echoes, in a minor way, that of the Audience Court and is similarly orientated. It is the nearest point of the complex to the town site of Kilwa itself, and the point most easily accessible from it, via cliff top paths. The most feasible explanation of this complex is that it represents a minor point of business and petition, more practical than the Audience Court: possibly the point where goods were received and tax exacted. Behind this complex there is a very large (4·60 m. square), deep well, masonry lined and roofed. Its size and positioning are strange—for it is far from the Palace where the water was needed, and which has anyway a well of its own. There is thus some doubt that it was in fact a well. The whole of the South Court is enclosed by three plain outside walls, each set at an angle to the respective range of rooms behind them. It is today impossible to determine the main entrance to the South Court. There is a small postern door in the centre of the south wing, and other wings possibly had similar doors, but they do not form the true court entrances—for they are too small. Possibly goods were brought up the steps at the south-west corner to the roof level and then carried along the roofs of the storage chambers to be lowered into the court wherever required—a perfectly practical proposition and one which would have increased the security of the court.

The only part of Husuni that has not been described here is the range of rooms constructed on the roof of the storage chambers in the north-west corner of the South

Court. These have been fully described in Chapter III when vaulted structures were considered. The six storage chambers at the north end of the west range and three storage chambers at the west end of the north range are of identical size (4·30 m. × 2·40 m.). Their thick (96 cms.) walls served to support an elaborately vaulted range of rooms on the upper floor above them, approached via the central staircases and with the flat roofs of the flanking chambers forming roof terraces that bound them. A reconstruction of the vaulted roofs of these rooms is shown in Fig. 69. As a visual climax, above the small square room at the end of the north-west long flanking chamber was the great conical fluted dome, its exterior ribbed; it must have dominated fittingly each vista of the Palace—seen from the north it would mark the end of all vistas southwards and eastwards across the Audience Court. It was near the cliff edge and gave visual emphasis to the crux of the Palace as seen from the beach and town approaches. From it, the Palace proper radiates northwards, and the great Court southwards, while behind it is ranged the great treble wing. From the upper floor and roof terraces again, it would end each vista. This remarkable dome, placed exactly to achieve its maximum effect, constitutes the only real entrance of the architecture of the coast into the realms of pure visual design and achieves its purpose admirably. The purpose of these rich apartments, with their flowering of decoration, visual design and spatial enterprise (still severely limited, but for the first time attempted), can be in little doubt. The great disadvantage of all coastal domestic planning is that, given the compactness of the basic house plan, its lack of windows in any but the main room, and the necessity for privacy, there is, in general, no satisfactory solution to the design of buildings that can be used for the routine of daily life, particularly if it is leisured, other than the courtyard with its blank walls and lack of view—a lack, no doubt, especially pointed at the magnificent site of Husuni. Nowhere, except possibly from the Pool, was there a view across the harbour entrance northwards. Only the Pavilion takes advantage of the fine view westwards to anchorage and town. This is remedied on the roof terraces. Fine views extend in every direction, taking in all parts of the Palace, especially the Audience Court below; the variety of domes, vaults and roof forms cuts down the necessity for blank supporting walls; and arched openings (of which several fragments remain), allowed light and air to penetrate to the core of the chambers, while height alone gave privacy, aided by low parapet walls. An additional benefit, conferred by height, was that the greatest effect was gained from any breeze. The evident great economic power of the owner of Husuni gave him the leisure that required numerous rooms for use for pleasure alone during the day, while providing the means to satisfy these requirements. The roof terraces are the result. Finally, the unique silhouette of the roof and its very varied shapes dominated the Palace and exclaimed the owner's power, not only to this part of the Palace, but beyond, especially to the shore below.

The problem of the position of the main public access to Husuni Kubwa remains unsolved. It seems clear that the northern staircase leading up from the shore to the northern tip of the headland could only have served the private living quarters of the Palace. The main public access is much more likely to have led almost directly to the Audience Court and the large rooms on its west side. A stair can be envisaged that could lead directly to the rooftop promenade of the Audience Court, while also serving the range of upper vaulted rooms (possibly entered via a hall under the great conical dome) and the walled service area outside the west side of the South Court, making this area suitable for the movement of goods from the South Court to the beach. There is no concrete evidence for this stair—cliff falls and erosion have badly damaged this area outside the Palace. Yet all planning considerations would seem to indicate that some such access may well have existed, and it would solve all the outstanding problems of communication. Such a stair is therefore shown in the reconstructions of Fig. 69 and Plates XIV and XV.

Eighteenth century domestic architecture

There are extensive remains of domestic buildings of the late eighteenth and nineteenth century along the coast. Major sites include the towns of Siu and Pate, several ruined houses on the island of Lamu in Kenya, several houses surrounding the late eighteenth century Palace of Kilwa and the remains of many large houses at Kua on Juani island. There are in addition many isolated stone built houses or remains of houses in many of the settlements along the coast. These ruined domestic buildings grade naturally into the architecture of the old parts of Zanzibari towns such as Zanzibar itself, Bagamoyo, Kilwa Kivinje, the earliest buildings of Mombasa and Dar es Salaam, and many others. No attempt will be made to describe these buildings, beyond showing that in the two sites most familiar to the author, Kilwa and Kua, resemblances to the early architecture remain.

In the main however, the standards of construction, decoration and design show the same marked deterioration on the earlier work so clear in the eighteenth century mosques. Complex plaster work mouldings decorate cornices and entire wall surfaces, while banks of niches in moulded plaster work frequently cover entire walls (especially in the Lamu area). Defensive works with loopholed parapet walls are frequently found.

Kilwa Palace

The residential core of the Palace of Kilwa (Fig. 78) is approached from a long narrow entrance hall, with benches along both its long aides. This leads, via a second smaller hall to an open central court from which a shallow stair or ramp ascends to the upper floor. The court is flanked by two rooms on each side which were probably bedrooms or servants' rooms. At the west end one enters an east facing suite of the normal early type—ante-room, main room, bedroom and washroom/latrine. The bedroom contains two buttress walls, one on each side, 1·30 m. high and 2·50 m. long. These probably supported timber cross pieces to form a wide shelf. This then would seem to be a bed—though both height and width are impractical. A similar structure exists in one of the "servants' bedrooms" of the court. To really consider these as beds may seem, however to distort the evidence too greatly. They are the logical successors to the "beds" of Gedi, Songo Mnara and Husuni Kubwa, and the position of the rooms in which they are found would seem to indicate that they were bedrooms. However, their true function must, at any rate in the Palace of Kilwa, remain an open question.

The main reception room is on the north side of the upper floor; niches in its outer wall, with four centred arched heads, alternate with square windows in a fashion typical of nineteenth century Zanzibar. Off this room, a latrine opens. The rooms above the two entrance halls were also important rooms with plaster work decoration and concrete roofs similar to those of the main reception room. The remaining rooms on the upper floor are of much poorer construction and finish and had only thatched roofs. Surrounding the core of the Palace is a massive solid battered wall to the north. This was later continued, on the west, as a simple outer skin wall (with an outer room added along part of its length) to end as a large solid bastion at the south-east. All served as defensive protection to the Palace core. The main courtyard is flanked by barracks and store rooms on its north and east sides, which provided further defence to the residential core. The upper walls of these rooms, and the barracks that occur on the south of the Palace were subsequently heightened by the addition of crude loopholed parapet walls, while a parapet wall containing gunports was added to the bastion top. This preoccupation with defensive work is a new feature on the coast. It is broadly contemporary with the erection of the Omani forts of Siu, Lamu and Kilwa itself, at a time when Oman was actively engaged in extending its political suzerainty over the coast.   Similar defensive work took place at the Palace of Songo Mnara.

Kilwa houses

The largest private house (Fig. 79A) within the Palace enclosure of Kilwa and contemporary with it, reflects many of the features of the Palace.   From a long narrow entrance hall, one enters a second smaller hall, with at least one bench along its wall, and from this the central court opens.   It again contains a very shallow stair leading to the upper floor, where the main room was situated (on the east side) with a washroom/latrine *en suite* at its south end.   This layout is repeated in simpler rooms below, on both east and west sides of the court.   There are two bedrooms on the ground floor at the south side of the court.   The washrooms/latrines contain vertical slit windows with splayed reveals, characteristic of the late eighteenth century.   The best example of them is found in a further house within the Palace enclosure (Fig. 79F) in what may well have been a bedroom, for it has the "buttress walls" found in the Palace bedrooms to support the "bed".   Externally, these slit windows are not themselves expressed, but the outer façade is decorated with blank rectangular panels, at window height and of window proportions, formed in moulded, painted plaster work.   Outside the bedroom, a long room has a washroom/latrine en suite and the same plan is found in the final illustrated house within the Palace enclosure (Fig. 76C).   The main room of this house contains many niches of differing designs, whose various arches so clearly reflect the varying, and to our eyes clashing, forms of the late eighteenth century.

Kua

The houses of Kua (Fig. 80) differ greatly from those of Kilwa, though retaining some of the most characteristic late eighteenth century features, notably the small slit windows and the long entrance halls or passages with benches along their sides.   They are "double houses", like those found much earlier at Gedi and Songo Mnara, with two identical adjoining halves—but the plans of the component halves are completely different from any plan yet described.   These two halves must represent the households of the two wives of the owner, unlike the Gedi and Songo Mnara houses where the division was by sexes.   Two typical plans of the largest houses (the "Palace" and the house to the north-west of it, Fig. 80) will be described.   From an entrance court or verandah two doors lead to the two halves of the house.   Each door leads to a long narrow L shaped passage (in one case lined with benches).   The short arm of the passage leads to the large main room (M), as usual decorated with wall niches, but lit only by slit windows.   From this room one enters a smaller private room (MP).   In the Palace a washroom/latrine (W) and possibly a storeroom also open off the main room. In one half, the store room (if it is such) can only be entered from a trap door high in the wall—a parallel to the system used at Gedi long before.   From the main room, one can also enter a large walled courtyard.   This description applied identically to each half of the plan.   The long arm of the L shaped passage finally gives on to a single very long ante-room (A), communal to both halves of the house.   The Palace also had an upper floor, reached from a stair in the entrance court.   Only in the Palace do latrines occur within the building.   In all other houses it seems that a washroom/latrine and an ancillary room were erected in a separate small building in each courtyard.   This is a logical conclusion to the process of development or separation whereby latrines, an integral part of the Songo Mnara houses, tend, in the late Gedi houses and even more at Mtwapa, to open off the house forecourt and not off living rooms.

The third Kua house illustrated is smaller and simpler than the others, but retains the same basis to its design.   There are two separate entrances, each leading to an ante-room at the north and south sides of the house.   These in turn give on to a short narrow passage, leading on the west to a decorated main room (M) and on the east to a smaller simpler room (MP).   Off the main room there is a bedroom (B) with the same strange buttress walls supporting a bed, previously seen in the Kilwa Palace and the Palace enclosure houses.   Both main rooms give on to a single large west court, in which the washroom/latrine was situated in a separate building.   The east court appears to have had no connection with the house, and has a self contained two roomed suite within it.

The Kua houses are extraordinary in the tortuous nature of their plans.   For the first time passages occur, splitting the typical plan in half.   The passage is duplicated in each house, which seems extraordinarily wasteful, when both ultimately lead from communal ante-room to communal entrance court.   The large walled courts are another seemingly extravagant feature for one would expect that in free standing perimeter walls of this nature (which do not support a roof), a timber, or wattle and daub, structure would serve equally well, if not better.   Yet, from an examination of the small scale published site plan covering the whole town of Kua,[1] it seems that these large walled courtyards, and probably the washhouses within them, were built of finer materials than the houses themselves, for the courts survive in pairs, while the house that stood between them has disappeared.   This strange reversal of normal practice is confirmed on the ground, where, in a superficial examination of the whole site, one certainly has the impression of many walled courts yet no sign of houses.

Mvuleni

The knowledge gained from the analysis of typical coastal houses of every period makes it easier to analyse certain atypical domestic buildings at Mvuleni, on the north-west coast of Zanzibar, and at Kilwa itself.

Two isolated and closely similar houses at Mvuleni (Fig. 81), each surrounded by high, straight, masonry walls enclosing rectangular courtyards, are ascribed to the Portuguese by strong local traditions, which have found their way into the literature on the subject.   These houses are built of the normal coral ragstone with simple, pointed arched doorways set in rectangular recesses and formed in very fine dressed coral.   The main rooms have the normal plain rectangular wall niches in both side and end walls, while one verandah shows evidence of a double row of fixings for wall hangings.   Throughout, the construction and decoration are therefore typical of the fifteenth or sixteenth centuries.   The plans are variants on the typical house plan of this period.   From a verandah one enters a long rectangular main room through a central door.   From the rear of this room doors lead to two small square bedrooms (in one house each contains the typical horizontal timber bed supports) while a further central door leads to a square lobby of similar size.   This lobby connects to a further rear lobby, again flanked by bedrooms, and so to a rear verandah.   Thus, in these houses, one has a double range of bedrooms and lobbies—a development on the sixteenth century Gedi houses, with their two roomed bedroom suites; yet also reminiscent of the domestic quarters of Husuni Kubwa (Fig. 68) which also has four bedrooms, two entered from each main room, though there they are interdigitated to form a single bedroom range.   The plans of the Mvuleni houses are thus a further variant on the typical house plan of the coast.   The axial planning is particularly strong with a vista through the entire house possible, via the series of central doors.   The core of one of these houses was flanked by suites of minor rooms on both sides, representing the main private rooms.

[1] Annual Report, Antiquities Division of Tanganyika, 1958.

Latrines occur at the end of verandahs—a position typical of the sixteenth, rather than the fifteenth century.

In one case, the "House by the Shore", four pillars rise above the central core, at first-floor level.   These are unlikely to have formed part of an upper floor, but most probably supported the main timbers of a thatched pitched roof, which were supported at the perimeter by the low buttress walls which project from the northern and southern sides of the house proper.   These four pillars are paralleled by the single northern pillar of the mosque of Takwa (Fig. 25) which was, therefore, very probably, also erected to form the central support of a pitched timber roof, probably in the seventeenth century.

The wall surrounding this house is loopholed on the side facing the sea.   In each group, three loopholes, one facing straight ahead with one angled sideways on each side of it, together provide an extensive field of fire.

These houses clearly belong to the main body of coastal domestic architecture, owing nothing to outside influences; while, typologically, it is most probable that they do indeed date from the period of Portuguese occupation of the coast during the sixteenth century.

Fifteenth century town houses

The complex masonry buildings (Fig. 75) immediately south of the Great Mosque of Kilwa have been revealed almost entirely by excavation and, except at the northern end, few walls survive above threshold level.   Finds show that the surviving structures belong, in the main, to the fifteenth century, with minor alterations and additions taking place in the sixteenth century.   The area was, however, occupied from the foundation of Kilwa and there is a great depth of occupation and building deposit ante-dating the standing buildings.   This, and the complex, irregular nature of the plans, is to be expected of an area which was, from the start, the centre of the town, immediately adjacent to the main congregational mosque.

In essence, the complex consists of two houses, each with two courtyards, and part of a third house (in the north east corner).   The whole complex is bounded on the west and south by early walls, considerably predating the houses themselves.   The western house (known as the South Building) is entered, at its north-western corner, through a monumental doorway at the head of the entrance stairs.   The entrance hall leads, via a lobby, to the main reception court, deeply sunken, with four steps lining the whole southern and eastern sides.   On the north there was, originally, an open arcade, probably somewhat similar to that surviving in the Palace court of Songo Mnara, while the whole of the eastern side of the court is flanked by a large main room with a raised seating dais at one end.   The whole arrangement echoes, on a smaller scale and somewhat crudely and irregularly, the reception arrangements of the Palaces of Husuni Kubwa and Songo Mnara.   As in the Audience Court of Husuni, there is a small tank or footbath at the corner of one flight of steps.   The court is considerably more elaborate than the reception court of a normal house.   The owner, who doubtless received his visitors in the eastern room (corresponding to the Pavilion of Husuni Kubwa and orientated like it, but unlike the main room of any domestic house) was certainly a person of some distinction, holding a position of authority.

From the south-east corner of the reception court, a narrow passage leads south to the domestic court.   This passage is flanked on each side by two rooms—the bedrooms of the house, arranged, as in sixteenth century Gedi, in two suites.   The domestic court was lined, as in the Palace of Gedi, by poorly constructed ranges of rooms, and contains a well.

This house has been considerably altered. The arcade was subdivided and a flight of stairs added to it, leading to an upper storey. The room at the north-east corner was blocked off and isolated from the house itself, an external door provided (opening off the narrow passage or road to the north) and a staircase built into it, leading again to an upper floor. A latrine was added at the northern end of the main reception room. The addition of an upper floor, with the consequent necessity of strengthening many walls or adding reinforcing linings to them to reduce the rafter spans, and the provision of staircases, is found throughout the later additions to the buildings of this complex.

East of the house described, there is a further house, more typical in plan (known as the South East Building). It is orientated eastwards and has sunken courtyards on both its east and west sides—the eastern one being considerably deeper than the western and lined by a flight of six steps. The surviving masonry collars to a series of up-right timber posts show that both courts were provided (at a late period of the building's occupation) with light timber roofs or awnings—a feature so far unparalleled elsewhere on the coast. The house itself consists of a main room to the east, giving onto three rooms—two bedrooms and a bedroom lobby (originally the central room, later transferred to the southern room). The lobby leads to the western main room and so through to the western court. Latrines occur off the southern end of both main rooms, while main private rooms open off both courtyard terraces at the northern end.

To the north of this house, an early, and so far unique, flagstone walk (which is much lower than the floor level of the house) probably continued on to join one which now passes along and under the east wall of the South Building. It remained in use and was later roofed when an upper floor was added—a modification that again required the addition of inner reinforcing wall linings on both northern and southern sides, to strengthen the roof support and narrow the spans. Stairs were also added, leading to the upper floor, from a room near the north-west corner of the house and from the north end of the east terrace.

The eastern court was used as a graveyard in the sixteenth century, when four small, poorly constructed tombs were placed in it. This court is flanked on its northern side by the retaining wall of a domestic court, part of a third house. The surviving portion of the latter house completes the complex in its north-east corner. It consists of the domestic court just mentioned, lined by the normal poorly constructed range of rooms on the northern side, with a well and latrine in the eastern corner, and a kitchen (with a typical, sunken, circular, earthenware hearth below two horizontal timbers which sup-ported cooking pots), lobby (connecting to an entrance court) and tank on the west side. The house was entered at the north-west corner, through a small hall leading to a large entrance court. This court did not have the normal sunken centre but, when the ubiquitous upper floor was added, raised walkways were built along its northern and eastern sides, leading to a flight of stairs giving onto the upper floor in its south east corner. At the same time a latrine (only accessible from the upper floor and not from the ground floor or court itself) was added to the south-west corner of the court.

Thus, in this extremely irregular complex of buildings one can discern three separate, self contained, domestic living units or houses. All have been extensively altered, and all have had an upper floor added to them—additions that have necessitated much adjustment and strengthening of the original structure. Two domestic courts, with wells, kitchen and poorly constructed ancillary rooms, are clearly discernible while the normal reception courts all have raised walkways on at least two sides and are flanked by raised benches or steps, providing ample seating for visitors. The complex illustrates the degree of improvisation and adaptation of basic house plans necessary in the congested centre of a town long occupied and built over. In spite of these severe difficulties, ample private courtyard space remained essential and it is clear that the life led in these houses was in no way modified, or different from, that provided by the larger, freer, yet more stereotyped, planning of a town such as Songo Mnara.

Husuni Ndogo

One building remains to be discussed—Husuni Ndogo (Fig. 70)—a massive walled enclosure, standing on a steep bluff, overlooking the sea, 75 m. east of Husuni Kubwa. This building is unique in East Africa and is quite without even the most tenuous local parallels. The little dateable material obtained from excavations within the enclosure indicate that it is contemporary with the great Palace of Husuni Kubwa—dating from the late thirteenth century.

Coral ragstone walls, over 1 m. thick, enclose a precise rectangle, 52 m. × 70 m., its main axis orientated 22° East of North. Solid bastions, with semicircular plinths and a six-sided superstructure (nine-sided at the corners), project from each corner, and at approximately 17 m. intervals along the sides. All the bastion quoins are formed in dressed coral. The only means of access to the walls or bastion tops appears to have been a single narrow stair towards the south-east corner. Though the walls still stand 2·50 m. high, the wall tops are now, of course, ruinous so the parapet details, if any, are lost. Internal buttress walls occurred round the entire perimeter of the enclosure at 4·30 m. intervals, projecting inwards 1·80 m. The present entrance, at the centre of the south wall, faces onto a blank inner wall—forming a bent entrance. Originally, however, the buttresses ran unbroken down the length of the south wall. Behind the inner entrance wall there is a well and nearby a small decorative octagonal tank, 2 m. in diameter. In the centre of the west wall a rectangular bastion contains a raised dais. There are no further original, or intelligible, structures within the enclosure.

The purpose of this very large enclosure remains unsolved. The security provided by the massive outer walls is the most immediately striking feature. It may, therefore, well have been built by the Sultan of thirteenth century Kilwa, owner of the nearby Palace of Husuni Kubwa, as a secure and easily regulated trading centre, within which individual traders could erect their own temporary booths or other structures: the internal buttresses providing a convenient means both of delimitation and attachment for such structures. Finds of crucibles in one area of the enclosure would seem to support such an interpretation and the building is clearly convenient for supervision from the Palace itself, while access to the great southern storage court of the Palace is also easy. Alternatively, it could possibly have been a barracks.[1]

It has been suggested[2] that part, at least, of Husuni Ndogo was a mosque. Between two internal buttresses, just off centre to the east of the centre of the north wall, extremely slight traces of an apsidal recess within the wall thickness have previously been discerned, well above ground level. The wall has collapsed to this level in this area. This apse, indicating the presence of a mihrab, was no longer discernible, even after particularly close examination, to the present author—who cannot, therefore, on the present evidence, support such an interpretation. Nevertheless, the flanking internal buttress walls at this point are set at a closer interval than elsewhere—the only interruption of their regular spacing. There is no parallel to a mosque or mihrab of this type, if it were such, elsewhere on the coast—but the whole design of Husuni Ndogo is unique. Its function therefore remains obscure, though the whole design is strongly reminiscent of buildings of much earlier date in the Near East. In this lies the great interest of Husuni Ndogo. These parallels are discussed in the following chapter.

1 See p. 114.
2 H. N. Chittick: Journal of African History, IV, 2. p. 188.

CHAPTER IX

ORIGINS OF THE COASTAL ARCHITECTURE

Any attempt here to seek the origins of the early architecture of the East African coast is hampered by the present author's limited knowledge, gained only from the more easily available literature, of Islamic architecture outside East Africa. In no one region of the Near East are there sufficiently numerous or detailed parallels to enable clear conclusions on the origins to be confirmed without doubt. This is probably largely due to the fact that, while studies of the early architecture of much of Islam have been made in great detail, the minor provincial architecture of the later mediaeval periods is little documented—and it is precisely from here that the sources of the coastal style must surely be derived. The builders of the East African mosques are much more likely to have drawn on their knowledge and experience of the recently erected provincial buildings of their homelands than on the earlier great monuments of the major cities—buildings whose scale, complex construction and elaborate finishes were little relevant to the much smaller settlements of the coast, with their much more limited material and human resources.

The fountainhead of all the post thirteenth century architecture of the coast is undoubtedly Husuni Kubwa. Its contemporary, Husuni Ndogo, though of a design and a building type never repeated locally, must have drawn its architectural inspiration from the same sources as Husuni Kubwa. This massive rectangular enclosure, with solid bastioned walls, is ultimately derived from the Roman castra or frontier fortresses of Syria. These formed the source of the designs of the desert palaces of the Umayyads, such as Minya, Qasr al Hair and Mshatta, dating from the first half of the eighth century, which developed during the latter half of the century, in Abbasid times, into the Great Palaces of Ukhaidir and, later, that of al Mutasim at Samarra. The same rectangular bastioned enclosure surrounded the Great Mosques of Raqqa and Samarra. In north-west Africa, the early ninth century *ribat*, or fortified monastery, of Susa has the same origins. There can be little doubt that Husuni Ndogo also owes its style ultimately to buildings such as these but the more immediate connecting links between these eighth century buildings and the thirteenth century East African building are still unknown.

The pointed arch occurs in early eighth century Umayyad buildings, and by mid century, at Mshatta, is of identical form to the typical East African arch, with the arch centres 1/5 span apart, a ratio which remained fairly constant thenceforth. In East Africa, prior to the eighteenth century, none of the other arch forms so characteristic of Islamic architecture, such as the horseshoe or four centred Persian arch, are ever found. The mid ninth century Palace of al Mutasim at Samarra has many further intriguing similarities to the Husuni buildings. It is built on a bluff overlooking the Tigris and approached by a monumental stair from the river. It is also arranged in a series of courts, whose layout is based on axial planning in very much the same way as that of Husuni Kubwa. Though of far larger size, scale and complexity, the basic handling of the plan units shows strong similarities to that of Husuni. An interesting detailed correspondence is found in the stucco dado of a mosque room near the throne room of Samarra, where the motif used is an inverted "fleur de lys",[1] whose somewhat rigid form is virtually identical to the carved coral "fleur de lys" of Husuni Kubwa (Fig. 72H). Part of the Palace complex of Samarra, set apart from the Palace proper, is a rectangular bastioned enclosure—the Barracks—closely similar to the great enclosure of Husuni Ndogo.

The decorative Pool of Husuni Kubwa has been compared in form to the ablution basin (probably twelfth century) of the Abbasid mosque of Harran in south-west Turkey[2]—this comparison is not certain and the relevant illustrations of the Harran basin are not available. However, the bath is certainly identical in form, though larger in size, to the small decorative marble pools, found with fountains at their centre in the main rooms of houses of Mamluke Egypt (1250–1517). In the Coptic museum of Cairo, a restoration of such a house, there is a series of such octagonal pools. All have a semicircular apse, containing an inset step, in each face of the octagon, and each pool is set in a square surround, with a raised triangular step across each corner of the square. Such extremely close identity to the Pool of Husuni Kubwa is a certain indication that they have a common origin—again however, the intermediate connecting links are unknown.

Several of the architectural features of Husuni Kubwa are found in widely differing areas of Islam—the ribbed (or melon) external surface form of the main conical dome is an extremely long lived and widespread form, as are several of the minor decorative motifs. The basic, polygonal, flat sided or tent shaped vault form of Husuni is, however, characteristic of Seljuk tower tombs or turbs and is, indeed, ultimately derived from tent forms of Turkish origin. Such tombs are found not only in Turkey and northern Iraq, but in Persia during the Seljuk period from the mid eleventh century to the end of the twelfth century. Two minarets of the al Azhar mosque, a building of the tenth century and later, in Cairo also echo this form.

It is more difficult to relate the other vault forms of the coast to any specific area of the Islamic homelands. The flat faced false pendentive, or Turkish triangle, is extremely rare in Persia. It does occur in a few twelfth century Seljuk cloister domes in the Jamia of Isfahan, and in the contemporary provincial Jamia of Sidih. The contemporary mosque of Ardistan has contiguous domical vaults, first used in Persia in Seljuk times, and here the pendentive is replaced by shallow groined squinches, a characteristic Seljuk form, supported on octagonal columns. The provincial mosques of Persia of this period (such as Sidih) are almost completely roofed with high crowned vaults. These features clearly relate to the Kilwa group of vaulted buildings. More significantly, certain basic features of Seljuk and subsequent building technique in Persia, such as the use of horizontal timber reinforcement in walling and of scaffold holes, left subsequently undisguised, would seem to confirm that the architecture of the coast is related to the Persian architecture of this period.

Though the Seljuk architecture of Persia is built almost entirely in brick—rubble and mortar construction with a plaster finish, so typical of East Africa, was used in Persia prior to the Seljuk period, particularly in the southern provinces. The Jamia of Shiraz was even reconstructed in the mid fourteenth century using rubble walling with cut and fitted stonework. It has been said of this period[3] "Persian builders scarcely understood inflexion. Most vistas in the arcades of mosques, for instance, simply peter out at the end. These buildings have a serial quality. The relation between a form and its neighbour is all important, that between a form and the whole infinitely

[1] H. C. Creswell: A Short Account of Early Muslim Architecture. Plate 52a.
[2] H. N. Chittick: Annual Report, Antiquities Division of Tanganyika, 1960, p. 8.
[3] E. Schroeder in A. U. Pope: Survey of Persian Art, Vol. VI, p. 999.

less so." No description could apply more completely and appositely to the architecture of East Africa. The trabeated columnar mosque plan in which the roof rests directly on piers or columns without the intermediary of arches—the "apadana" type of plan—is of indigenous Persian origin, derived from Achaemanid and Sassanian origins, continued there, if only rarely, in such mosques as the Jamia of Shiraz and Isfahan and, at the end of the fourteenth century, at Samarkand. The many columned, unmodulated mosque plan is, of course, the only type of mosque found in East Africa.

The most frequent mosque plan in the Near East and India—the "madrassa" type—in which arcades surround a great central court with great iwans (barrel vaulted halls with openings at one end) at the centre of each side—is completely unknown in East Africa. Their characteristic features, such as great unified spaces dominated by a single central feature, or carefully composed façades with great central doorways, are quite alien to the coast. It is the complete contrast between such features and the unmodulated architecture of the coast, in which no mosque (except for the early form of the Great Mosque at Kilwa) had a central court and in which composition about a dominant feature is absolutely unknown, that makes the architecture of East Africa appear superficially to have not the least affinity with Islamic architecture of the Near East or India.

The fifteenth century vaulted extensions to the Great Mosque of Kilwa have been compared to the Jamia of Gulbarga, a major monument of Bahmanid India, completed in A.D. 1367—mainly because this is the only other widely known early mosque without a courtyard and entirely roofed by a series of small domes. However, this is a modulated, symmetrical design with a large, 12 m. diameter dome in front of the mihrab, 8 m. diameter lesser domes in each of the four corners, and sixty three 4·50 m. diameter minor domes roofing the court. This is a design stemming from an approach basically different from that of East Africa unless one envisages the fifteenth century extensions to the Great Mosque of Kilwa as merely the roofing of a pre-existing courtyard, with the major ancillary units requiring architectural differentiation, such as the mosque proper, already existing and therefore not open to such differentiation. This is a legitimate approach and would bring the design of Gulbarga and Kilwa closer together. Though Gulbarga and Kilwa have this superficial resemblance, they differ widely in detail—the main dome of Gulbarga rests on a square clerestory, the perimeter arches are supported on square piers which lack capitals, and the wide arches have their springing at a markedly low level. The vaults rise from flat corbelled pendentives, except in the case of the main dome where floriate squinches occur, a feature quite different from the groined squinches of Kilwa. However, the structural arches are ogival in form and the profile of the domes is very similar to that of Kilwa. The architect of Gulbarga, Rafi, came from Kazvin in northern Persia of a noted family of architects and the design of this mosque is largely individual to him, for it was never subsequently repeated.

There are, nevertheless, further resemblances between the East African and Indian Islamic architecture. The simple, pointed, ogival or nicked arches, the flat faced false or corbelled pendentive, and the method of transition between octagon and circular dome seat achieved by the varying projection of multiple stonework cornices (the latter so characteristic of the Kilwa domed buildings) are all characteristic of India. In India, like East Africa, the otherwise ubiquitous Islamic stalactite vaulting is never found—though in East Africa this can be easily explained as due to lack of skill, and the technical complexities involved.

Sufficient comparisons have been made to show the extreme difficulty, without visiting the Near East or India, of finding sufficiently detailed and extensive comparisons between the architectural style of the coast and that of any single region abroad. For every single correspondence noted, the buildings abroad show, in almost every case, numerous basic features completely different to those of the coastal buildings and derived from a fundamentally different background and approach.   It is therefore of little value to enumerate further isolated points of comparison.   For valid conclusions, one must be able to show that numerous comparisons, drawn from many buildings of a homogeneous architectural region and period abroad, are closely similar to the basic motifs that go to make up the architectural style of the coast.   This has, so far, proved impossible.

These difficulties do, however, tend to confirm what is already clearly apparent: that the architectural style of East Africa before the eighteenth century is, to a large extent, indigenous to the coast.   Beneath the basic unity of the coastal architecture, there are several minor regional variants.   Square piers, octagonal columns, raised arch archivolts, recesses in the pilasters framing the mihrab: all are minor features clearly confined to certain limited areas of the coast and following discernible regional patterns.   Nevertheless, the architecture is a homogeneous entity, and the minor variants are of no fundamental significance.   It is an architectural style, perhaps limited in its aims and satisfied with a standardized and unadventurous technical competence sufficient only to such aims, never seeking the imaginative or inventive new solution.   Yet it certainly progresses and develops, extremely slowly but steadily, and without outside influence.   The only really significant changes, after the thirteenth century, are probably the replacement of the false pendentive and conical vaults of Husuni Kubwa, Mwana and Ungwana by the groined squinch and curved domes of the Kilwa group of buildings of the fifteenth century, and the introduction of the trefoliate inner mihrab arch in the neo-classic mosques of the late seventeenth century.

No doubt the innate strength that enabled this individual style of building to arise, survive and develop is largely due to the complete and masterful exploitation of the very limited, yet so easily available, varieties of local building material.   For the style is not only individual but assured.   The refinement, yet simplicity, of the early arch and moulding forms; the individual, yet uniform, planning of all domestic buildings; the technical competence of highly skilled artisans, working in a clearly defined and fixed conservative tradition of craftsmanship (and never tempted to step out of its controlling influence to initiate their own individual techniques or designs): all contribute to the homogeneity and assurance of what appears, more and more clearly, to be an in-digenous East African architecture.   The self-reliance of the architecture is confirmed by the presence of imported plaques (such as those of the mosque of Fakhr ad Din, Mogadishu and the Sultansmausoleum, Kilwa) illustrating architectural features very different to those of the coast.   The coastal architecture remained completely unaffected by even such concrete evidence, valued highly for its intrinsic and decorative appeal, yet with no further effect on the architecture.

The few buildings that predate Husuni Kubwa may have been of differing style to the subsequent architecture—certainly the mihrab of Kaole is quite different from any other surviving, while the design of the Tower of the Jamia of Mogadishu, and its contemporaries, is never repeated after the thirteenth century.   The coursed, and even squared, rubble wall is characteristic of this period.   Husuni Kubwa initiates the true architectural style of the coast with a variety and splendour never again equalled.   This is proof that the coastal architecture did draw its inspiration and initial impetus from abroad.   But thereafter, it followed its own course, supported by the skills of artisans working and exploiting a single basic material to its limits.   Complete mastery over their material; restrained, yet highly competently handled, decoration;

widespread desire for, and recognition of the value of, compactly and uniformly designed private houses, in which a leisured and secluded domestic life was possible in the spacious courtyards of even the most congested town centre; the value set on sound construction, and proper sanitation: all show that the architecture of the early Islamic settlements of East Africa clearly reflects a limited, unadventurous and provincial but, nevertheless, competent, comfortable and satisfying life, conscious of beauty for its own sake (as shown in its display of porcelain and the wall hangings in the major rooms of every house). At least once, at Husuni Kubwa, it rises far above the norm, to delight in the advantages of an ideal site in which climate, views, ample space and means are all exploited to the full.

APPENDIX I

DETAILED STUDY OF SONGO MNARA

Songo Mnara Palace

The plan of the Palace of Songo Mnara (Fig. 73, Plate XVI) is most easily compre-hended when it is realised that it is not a "Palace" in any usual sense of the word but rather 15 adjoining, closely connected houses, which have been given a certain surface unity by the addition of a monumental façade and vaulted arcade to the central court. The original structure consisted of six standard houses (nos. 13, 14, 15, 10, 9, 7) ringing the court on the north and east. To the south, there were four minor houses (3, 4, 5, 6). Between houses 4 and 5 on the south side of the court, and exactly opposite the long entrance passage, there was a square room supporting a dome. The entrance passage and this domed room survive from the earliest period of the Palace. The original Palace had a court but of differing form to that which now exists. In order to give this original court, at the core of the Palace, a design more suitable to its importance, single rows of apartments with monumental central doors were built on the east and west sides (house 1: B1, B2, B3, house 2: M) and a vaulted arcade built round three sides of the court. This arcade now only survives on the southern side. These altera-tions entailed moving the axis of the court 2 m. to the east, so the earlier axis of the entrance passage and domed room, mentioned above, is no longer the central axis of the court. This led to serious difficulties in relating the monumental southern door of the court to the domed chamber behind it and also in providing access to house 5. Probably at this time a series of rooms whose purpose is unknown was added at the south-east end outside the external south and east walls of house 7, and the minor house 8 built.

In the eighteenth century the Palace complex was reoccupied and numerous houses appear to have had a second storey added to them. These additions are placed in this century almost entirely because their workmanship is very noticeably inferior to that of the earlier period. (They also frequently have one characteristic feature found in many late eighteenth century buildings (e.g. Makutani Palace, Kilwa): a narrow vertical slit window with splayed reveals. These windows often occur in a horizontal series.) At this time house 10 had already largely fallen into ruin, or was purposely destroyed, and the atypical and irregular houses 11 and 12 were fitted into the available space. Above these two houses, and extending over house 8, a large upper storey was added, approached from two staircases (in house 11A and the court of house 7). It is too ruinous and in-accessible for a satisfactory plan to be established. An upper storey was also added to house 5 (in the south-west corner). By this time the eastern and western vaulted arcades had collapsed. They were replaced by poorly constructed outer rooms (1A and 2A). The apartments on the east and west sides of the main court were also extensively altered, as was House 13. Outside the Palace, the eighteenth century work included the addition of a large house in front of house 18 and extending over the east and west wings of this house. The quadrant shaped latrine ducts characteristic of the eighteenth century give evidence of this. Alterations or additions also took place

Plate XVI. Central court, Palace of Songo Mnara. The coarse workmanship of the eighteenth century arcade in the foreground contrasts strongly with the fine fifteenth century arched doorways in the rear.

Plate XV. Reconstruction of the thirteenth century Palace of Husuni Kubwa, viewed from the north-east.

in front of the washroom of house 38—where a narrow cubicle received a grid of the typical slit windows of eighteenth century houses. This has led several writers rather romantically to describe this, and house 37, as the "guard house"—a term which has even less validity than the term "Palace" at Songo Mnara. They are quite standard houses, with late eighteenth century additions, lit in a standard way for that period. The slit windows were certainly not loopholes. However, many of the outer Palace walls were heightened by rough, unplastered, loopholed, parapet walls (as was house 17) at this time. Defensive work of very similar character occurs in the upper outer walls of the Palace at Kilwa.

House plans

The house plans of Songo Mnara described in Chapter VIII are almost completely standardized (Fig. 74). Houses 7, 9, 14, 16, 17, 18, 23, 30, 37 (in this case the caretaker seems to have occupied the entire minor house 38), 43 and 48 are typical of the standard house. Smaller examples which lack the normal courtyard wings or, if isolated, the stone walled courtyard itself are 19, 22, 26, 40, 41, 46. These grade into the typical isolated minor houses of 15, 24, 28, 29, (besides those of 1, 2, 3, 4, 5, 6, 8, within the Palace itself). The large typical double house is represented by houses no. 21, 34 and 45, while examples of doubling on a much smaller scale, in minor houses without courtyards, are found in houses 32, 33, 39, 42 and 44.

The houses numbered 10, 11, 12, 20, 36, 47 are too atypical to fit into any of these groupings, in most cases because they are later additions and have had to be adapted to fit difficult and irregular spaces. Their planning basis is, however, quite clearly the same as that of the more normal houses.

SELECTED BIBLIOGRAPHY

Abbreviation: T.N.R.: Tanganyika Notes and Records.

AXELSON, E. South East Africa, 1488–1530. London. 1940.

The Portuguese in South East Africa, 1600–1700. Johannesburg. 1960.

BAUMANN, O. Mafia. 1896. (Reprinted T.N.R. 46. 1957).

BUCHANAN, L. A. C. The Ancient Monuments of Pemba. Zanzibar. 1932.

BURTON, R. F. Zanzibar: City Island and Coast. London. 1872.

CERULLI, E. Somalia. Rome. 1957.

CHITTICK, H. N. Annual Reports of the Antiquities Division of Tanganyika, 1957–1961.

Annual Reports of the British Institute of History and Archaeology in East Africa, 1959–1962, 1963.

Notes on Kilwa. T.N.R., No. 53. 1959.

Kisimani Mafia. Occasional Paper, Antiquities Division of Tanganyika. 1961.

Kilwa and the Arab Settlement of the East African Coast. Journal of African History. IV. 2. 1963.

CRESWELL, K. A. C. Early Muslim Architecture. 2 vols. Oxford, 1932–1940.

A Short Account of Early Muslim Architecture. Penguin. 1958.

DORMAN, M. H. The Kilwa Civilization. T.N.R., No. 6. 1938.

FERGUSSON, J. History of Indian and Eastern Architecture. J. Murray. 1910.

FLURY, S. The Kufic Inscriptions of Kizimkazi Mosque, Zanzibar. Journal of the Royal Asiatic Society. 1922.

GIBB, H. A. R. (ed.) The Travels of Ibn Battuta. Hakluyt Society. 1919.

GRAY, J. M. History of Zanzibar from the Middle Ages to 1856. Oxford. 1962.

Kilwa in 1812. T.N.R., No. 24. 1947.

A History of Kilwa. T.N.R., Nos. 31–32. 1951–1952.

The French at Kilwa. T.N.R., No. 44. 1956.

GRENVILLE, G. S. P. FREEMAN- Mediaeval History of the Coast of Tanganyika. Oxford University Press. 1962.

The East African Coast. Select Documents. Oxford. 1962.

In: History of East Africa. Vol. 1. (Ed. Oliver, Mathew). Oxford. 1962.

Mediaeval Mosques of Tanganyika. T.N.R., No. 36. 1954.

Recent Archaeological Work on the Tanganyika Coast. Man. LVIII. 1958.

East African Coinage. T.N.R., Nos. 45. 1956, and 53. 1959.

The Chronology of the Sultans of Kilwa. T.N.R., No. 50. 1958.

GROTTANELLI, V. L.   Missione Grottanelli nell'Oltreguiba. R.A. XXXIX. Rome. 1951–1952.
Pescatori dell' Oceano Indiano. Rome. 1955.

GUILLAIN, M.   Documents sur l'histoire, la géographie et le commerce de l'Afrique orientale. Paris. 1856.

HAVELL, E. B.   Indian Architecture. Murray. 1927.

INGRAMS, W. H.   Zanzibar, its History and People. London. 1931.

KIRKMAN, J. S.   The Arab City of Gedi. Excavations at the Great Mosque. Oxford. 1954.
Gedi—The Palace. Hague. 1963.
Culture of the Kenya Coast in the Later Middle Ages. South African Archaeological Bulletin. XI. 44. 1956.
Historical Archaeology in Kenya. Antiquaries Journal. XXXVII. 1957.
Takwa. Ars Orientalis. II. 1957.
The Pillars of Malindi and Mambrui. Oriental Art. 1958.
Mnarani. Ars Orientalis. III. 1959.
Ras Mkumbuu. T.N.R., No. 53. 1959.
Gedi—The Tomb of the Dated Inscription. Journal of the Royal Anthropological Institute. 1960.

MARCAIS, G.   L'Architecture Musulmane d'Occident. Paris. 1954.

MATHEW, G.   In: History of East Africa. Vol. 1. (Ed. Oliver, Mathew). Oxford. 1962.
Tanganyika's First Colonists. East African Annual, 1951–1952 (with J. P. Moffett).
Recent Discoveries in East African Archaeology. Antiquity. Vol. XXVII. Dec., 1953.
The Culture of the East African Coast in the Seventeenth and Eighteenth Centuries. Man. LVI. 1956.
Chinese Porcelain in East Africa and on the Coast of South Arabia. Oriental Art. II. 1956.
Songo Mnara. T.N.R., No. 53. 1959.
In: Conferences on African History and Archaeology, Reports. School of Oriental and African Studies, London. 1953, 1957.

OWEN, W. F. W.   Narrative of Voyages. New York. 1833.

PEARCE, F. B.   Zanzibar, the Island Metropolis. London. 1920.

POPE, A. U.   A Survey of Persian Art. Vol. VI. Oxford University Press. 1939.

PRINS, A. J. H.   The Swahili Speaking Peoples of Zanzibar and the East African Coast. London. 1961.

PRIOR, J.   Voyage along the Eastern Coast of Africa in the Nisus frigate. London. 1819.

RICHMOND, E. T.   Moslem Architecture. Royal Asiatic Society. 1926.

ROSINTAL, J.   Pendentives, Trompes et Stalactites dans l'architecture orientale. Paris. 1928.

RUMPLER, M.   La Coupole dans l'architecture byzantine et musulmane. Strasbourg. 1956.

SCHACHT, J.   An Unknown Type of Minbar and its Historical Significance. Ars Orientalis. II. 1957.
Further Notes on Minbars. Ars Orientalis. III. 1959.

STIGAND, C. H.   The Land of Zinj. London. 1913.

STRANDES, J.   The Portuguese Period in East Africa. (Ed. Wallwork and Kirkman). Nairobi. 1961.

STUHLMANN, F.   Beitrage zur Kulturgeschichte von Ostafrika.   Berlin.   1909.

THEAL, G. M.   Records of South Eastern Africa.   9 vols.   Cape Town, 1898–
                         1903.

VELTEN, C.   Prosa und Poësie der Suahili.   Berlin.   1907.

VOELTZKOW, A.   Reisen in Ost-Afrika in den Jahren 1903–1905.

WALKER, J.   History and Coinage of the Sultans of Kilwa.   Numismatic
                         Chronicle.   1936.   (Reprinted T.N.R., No. 45.   1956).

WHEELER, R. E. M.   Archaeology in East Africa.   T.N.R., No. 40.   1955.

WILBER, D. N.   The Architecture of Islamic Iran.   Princetown.   1955.

———   A Guide to Zanzibar.   Zanzibar.   1961.

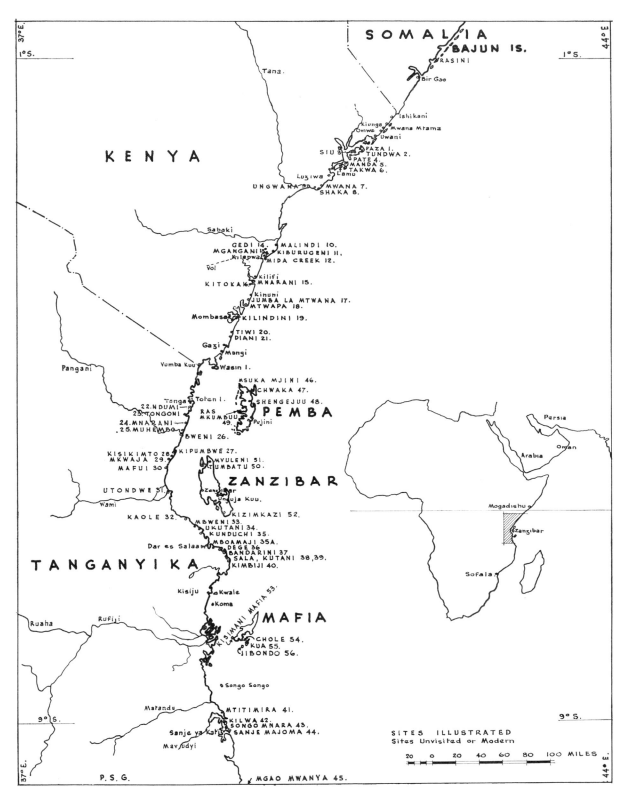

Fig. 1

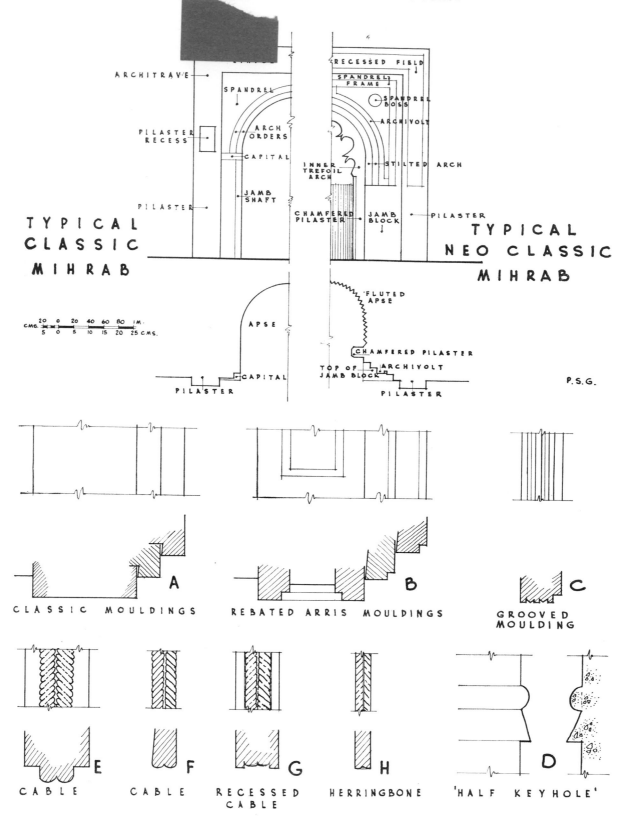

Fig. 2

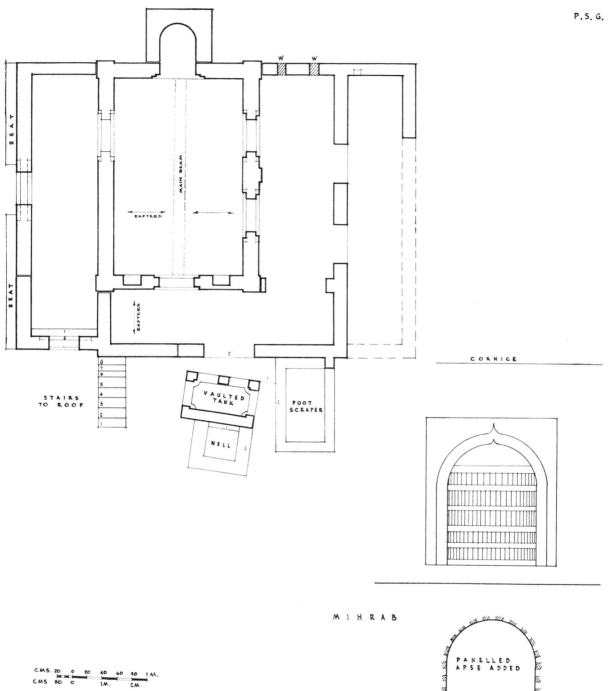

CORNICE

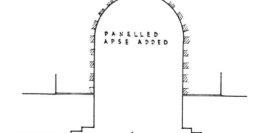

MIHRAB

32.
EARLY MOSQUE
KAOLE

Fig. 3

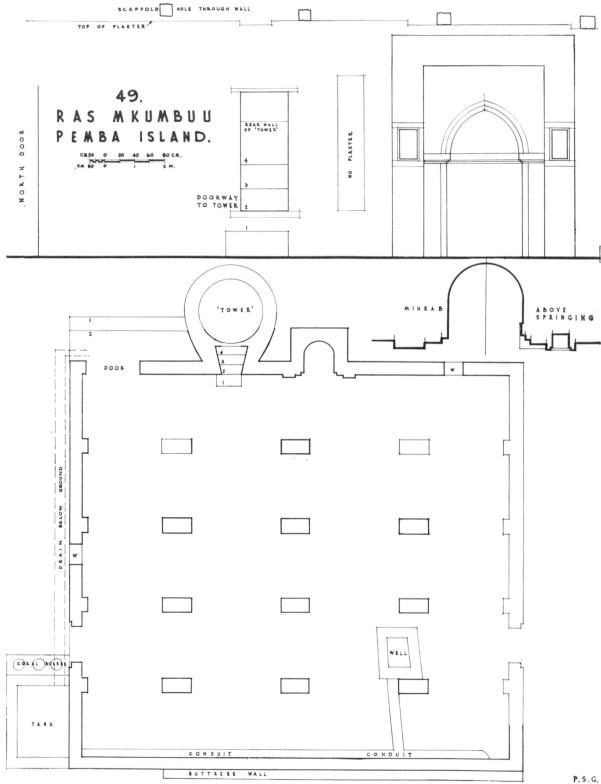

Fig. 4

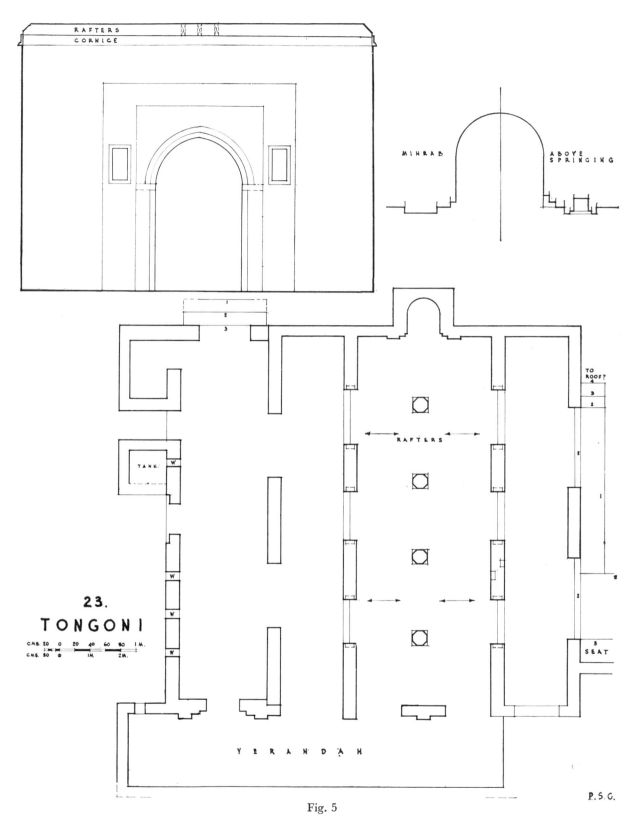

Fig. 5

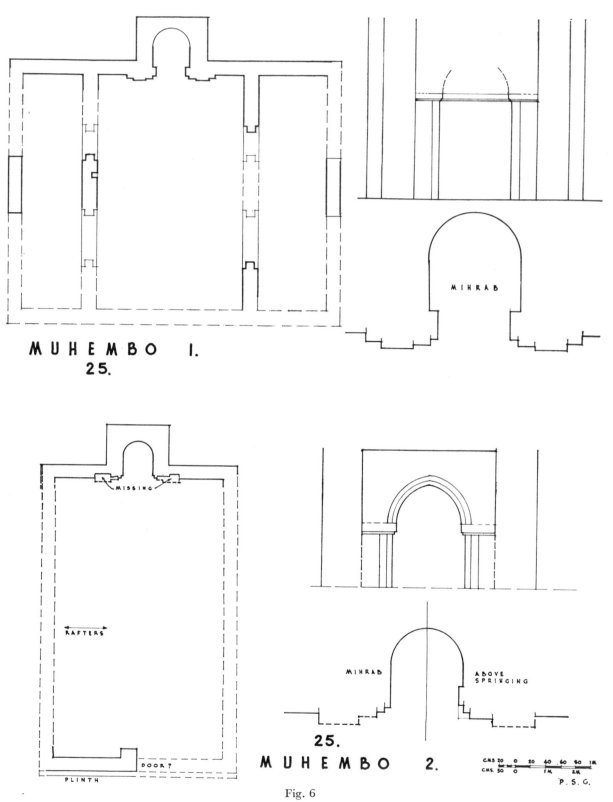

Fig. 6

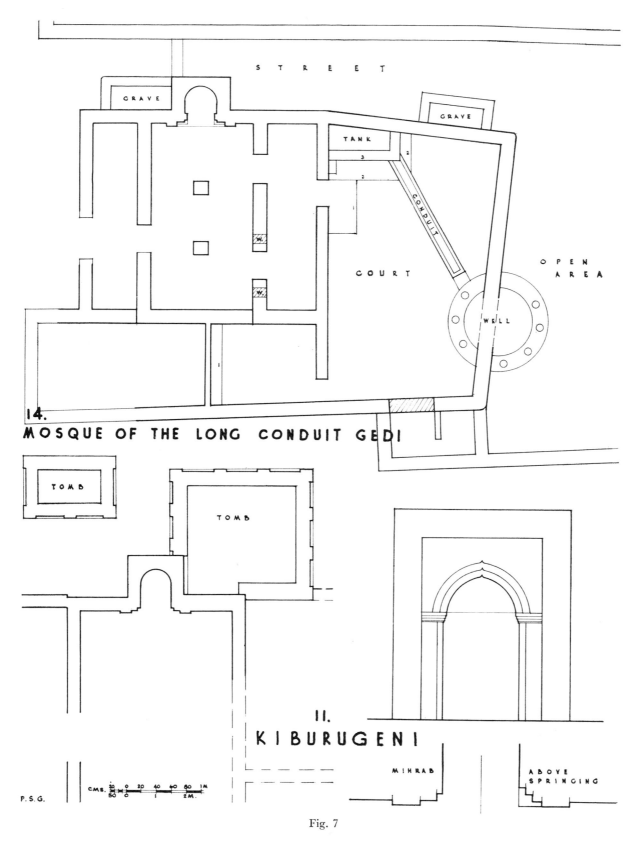

14.
MOSQUE OF THE LONG CONDUIT GEDI

11.
KIBURUGENI

Fig. 7

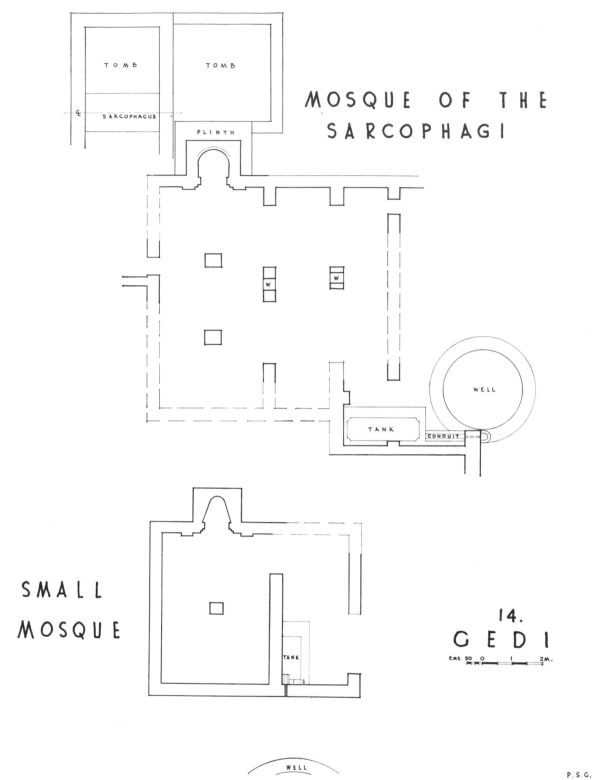

Fig. 8

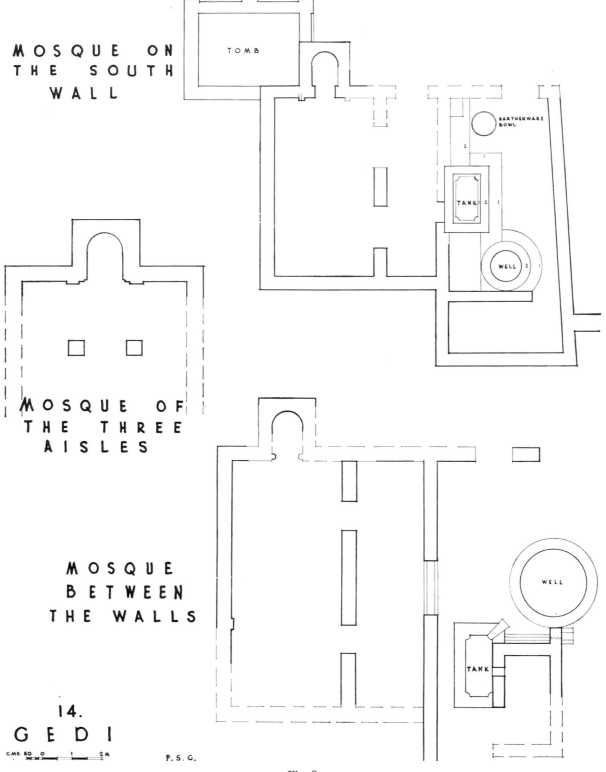

MOSQUE ON
THE SOUTH
WALL

TOMB

EARTHENWARE
BOWL

TANK

WELL

MOSQUE OF
THE THREE
AISLES

MOSQUE
BETWEEN
THE WALLS

WELL

TANK

14.
GEDI

CMS. 50 0   I   2 M

P. S. G.

Fig. 9

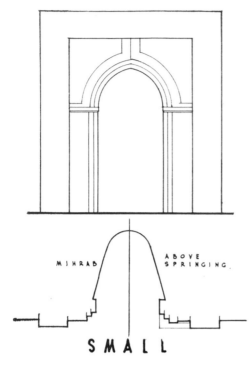

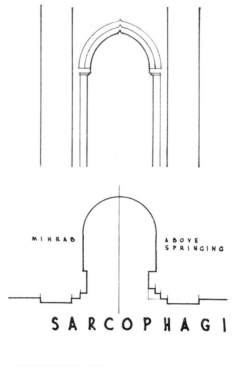

SMALL

SARCOPHAGI

THE MINOR MOSQUES, GEDI

14.

20 CMS. 0 20 40 60 80 1M.

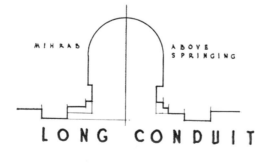

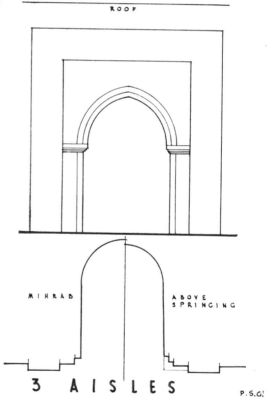

LONG CONDUIT

3 AISLES

P.S.G.

Fig. 10

DOMED MOSQUE, MWANA

7.

MIHRAB

WINDOW

RAIN SPOUT

ABOVE SPRINGING

MIHRAB

MIHRAB

WINDOW

WINDOW

WINDOW

CMS. 20 0 20 40 60 80 1M.
50 0 1M 2M.

P. S. G.

Fig. 11

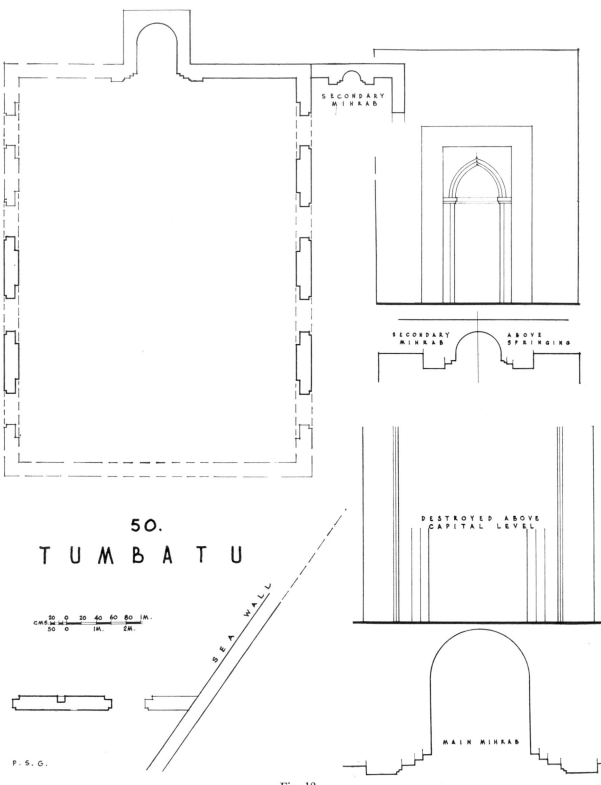

50.

TUMBATU

SECONDARY MIHRAB

SECONDARY MIHRAB   ABOVE SPRINGING

DESTROYED ABOVE CAPITAL LEVEL

MAIN MIHRAB

SEA WALL

20 0 20 40 60 80 1M.
CMS.
50 0   1M.   2M.

P. S. G.

Fig. 12

GREAT MOSQUE
KILWA
42.

52.
KISIMANI MAFIA

P.S.G.

Fig. 13

SMALL DOMED MOSQUE KILWA

CMS. 20 0 20 40 60 80

Fig. 14

SECTION

EXTERNAL
ELEVATION

SONGO MNARA PALACE ARCADE

CMS. 20 0 20 40 60 80 1M.

P.S.G.

Fig. 16

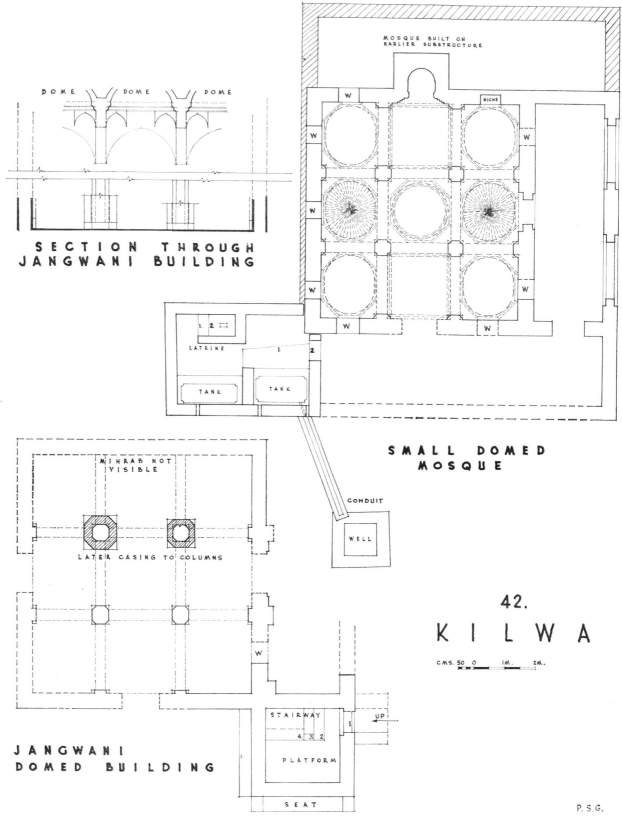

DOME   DOME   DOME

SECTION THROUGH
JANGWANI BUILDING

MOSQUE BUILT ON
EARLIER SUBSTRUCTURE

W   NICHE

W   W

W   W

W   W

W   W

LATRINE   1   2

TANK   TANK

SMALL DOMED
MOSQUE

CONDUIT

WELL

MIHRAB NOT
VISIBLE

LATER CASING TO COLUMNS

42.

K I L W A

CMS. 50 0   1M.   2M.

W

STAIRWAY   UP

4 3 2

JANGWANI
DOMED BUILDING

PLATFORM

SEAT

P. S. G.

Fig. 17

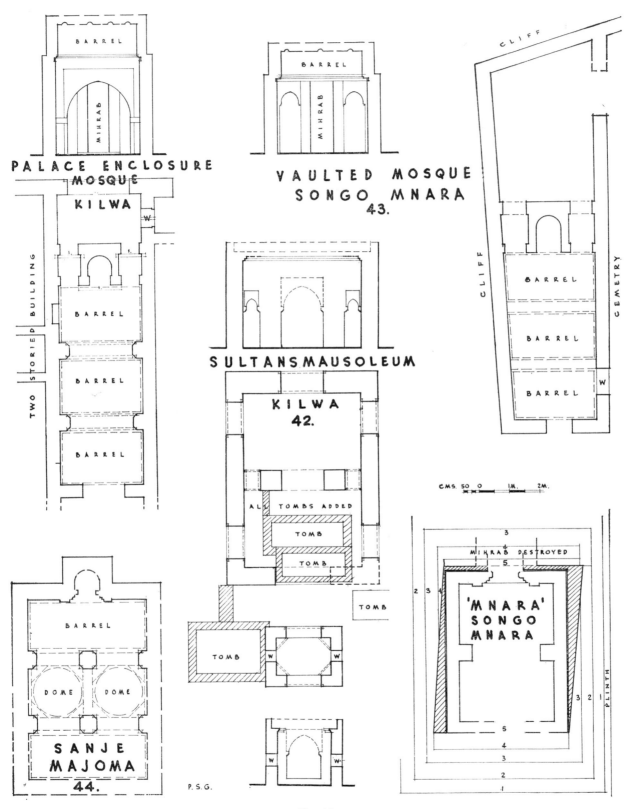

PALACE ENCLOSURE MOSQUE KILWA

VAULTED MOSQUE SONGO MNARA 43.

SULTANSMAUSOLEUM KILWA 42.

SANJE MAJOMA 44.

'MNARA' SONGO MNARA

P.S.G.

Fig. 18

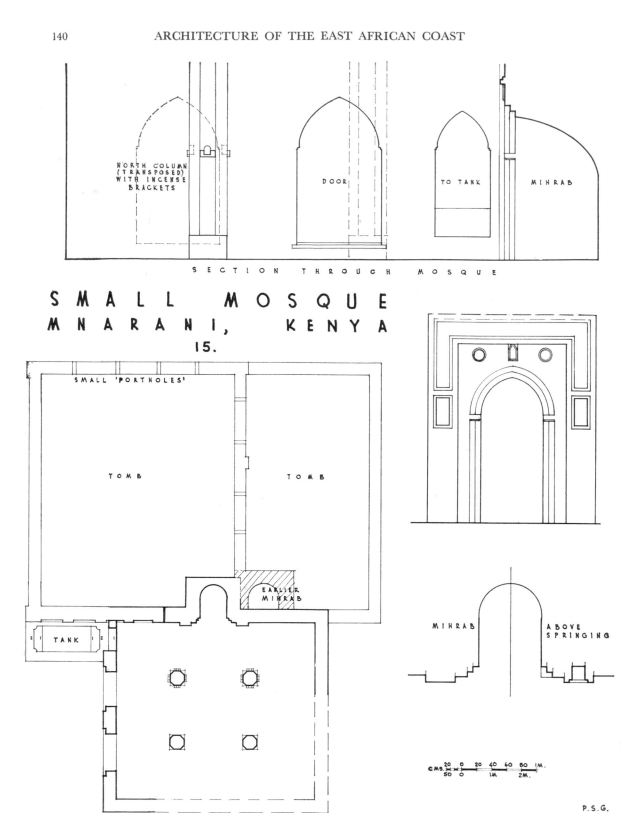

Fig. 19

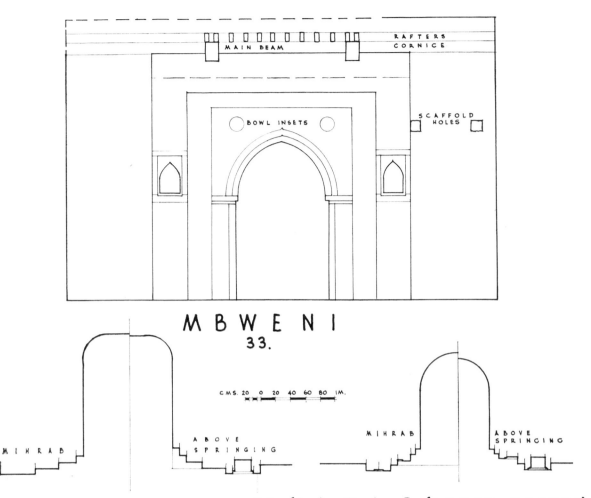

MBWENI
33.

32. KAOLE (LATER MOSQUE)

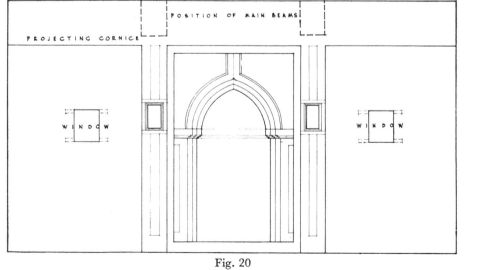

Fig. 20

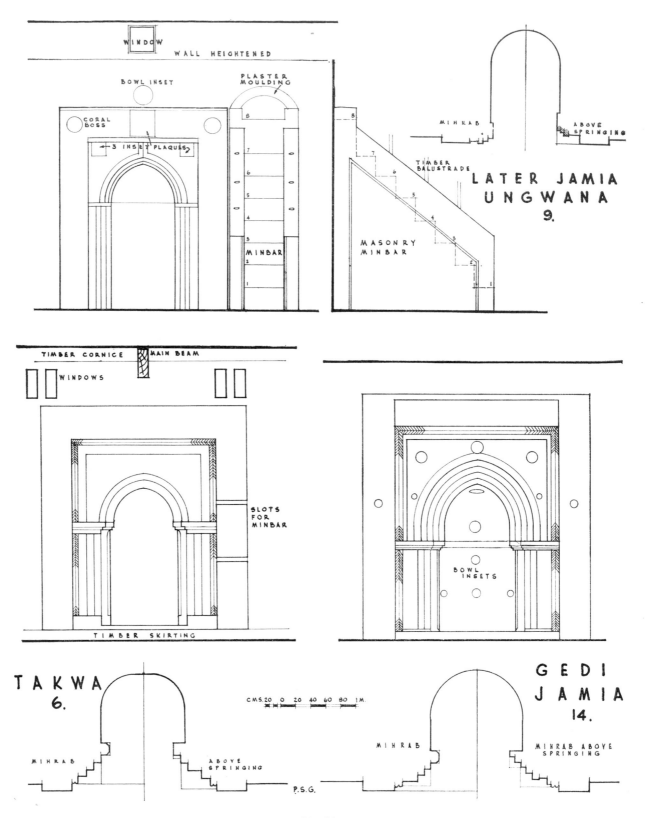

Fig. 21

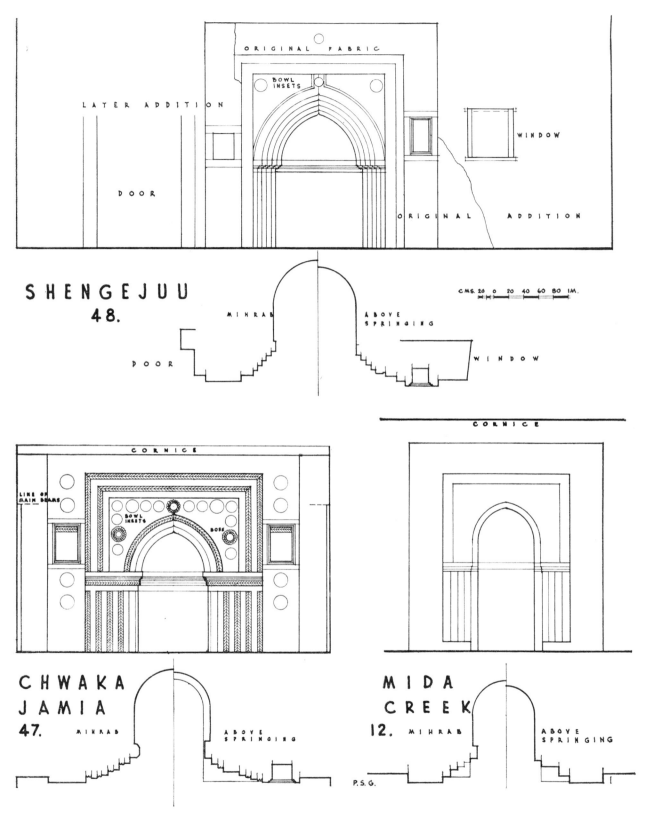

Fig. 22

144

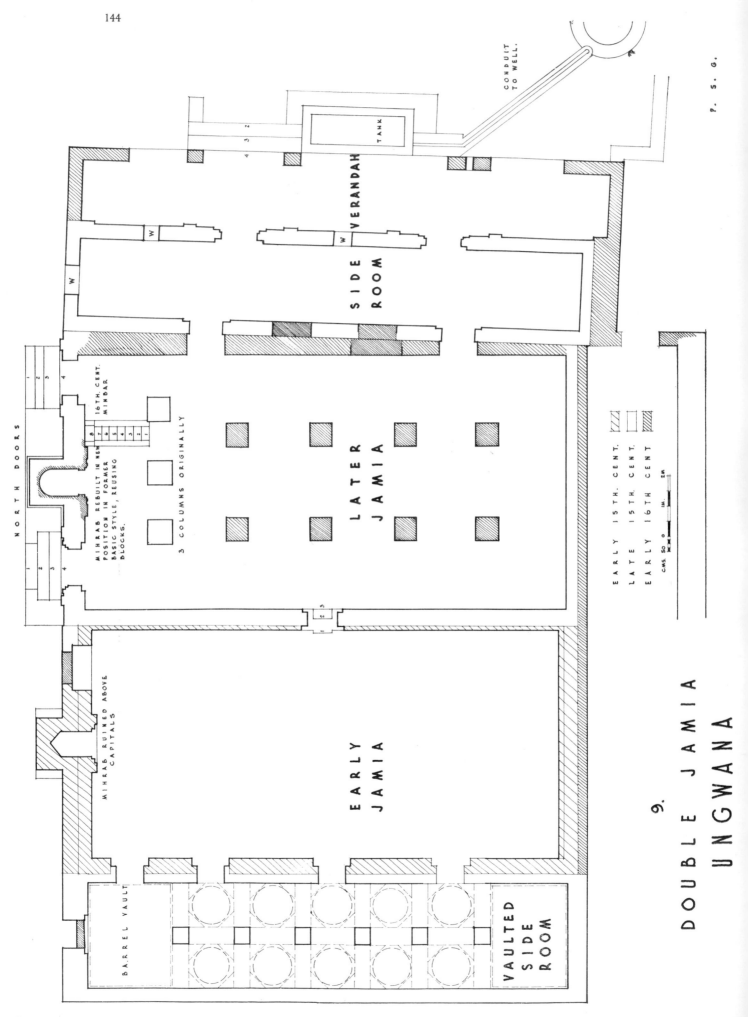

Fig. 23

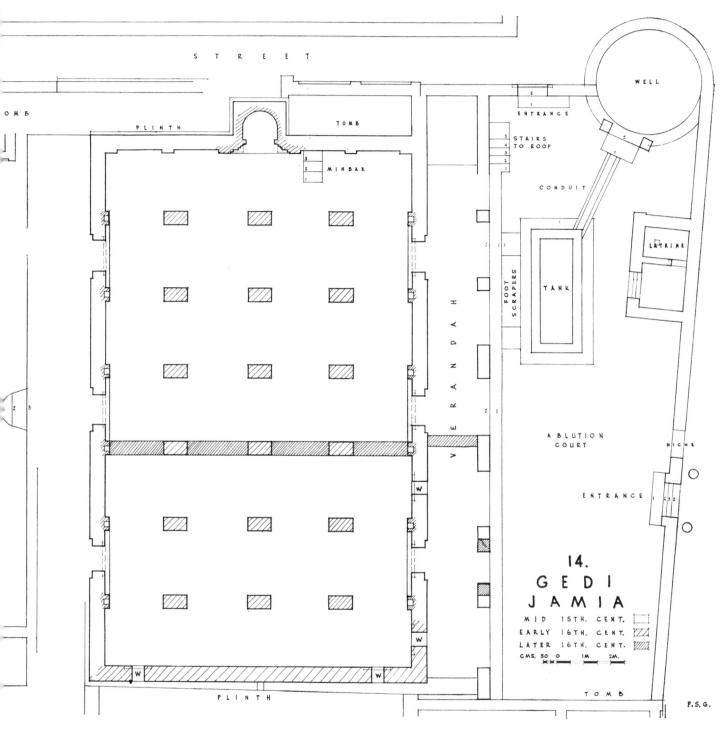

Fig. 24

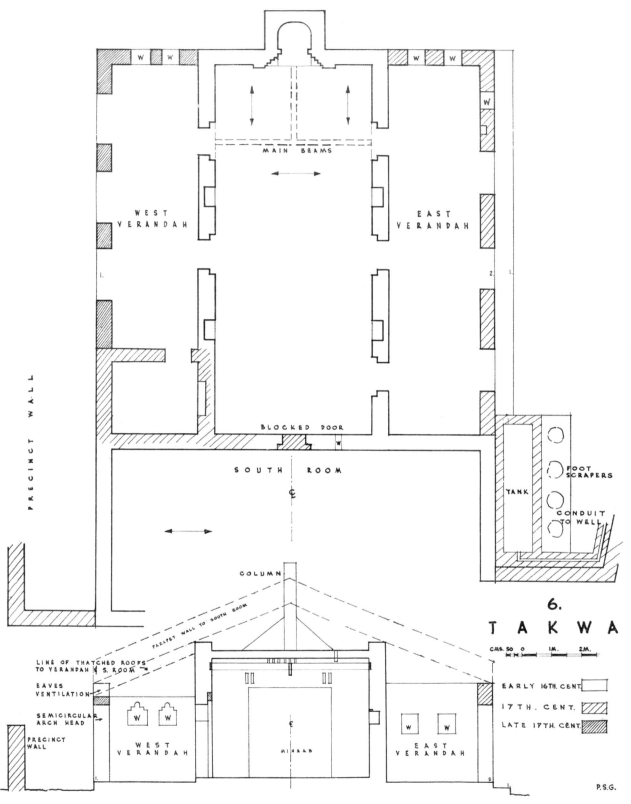

Fig. 25

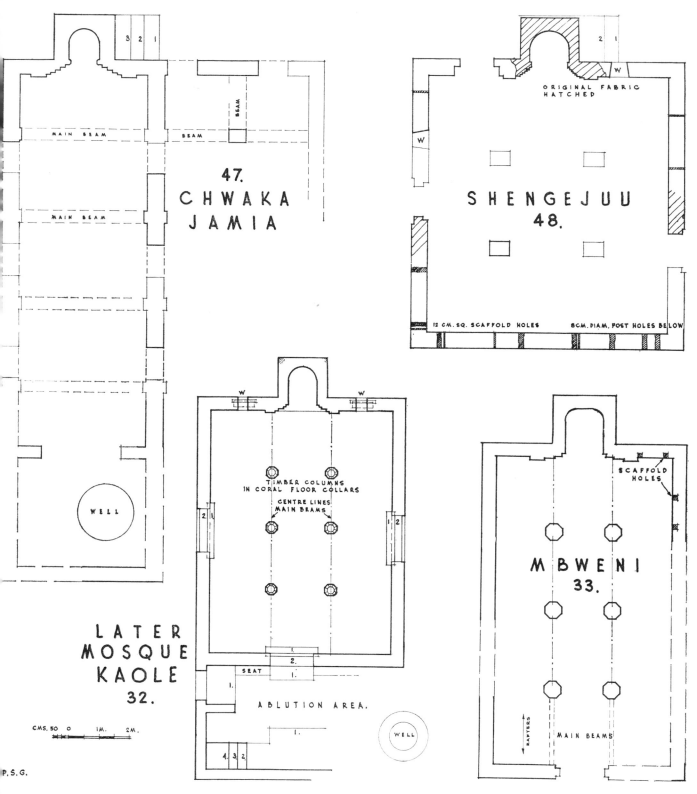

Fig. 26

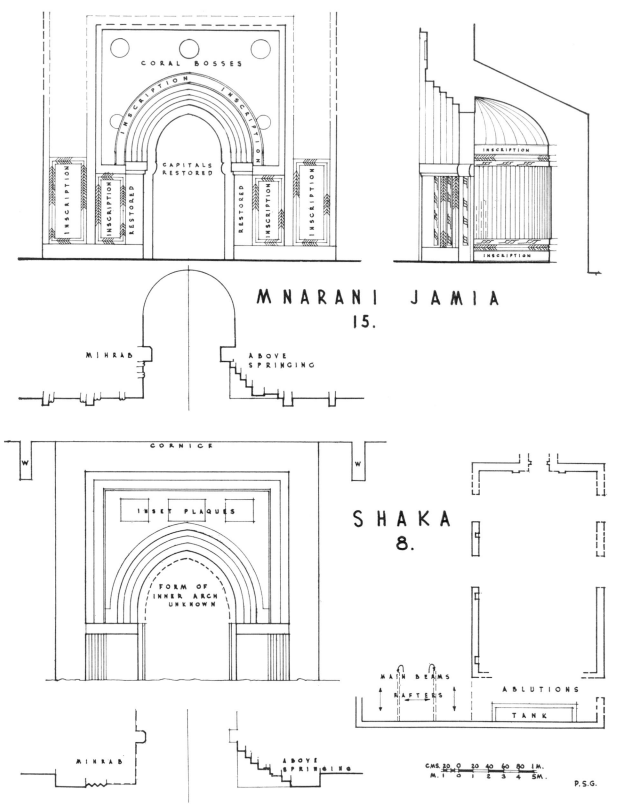

Fig. 27

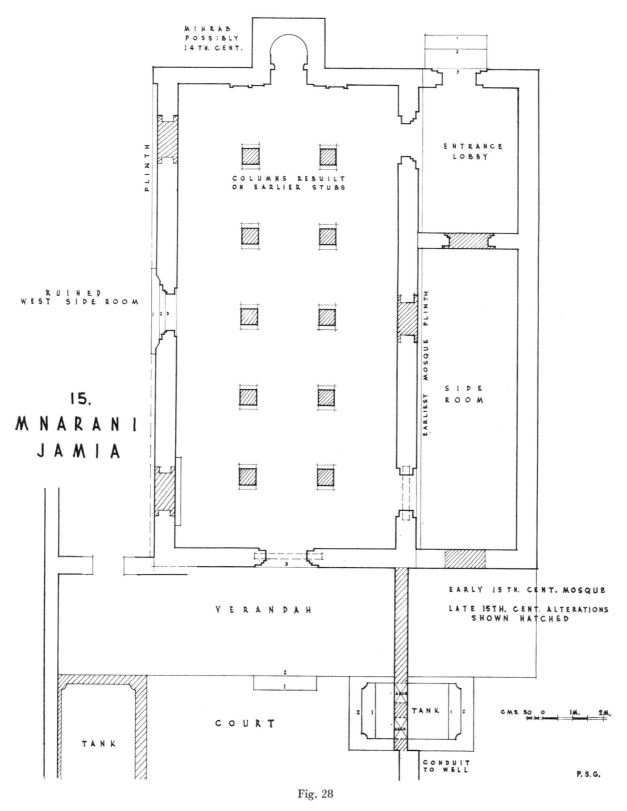

MIHRAB
POSSIBLY
14TH. CENT.

PLINTH

ENTRANCE
LOBBY

COLUMNS REBUILT
ON EARLIER STUBS

RUINED
WEST SIDE ROOM

EARLIEST MOSQUE PLINTH

SIDE
ROOM

15.

MNARANI
JAMIA

VERANDAH

EARLY 15TH. CENT. MOSQUE

LATE 15TH. CENT. ALTERATIONS
SHOWN HATCHED

COURT

TANK

TANK

CONDUIT
TO WELL

CMS. 50 0 1M. 2M.

P. S. G.

Fig. 28

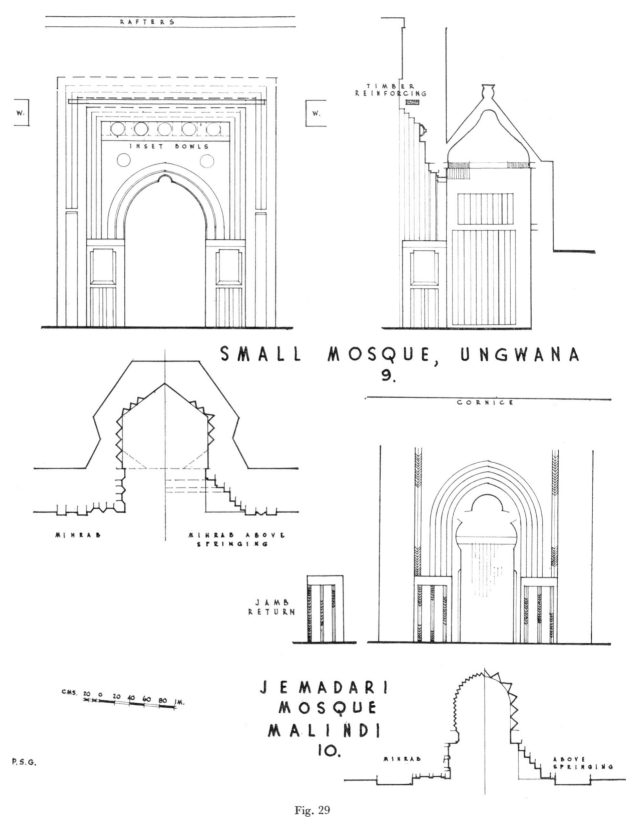

RAFTERS

W.

W.

TIMBER
REINFORCING

INSET BOWLS

SMALL MOSQUE, UNGWANA
9.

CORNICE

MIHRAB

MIHRAB ABOVE
SPRINGING

JAMB
RETURN

CMS. 20 0 20 40 60 80 1M.

P.S.G.

JEMADARI
MOSQUE
MALINDI
10.

MIHRAB

ABOVE
SPRINGING

Fig. 29

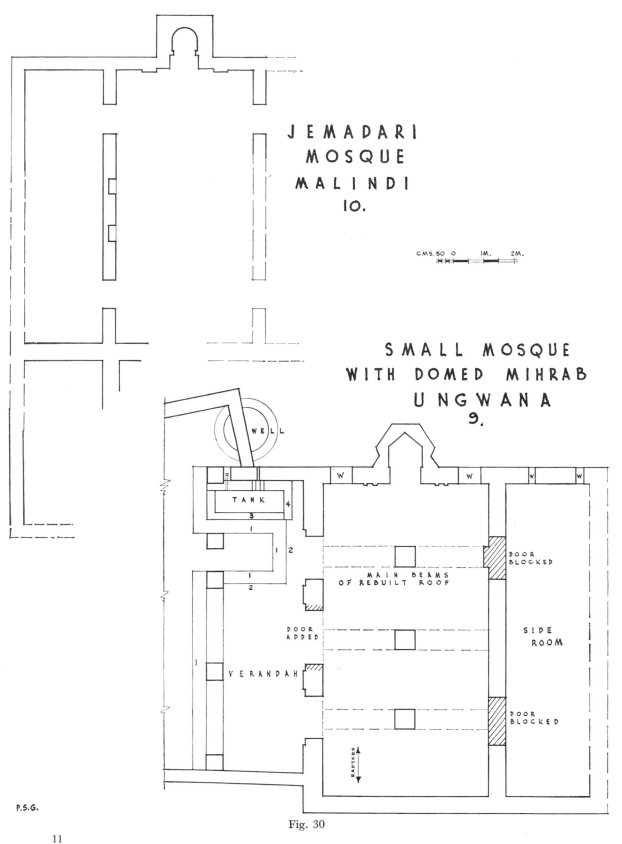

JEMADARI
MOSQUE
MALINDI
10.

CMS.50 0   1M.   2M.

SMALL MOSQUE
WITH DOMED MIHRAB
UNGWANA
9.

WELL

TANK 4
3
1
1 2
1
2

MAIN BEAMS
OF REBUILT ROOF

DOOR
BLOCKED

SIDE
ROOM

DOOR
ADDED

DOOR
BLOCKED

1

VERANDAH

RAFTERS

W   W   W W

P.S.G.

Fig. 30

11

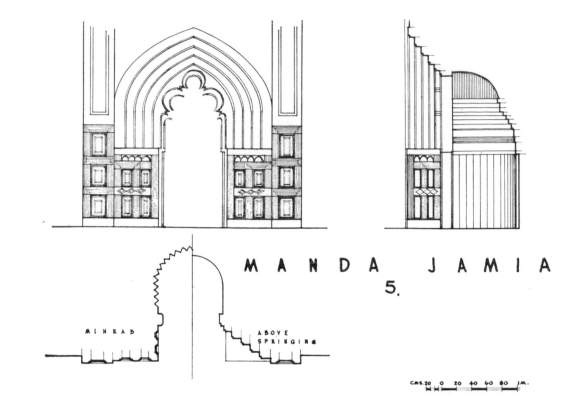

MANDA JAMIA

5.

ABOVE
SPRINGING

MIHRAB

CMS.20 0 20 40 60 80 1M.

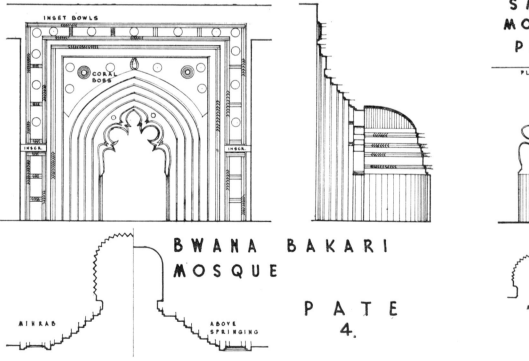

INSET BOWLS

CORAL
BOSS

INSCR.   INSCR.

BWANA BAKARI
MOSQUE

PATE
4.

SMALL
MOSQUE
PATE

PLASTER FRIEZE

MIHRAB

ABOVE
SPRINGING

MIHRAB

P.S.G.

Fig. 31

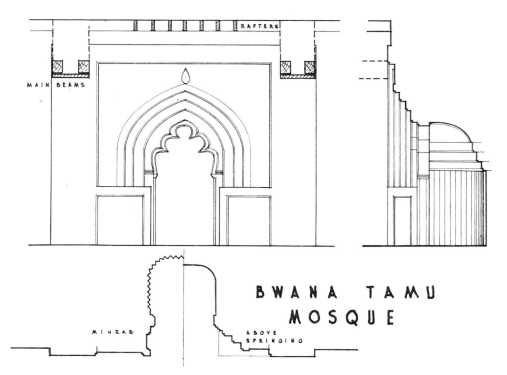

BWANA TAMU
MOSQUE

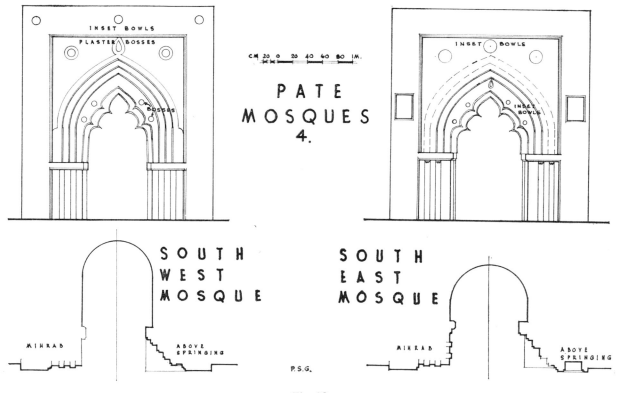

PATE
MOSQUES
4.

SOUTH
WEST
MOSQUE

SOUTH
EAST
MOSQUE

P.S.G.

Fig. 32

SHALA FATANI
FAZA 1.

SIU
FORT

MIHRAB

MIHRAB ABOVE
SPRINGING

MIHRAB

ABOVE
SPRINGING

CMS. 20 0 20 40 60 80 1M.

PLASTER   BOSSES

CORAL   BOSSES

JAMB
RETURNS

MOSQUE
WITH
MNARA

SIU
3.

JAMIA

MIHRAB

MIHRAB ABOVE
SPRINGING

MIHRAB

ABOVE
SPRINGING

P.S.G.

Fig. 33

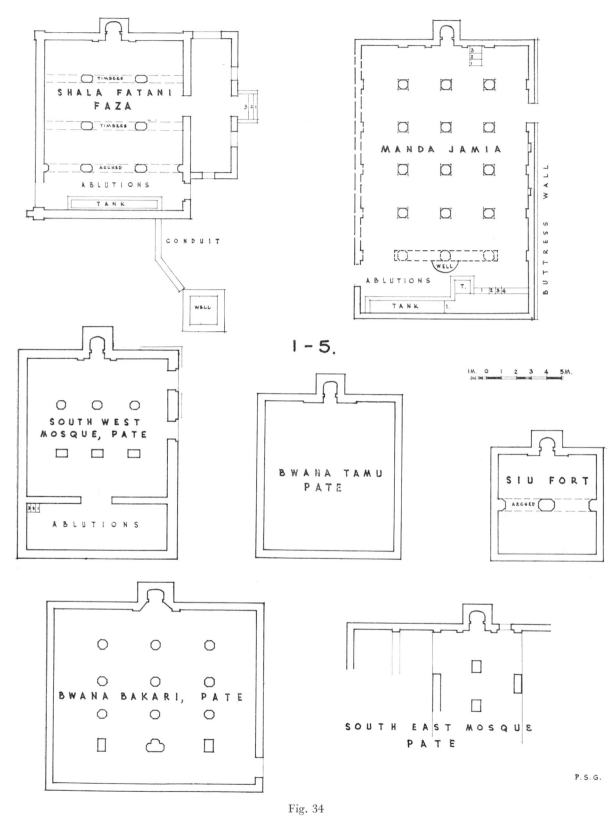

Fig. 34

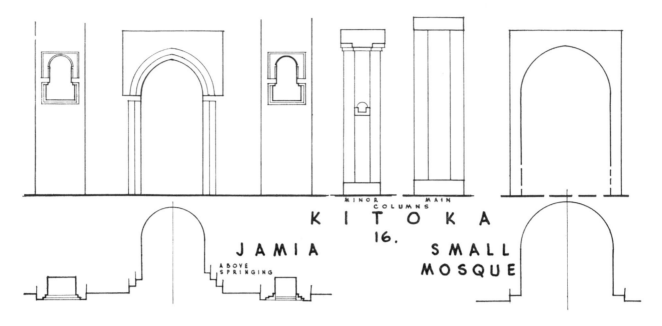

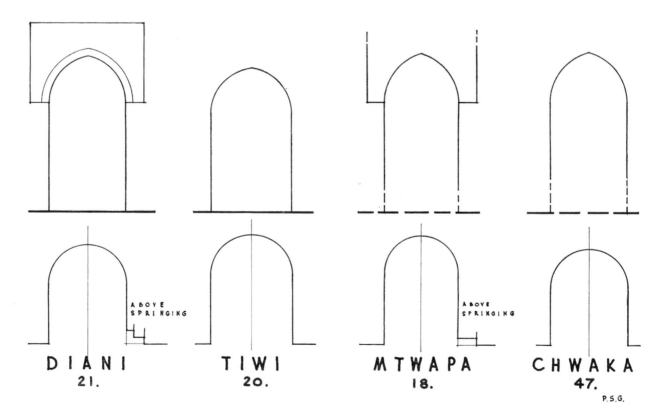

Fig. 35

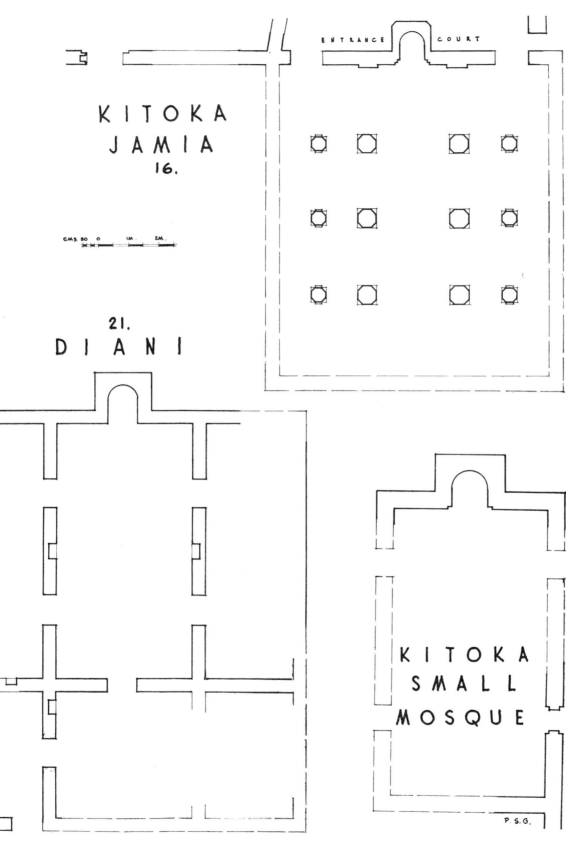

KITOKA
JAMIA
16.

CMS. 50 0   1M.   2M.

ENTRANCE   COURT

21.
DIANI

KITOKA
SMALL
MOSQUE

P. S.G.

Fig. 36

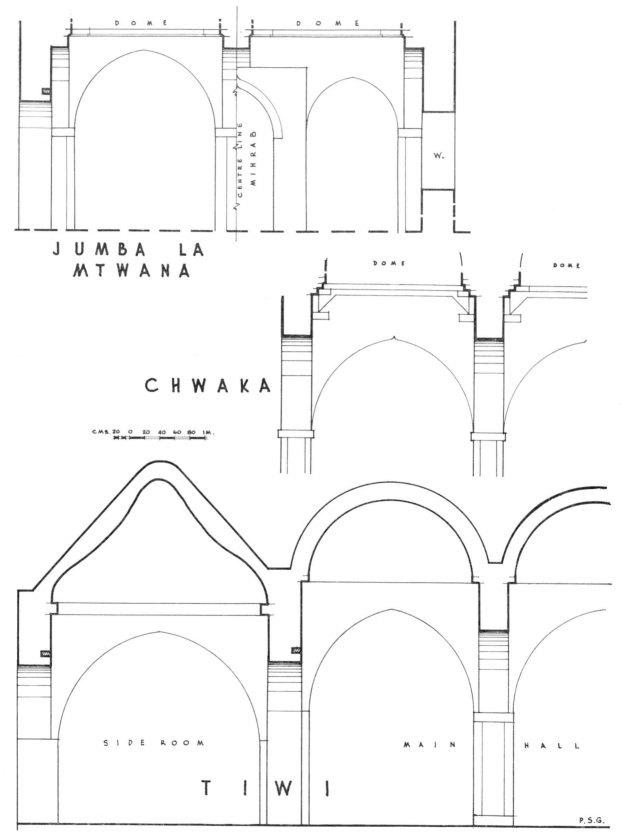

Fig. 37

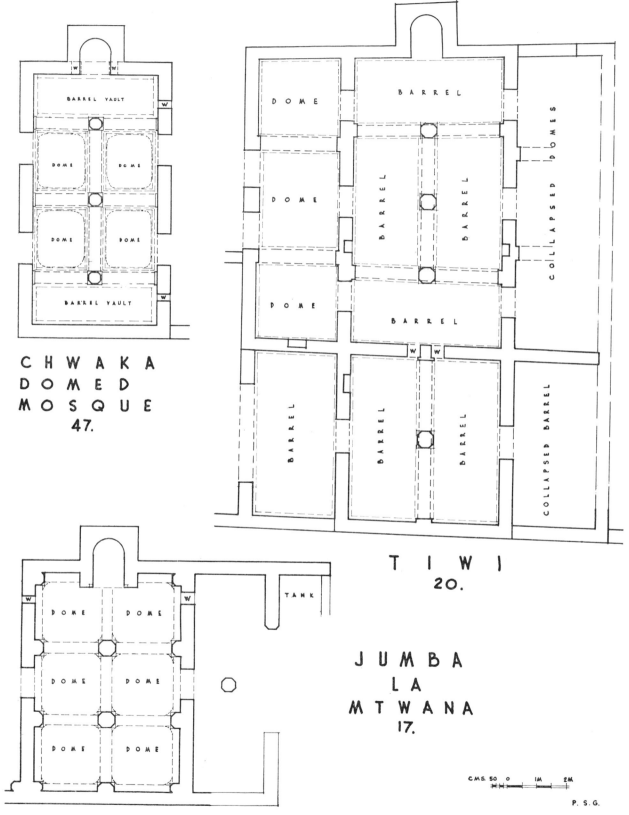

CHWAKA
DOMED
MOSQUE
47.

TIWI
20.

JUMBA
LA
MTWANA
17.

CMS. 50 0 IM 2M

P. S. G.

Fig. 38

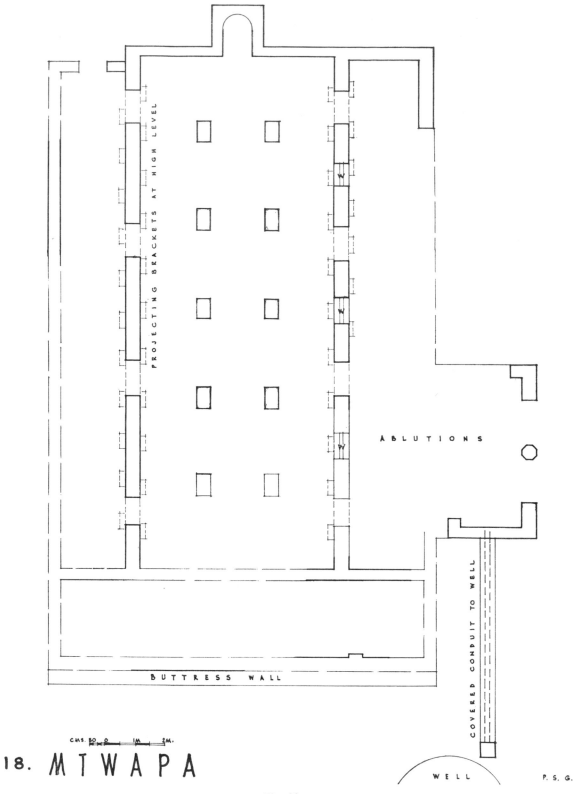

18. M T W A P A

Fig. 39

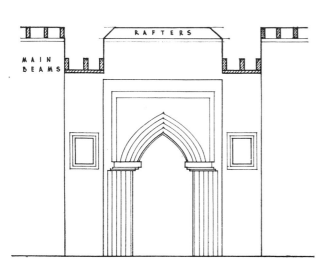

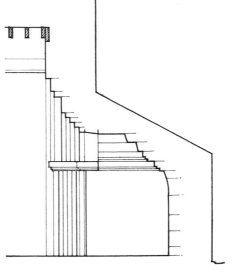

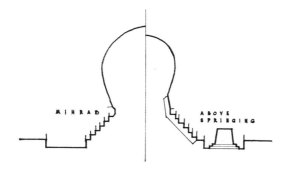

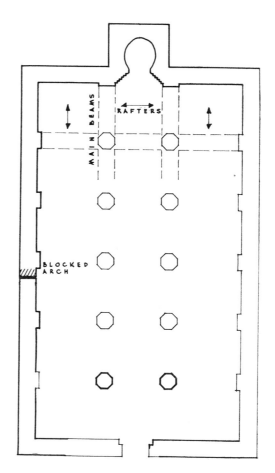

40.
KIMBIJI

P. S. G.

Fig. 40

WINDOW

SKIRTING

SCAFFOLD
HOLE

SOUTH DOOR

D E G E
3 6.

MIHRAB   ABOVE
                SPRINGING

ABOVE
SPRINGING

W   W

EXTENSION

ARCHED
WINDOW
W   W

B A N D A R I N I
37.

CMS 20 0 20 40 60 80 1M.
     50 0   1M.   2M.

MIHRAB   ABOVE
                SPRINGING

P. S. G.

Fig. 41

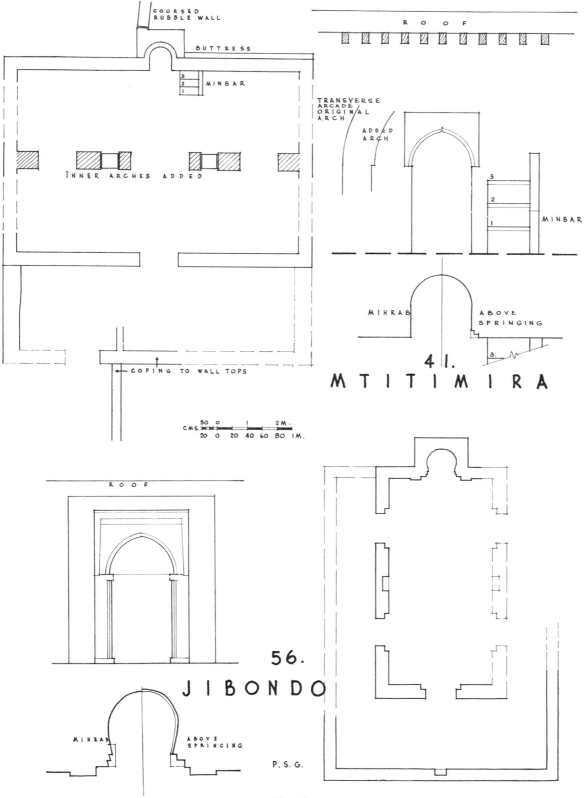

41.

M T I T I M I R A

56.

J I B O N D O

P. S. G.

Fig. 42

Fig. 43

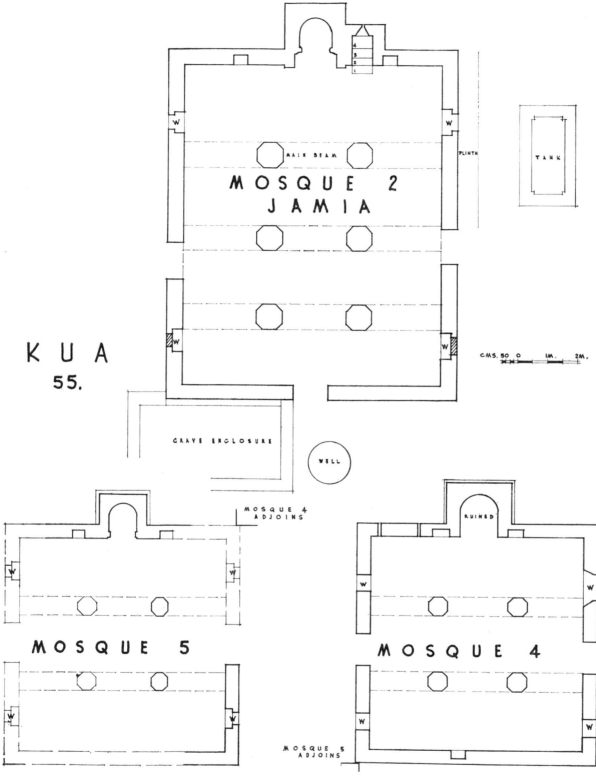

MOSQUE 2
JAMIA

TANK

PLINTH

MAIN BEAM

W

W

CMS. 50 0   1M.   2M.

K U A
55.

GRAVE ENCLOSURE

WELL

MOSQUE 4
ADJOINS

MOSQUE 5

MOSQUE 4

RUINED

W

W

W

W

W

W

W

W

MOSQUE 5
ADJOINS

Fig. 44

Fig. 45

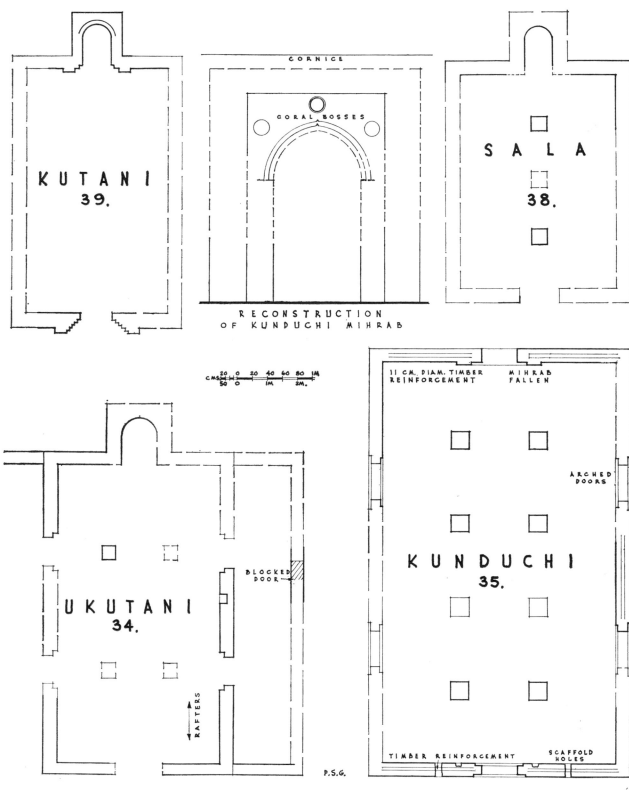

KUTANI
39.

CORNICE

CORAL BOSSES

RECONSTRUCTION
OF KUNDUCHI MIHRAB

SALA
38.

CMS. 20 0 20 40 60 80 1M
50 0   1M   2M.

UKUTANI
34.

BLOCKED
DOOR

RAFTERS

11 CM. DIAM. TIMBER
REINFORCEMENT

MIHRAB
FALLEN

ARCHED
DOORS

KUNDUCHI
35.

TIMBER REINFORCEMENT

SCAFFOLD
HOLES

P.S.G.

Fig. 46

12

Fig. 47

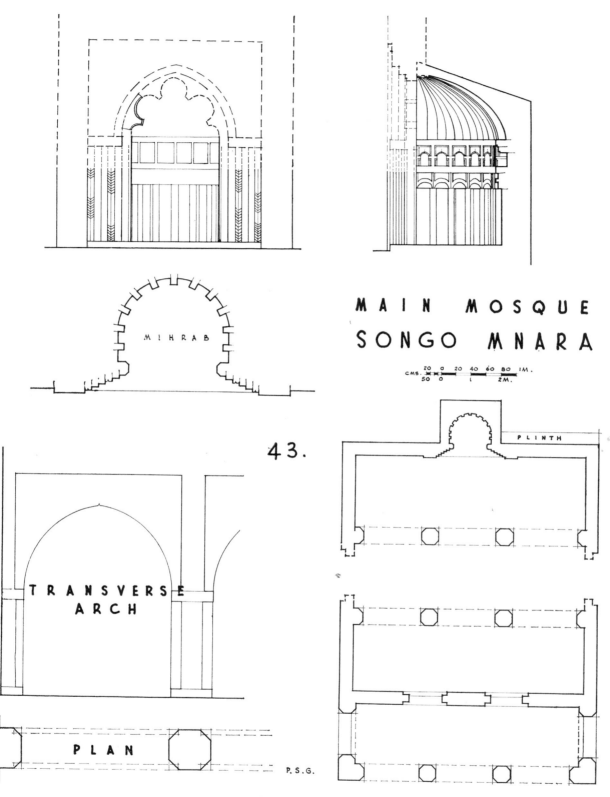

MIHRAB

MAIN MOSQUE
SONGO MNARA

CMS. 20 0 20 40 60 80 1M.
50 0 1 2M.

43.

PLINTH

TRANSVERSE
ARCH

PLAN

P. S. G.

Fig. 48

Fig. 49

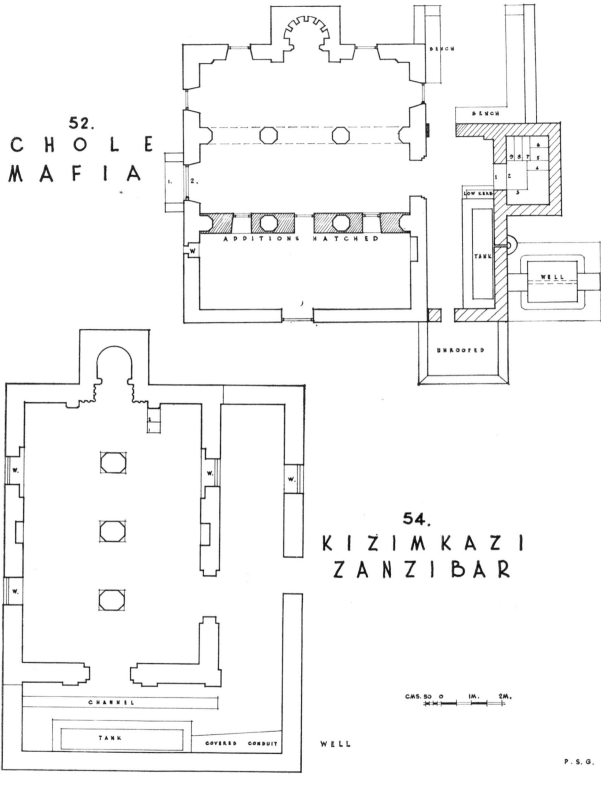

52.
CHOLE
MAFIA

ADDITIONS HATCHED

BENCH

BENCH

LOW KERB

TANK

WELL

UNROOFED

54.
KIZIMKAZI
ZANZIBAR

CHANNEL

TANK

COVERED CONDUIT

WELL

CMS. 50 0   1M.   2M.

P. S. G.

Fig. 50

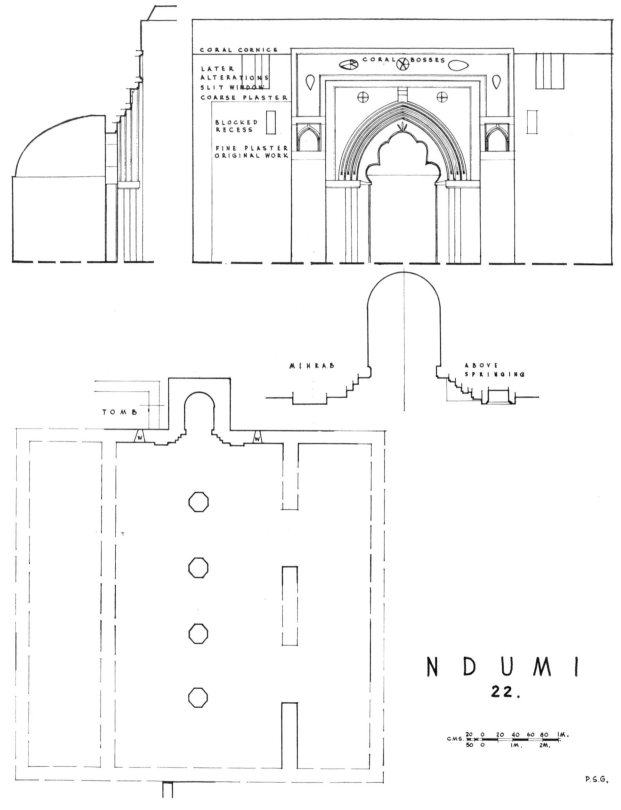

CORAL CORNICE

CORAL BOSSES

LATER
ALTERATIONS
SLIT WINDOW

COARSE PLASTER

BLOCKED
RECESS

FINE PLASTER
ORIGINAL WORK

MIHRAB

ABOVE
SPRINGING

TOMB

N D U M I
22.

CMS. 20 0 20 40 60 80 1M.
50 0 1M. 2M.

P.S.G.

Fig. 51

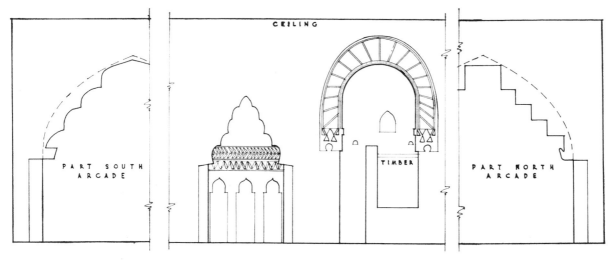

CEILING

PART SOUTH ARCADE

TIMBER

PART NORTH ARCADE

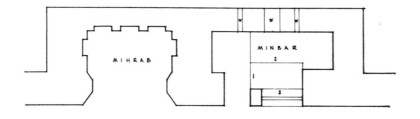

MIHRAB

MINBAR

35A.
MBOAMAJI

CMS. 20 0 20 40 60 80 1M.
50 0 1M. 2M.

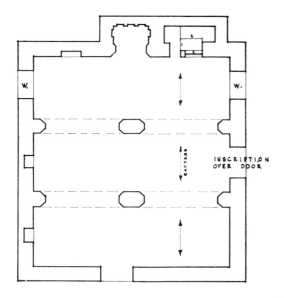

W.   W.

INSCRIPTION
OVER DOOR

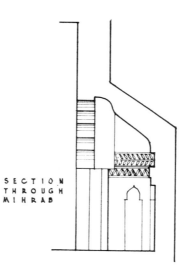

SECTION
THROUGH
MIHRAB

P.S.G.

Fig. 52

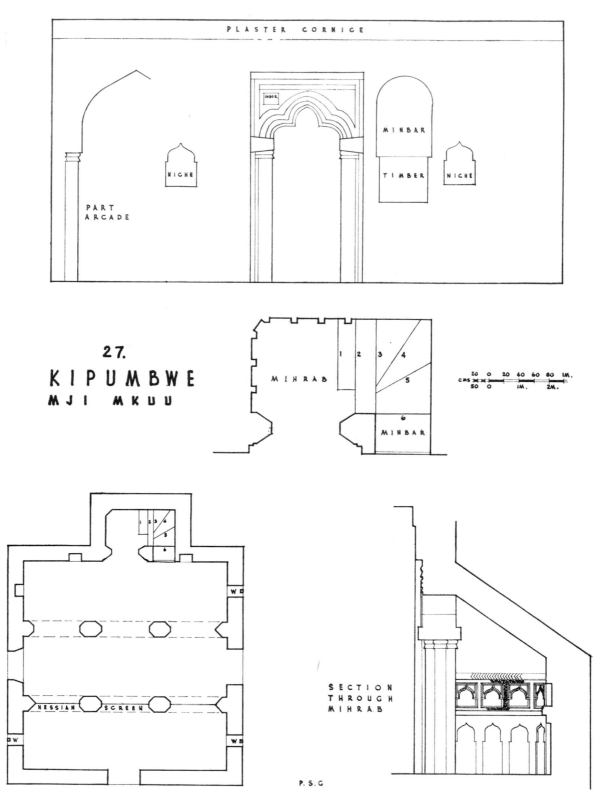

PLASTER CORNICE

INSCR.

MINBAR

TIMBER

NICHE

NICHE

PART
ARCADE

27.
KIPUMBWE
MJI MKUU

MIHRAB

1 2 3 4

5

6

MINBAR

20 0 20 40 60 80 1M.
CMS
50 0   1M.   2M.

W

HESSIAN SCREEN

W

W

SECTION
THROUGH
MIHRAB

P. S. G

Fig. 53

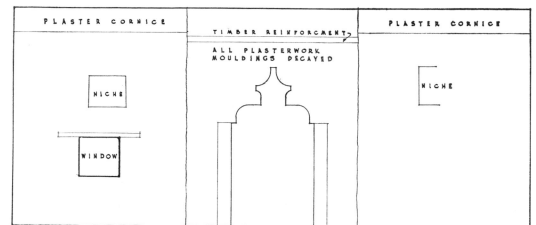

PLASTER CORNICE

TIMBER REINFORCEMENT

ALL PLASTERWORK
MOULDINGS DECAYED

PLASTER CORNICE

NICHE

WINDOW

NICHE

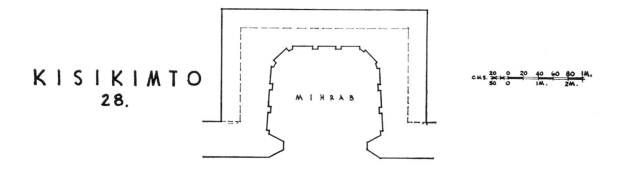

K I S I K I M T O
28.

MIHRAB

CMS.

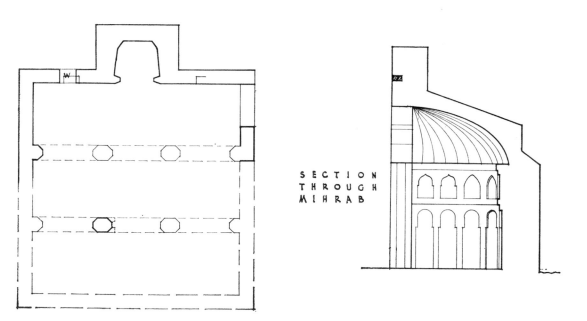

SECTION
THROUGH
MIHRAB

P.S.G.

Fig. 54

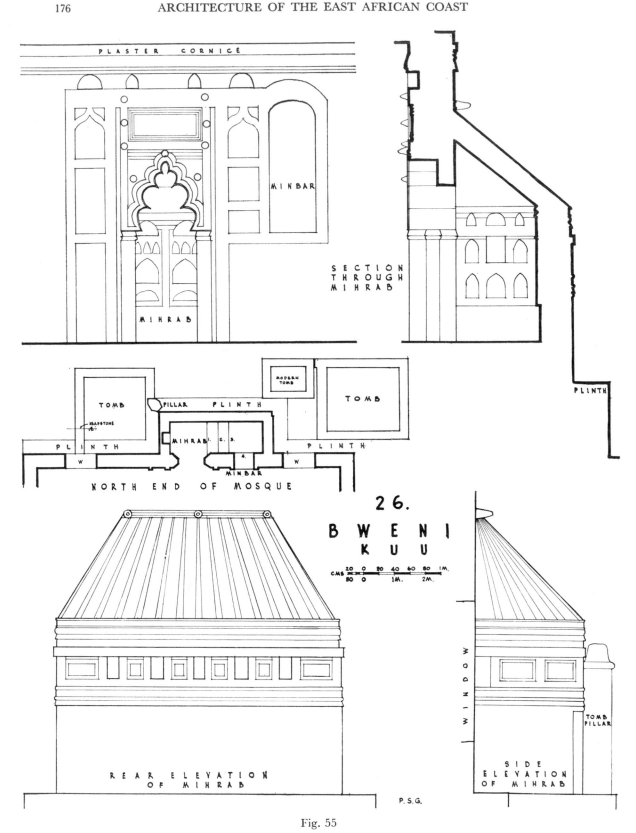

PLASTER CORNICE

MINBAR

MIHRAB

SECTION
THROUGH
MIHRAB

PLINTH

TOMB

PILLAR   PLINTH

MODERN
TOMB

TOMB

HEADSTONE

PLINTH

MIHRAB 1. 2. 3.

PLINTH

W

4.

W

MINBAR

NORTH END OF MOSQUE

26.

B W E N I
K U U

CMS 20 0 20 40 60 80 1M.
50 0   1M.   2M.

WINDOW

TOMB
PILLAR

REAR ELEVATION
OF MIHRAB

P. S. G.

SIDE
ELEVATION
OF MIHRAB

Fig. 55

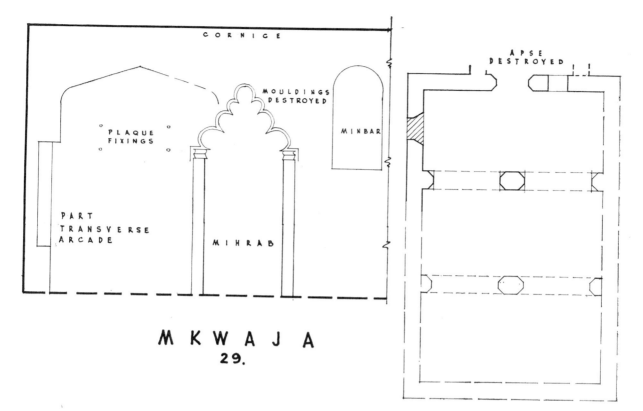

M K W A J A
29.

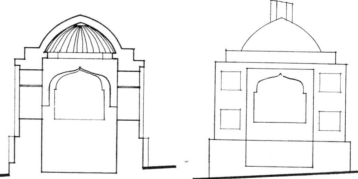

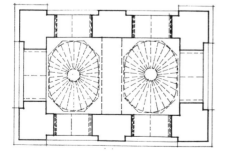

D O M E D   T O M B
M A L I N D I   C E M E T E R Y
K I L W A
42.

P.S.G.

Fig. 56

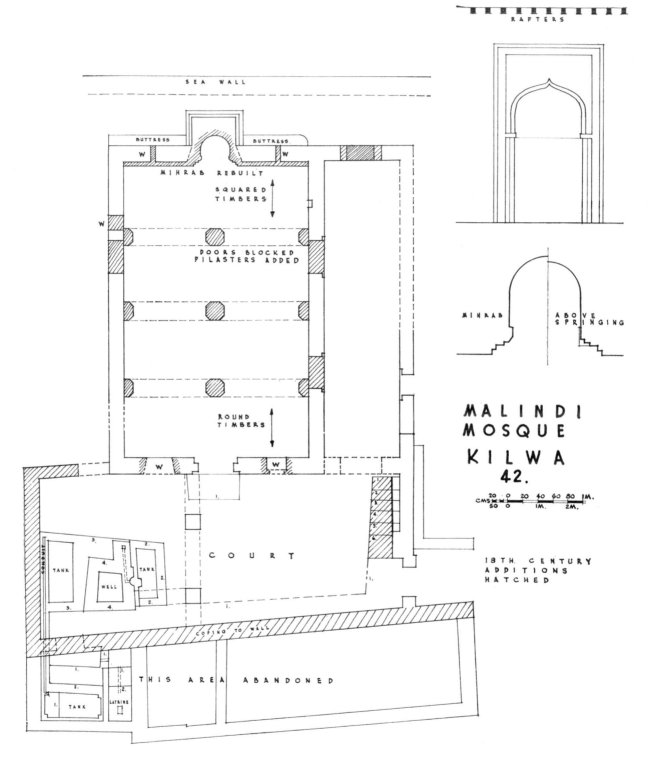

Fig. 57

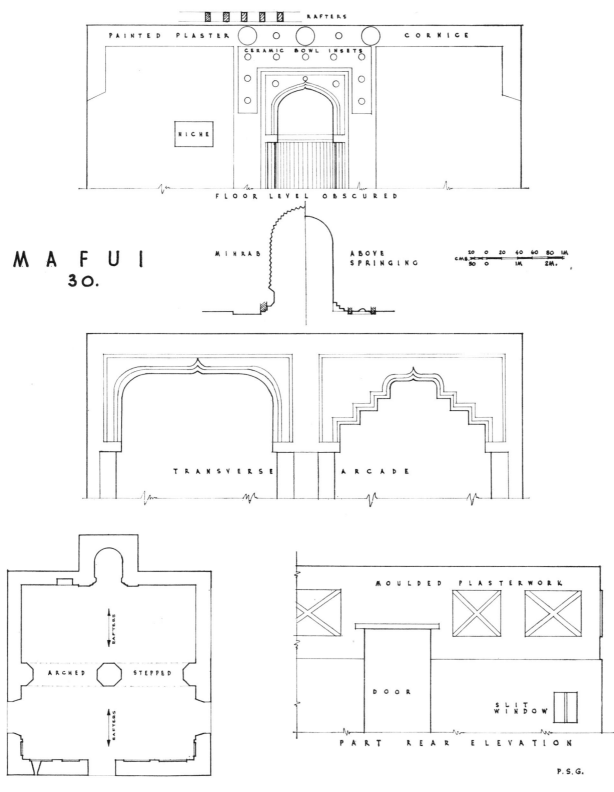

MAFUI
30.

Fig. 58

Fig. 59

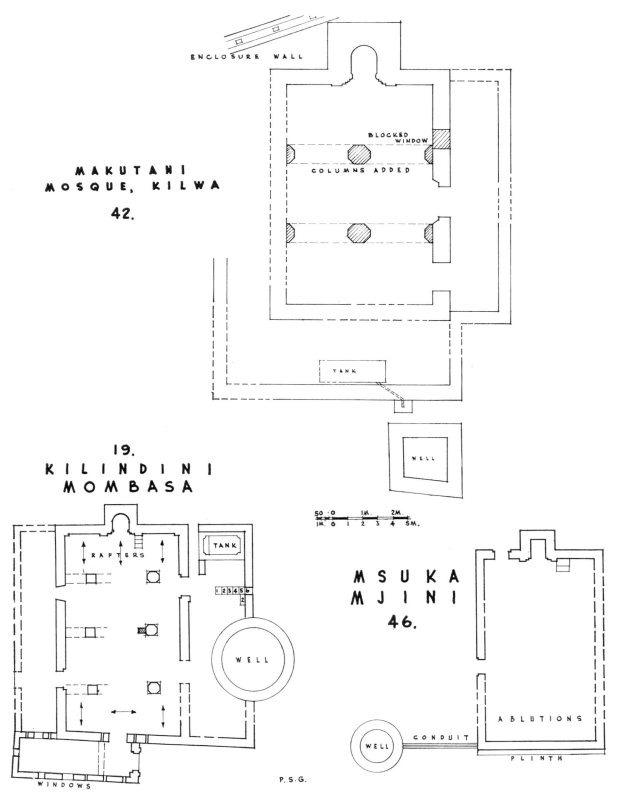

ENCLOSURE WALL

BLOCKED WINDOW

MAKUTANI MOSQUE, KILWA

42.

COLUMNS ADDED

TANK

WELL

19.

KILINDINI MOMBASA

RAFTERS

TANK

1 2 3 4 5 6
2

WELL

MSUKA MJINI

46.

50·0   1M.   2M.
1M. 0 1 2 3 4 5M.

WELL

WINDOWS

P. S. G.

ABLUTIONS

WELL   CONDUIT

PLINTH

Fig. 60

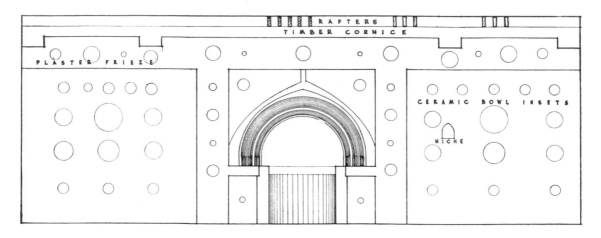

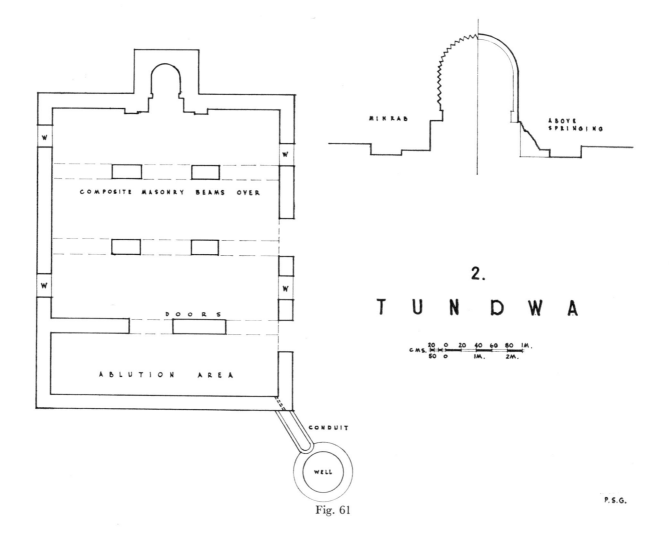

Fig. 61

2.

TUNDWA

P.S.G.

CORAL BOSS
& PLASTER
MOULDINGS

MIHRAB ABOVE SPRINGING

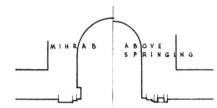
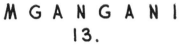

MGANGANI
13.

CMS. 20 0 20 40 60 80 1M.

ALL MOULDINGS
IN CARVED
CORAL

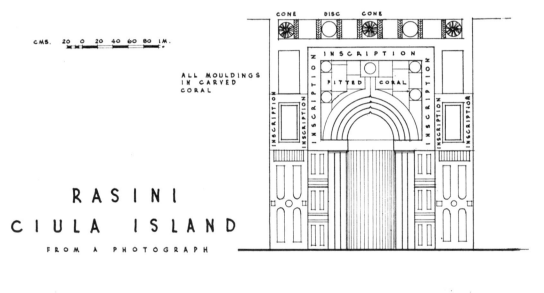

CONE DISC CONE

INSCRIPTION

PITTED CORAL

RASINI
CIULA ISLAND
FROM A PHOTOGRAPH

MIHRAB ABOVE SPRINGING

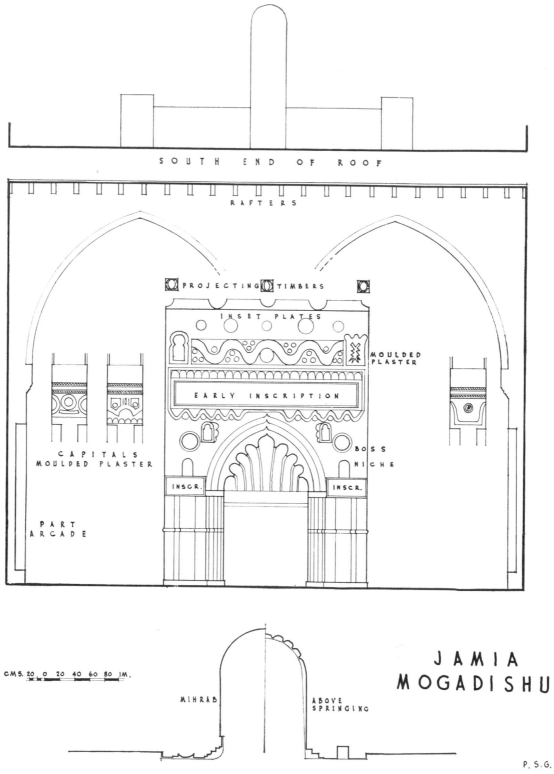

SOUTH   END   OF   ROOF

RAFTERS

PROJECTING TIMBERS

INSET PLATES

MOULDED PLASTER

EARLY INSCRIPTION

CAPITALS
MOULDED PLASTER

BOSS

NICHE

INSCR.   INSCR.

PART
ARCADE

CMS. 20 0 20 40 60 80 1M.

MIHRAB

ABOVE
SPRINGING

JAMIA
MOGADISHU

P. S. G.

Fig. 63

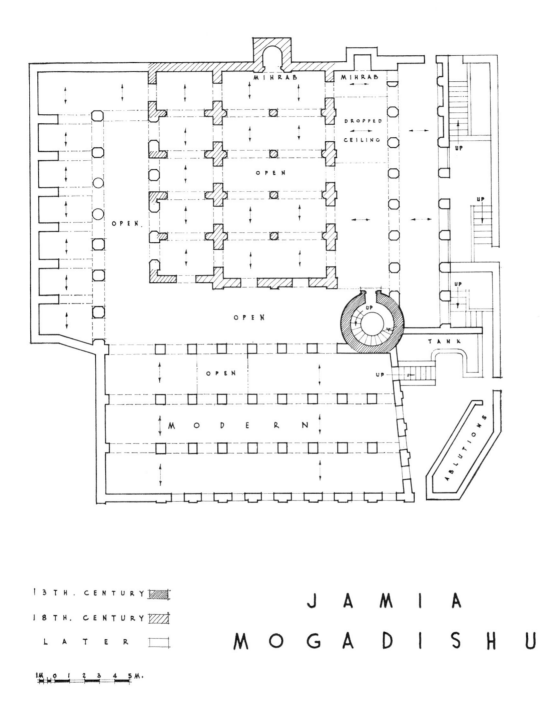

JAMIA
MOGADISHU

13TH. CENTURY
18TH. CENTURY
LATER

1M. 0 1 2 3 4 5M.

P. S. G.

Fig. 64

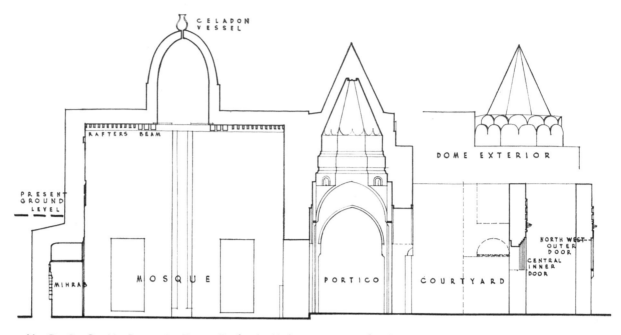

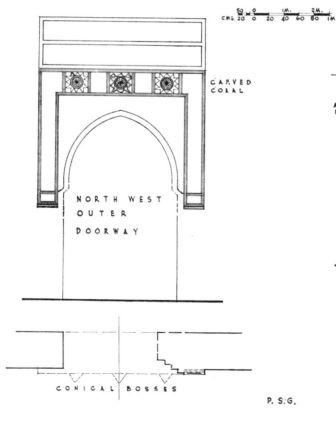

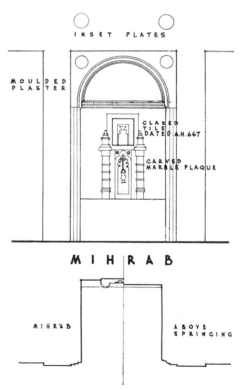

MOSQUE OF FAKHR AD DIN, MOGADISHU

Fig. 65

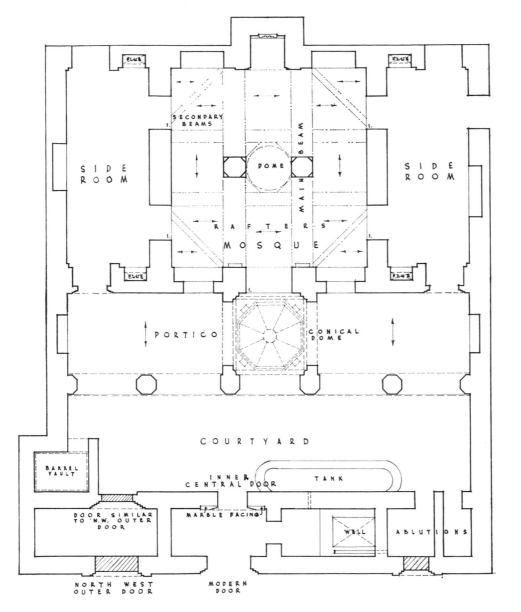

MOSQUE OF
FAKHR AD DIN
MOGADISHU

50 0   1M.   2M.

P.S.G.

Fig. 66

13*

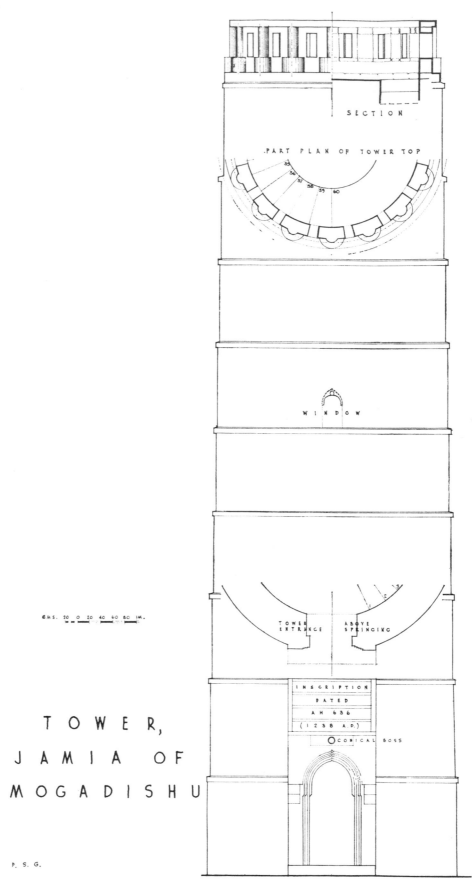

SECTION

PART PLAN OF TOWER TOP

WINDOW

CMS. 20 0 20 40 60 80 1M.

TOWER
ENTRANCE

ABOVE
SPRINGING

INSCRIPTION
DATED
AH 636
(1238 A.D.)

 CONICAL BOSS

TOWER,
JAMIA OF
MOGADISHU

P. S. G.

Fig. 67

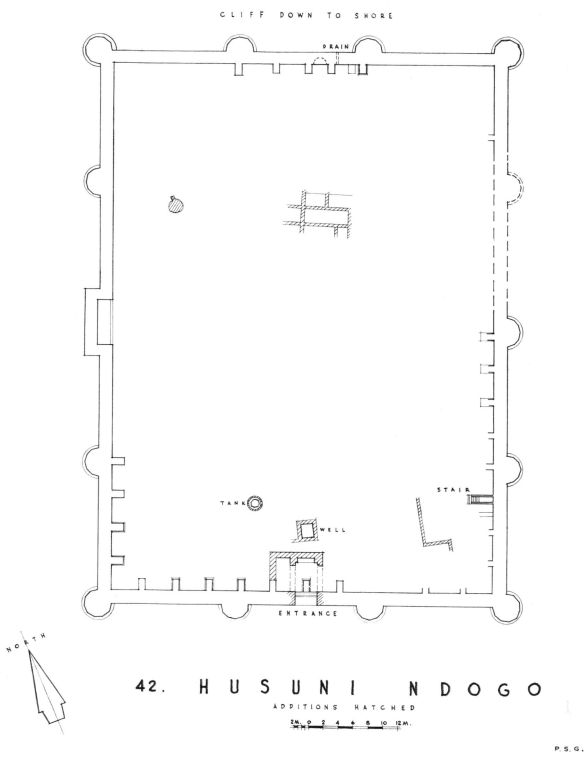

CLIFF DOWN TO SHORE

DRAIN

TANK

WELL

STAIR

ENTRANCE

NORTH

42. H U S U N I   N D O G O

ADDITIONS HATCHED

2M. 0 2 4 6 8 10 12M.

P.S.G.

Fig. 70

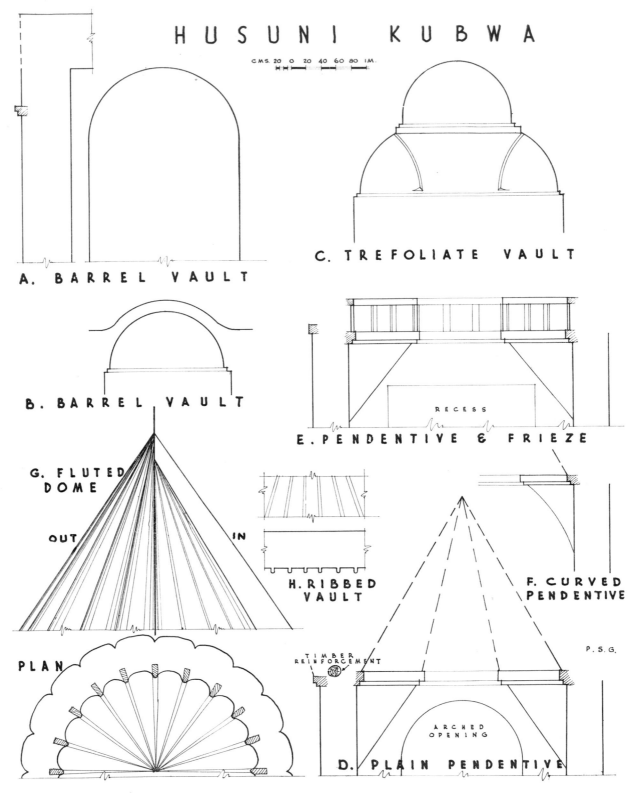

HUSUNI KUBWA

CMS. 20 0 20 40 60 80 1M.

A. BARREL VAULT

C. TREFOLIATE VAULT

B. BARREL VAULT

E. PENDENTIVE & FRIEZE

RECESS

G. FLUTED DOME

OUT   IN

H. RIBBED VAULT

F. CURVED PENDENTIVE

PLAN

TIMBER REINFORCEMENT

ARCHED OPENING

D. PLAIN PENDENTIVE

P.S.G.

Fig. 71

A. CHAMFERED FRAME

B. CEILING BRACKETS

RAFTER RAFTER RAFTER

TIMBER CORNICE

RAFTER

SECTION

PLAN

F.

G.

D. ARCADING E

CMS. 5 0 5 10 15 20 25 CMS.

PLAN

PLAN

HUSUNI KUBWA CARVED MOTIFS

MOTIF G.

H. 'FLEUR DE LYS'

GABLE ENDS OF BARREL VAULTS

CMS. 20 0 20 40 60 80 CMS.

PLAN

SECTION

SECTION

J. UNGWANA TILE

I. TILING

CMS. 5 0 5 10 15 20 25 CMS.

P. S. G.

DENTELLE PATTERN

K. DART MOTIF

Fig. 72

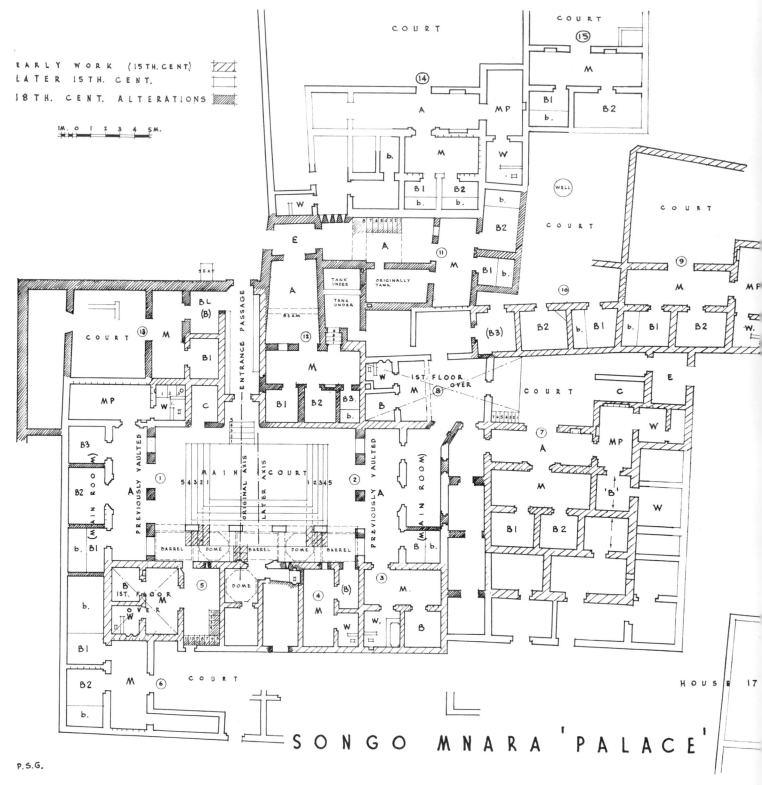

EARLY WORK (15TH. CENT.)
LATER 15TH. CENT.
18TH. CENT. ALTERATIONS

1M. 0 1 2 3 4 5M.

SONGO MNARA 'PALACE'

P.S.G.

Fig. 73

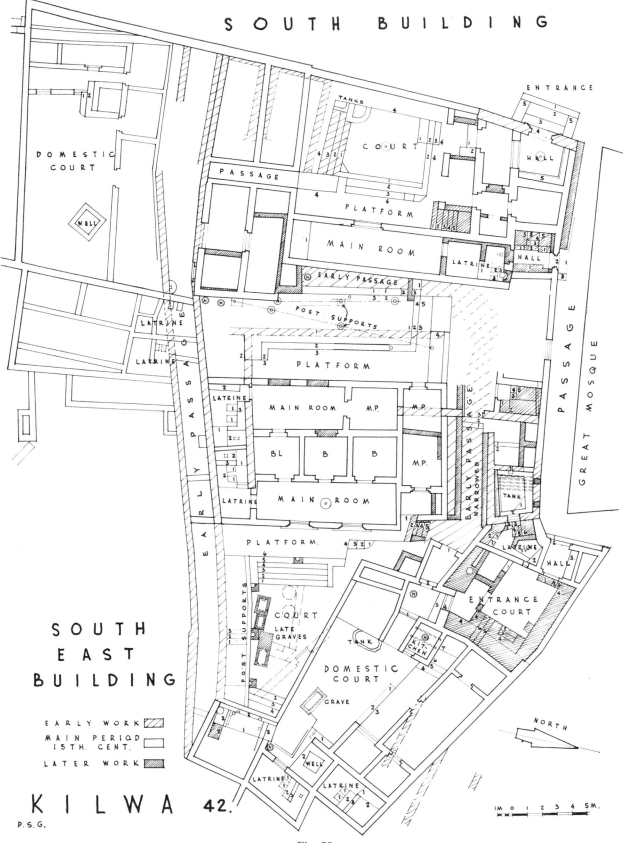

Fig. 75

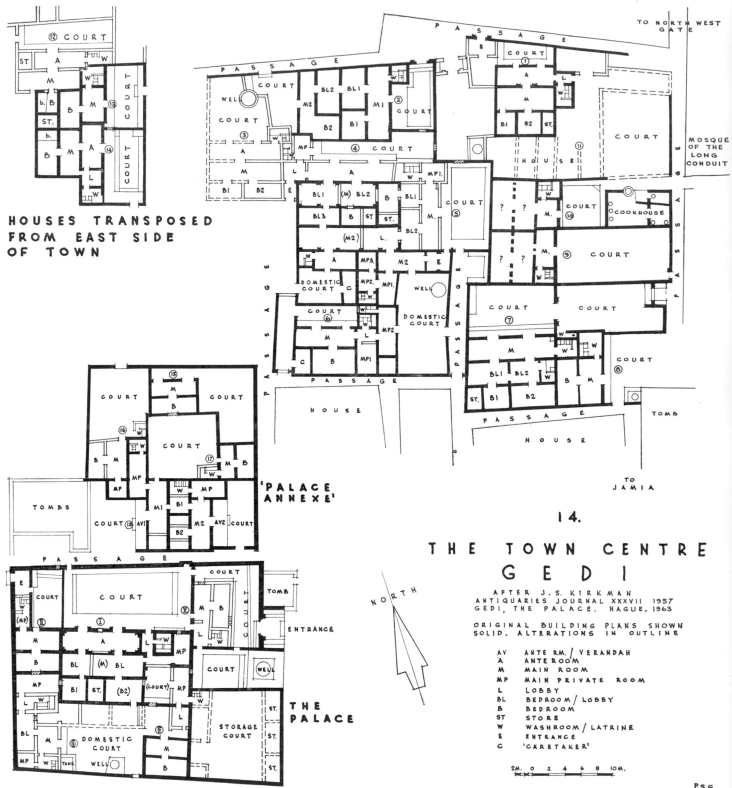

HOUSES TRANSPOSED
FROM EAST SIDE
OF TOWN

'PALACE
ANNEXE'

THE
PALACE

14.

THE TOWN CENTRE
GEDI

AFTER J. S. KIRKMAN
ANTIQUARIES JOURNAL XXXVII 1957
GEDI, THE PALACE. HAGUE, 1963

ORIGINAL BUILDING PLANS SHOWN
SOLID. ALTERATIONS IN OUTLINE

AV   ANTE RM./VERANDAH
A   ANTEROOM
M   MAIN ROOM
MP   MAIN PRIVATE ROOM
L   LOBBY
BL   BEDROOM/LOBBY
B   BEDROOM
ST   STORE
W   WASHROOM/LATRINE
E   ENTRANCE
C   'CARETAKER'

2M. 0 2 4 6 8 10M.

P.S.G.

Fig. 76

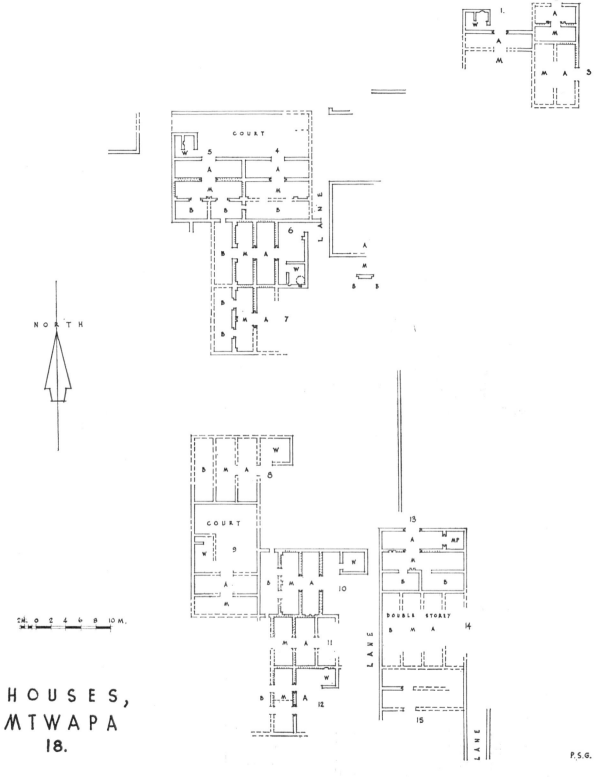

HOUSES,
MTWAPA
18.

Fig. 77

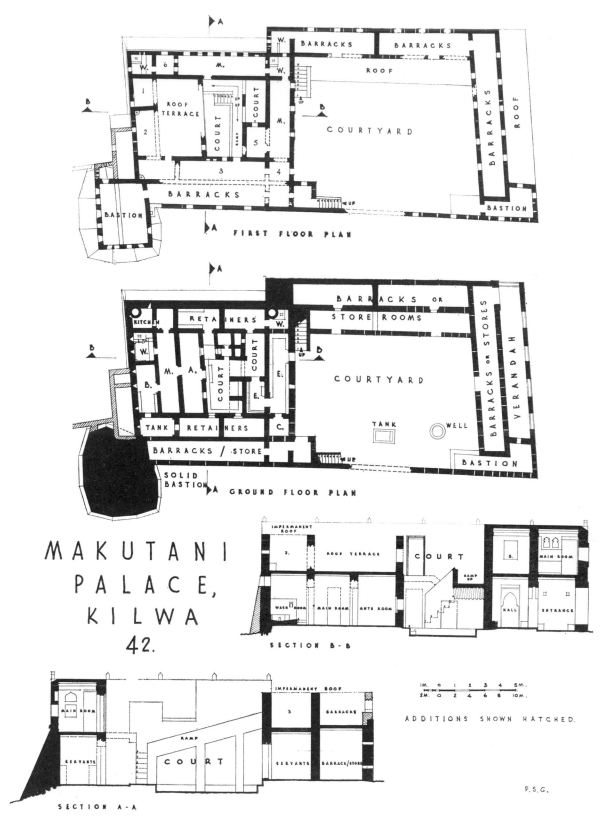

MAKUTANI
PALACE,
KILWA
42.

Fig. 78

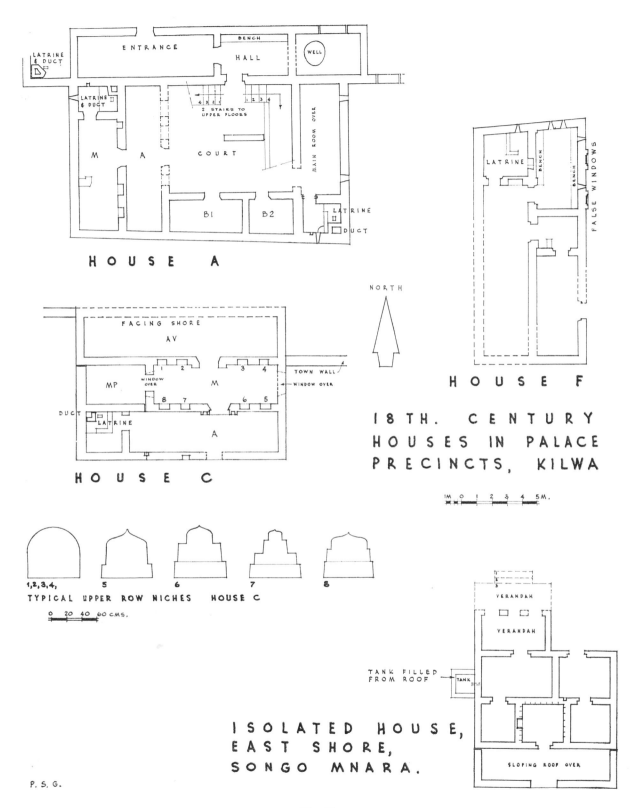

HOUSE A

HOUSE C

HOUSE F

18TH. CENTURY
HOUSES IN PALACE
PRECINCTS, KILWA

TYPICAL UPPER ROW NICHES   HOUSE C

0   20   40   60 CMS.

ISOLATED HOUSE,
EAST SHORE,
SONGO MNARA.

P. S. G.

Fig. 79

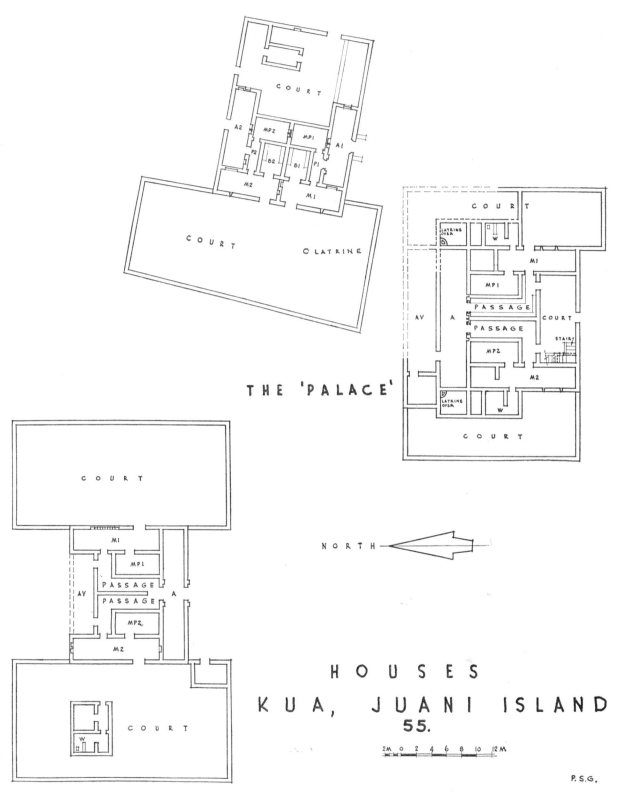

THE 'PALACE'

NORTH

HOUSES
KUA, JUANI ISLAND
55.

2M 0 2 4 6 8 10 12M

P.S.G.

Fig. 80

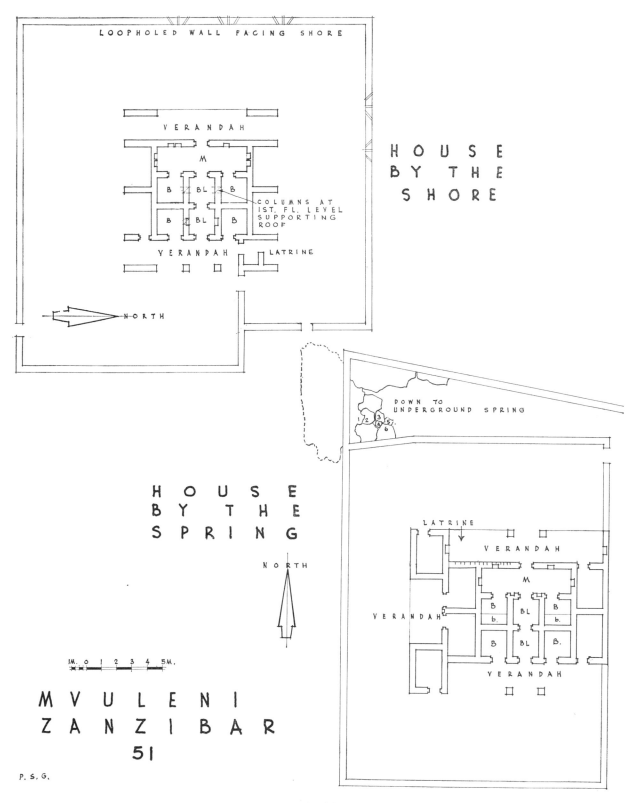

LOOPHOLED WALL FACING SHORE

VERANDAH

M

B BL B

COLUMNS AT
1ST. FL. LEVEL
SUPPORTING
ROOF

B BL B

VERANDAH   LATRINE

NORTH

HOUSE
BY THE
SHORE

HOUSE
BY THE
SPRING

NORTH

DOWN TO
UNDERGROUND SPRING

1 2 3 5
4 6

LATRINE

VERANDAH

M

VERANDAH
B BL B
b.   b.

B BL B.

VERANDAH

1M. 0 1 2 3 4 5M.

MVULENI
ZANZIBAR
51

P. S. G.

Fig. 81

A. MARBLE DOOR FACING
FAKHR AD DIN, MOGADISHU

HUSUNI KUBWA BOSSES
42.

D. UNGWANA
9.

CMS. 2 0 2 4 6 8 10 CMS.

F. MNARANI MIHRAB MOULDING 15.

BOSSES WITH PALMETTE MOTIFS

E. S.E. BUILDING
KILWA
42.

G. MNARANI
SOUTH DOOR 15.

P.S.G.

H. MNARANI MIHRAB
15.

Fig. 82

B. MNARANI 15.

A. MOMBASA GRAVESTONE
866 A.H. 1476 A.D. 19.

C. MNARANI 15.

D. MNARANI TOMB D
15.

E. MNARANI TOMB G.
15.

F. MNARANI TOMB C.
15.

G. MNARANI TOMB B
15.

H. TOMB NEAR 14.
GEDI PALACE

BOSSES WITH INTERLACE MOTIFS.

CMS. 2 0 2 4 6 8 10 12 CMS. APPROX.

P.S.G.

I. KILWA SMALL
DOMED MOSQUE
42.

J. MAKUTANI PALACE
42.

K. SIU MOSQUE
WITH MNARA
3.

Fig. 83

P. S. G.

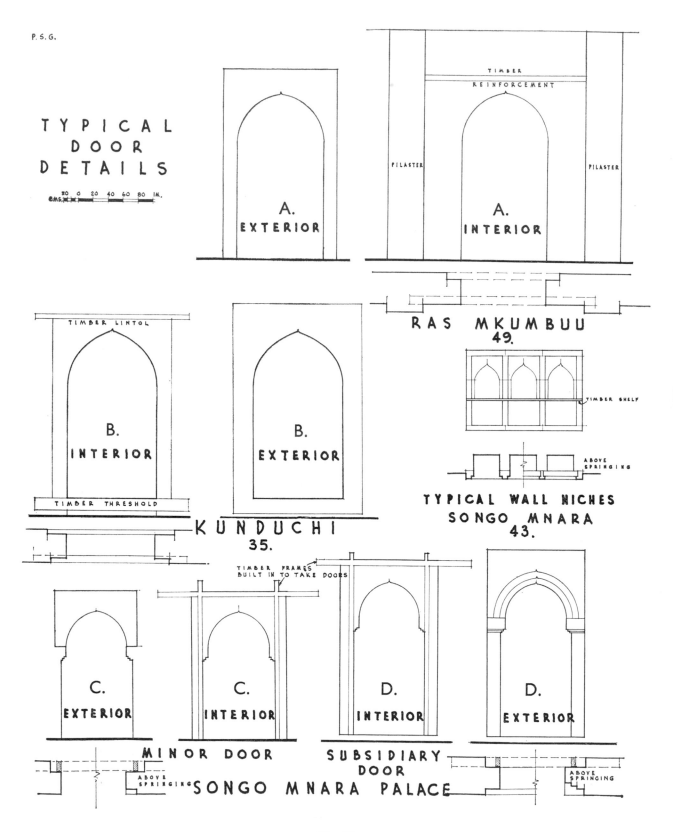

TYPICAL DOOR DETAILS

A. EXTERIOR

A. INTERIOR

TIMBER REINFORCEMENT

PILASTER   PILASTER

RAS MKUMBUU
49.

TIMBER LINTOL

B. INTERIOR

B. EXTERIOR

TIMBER THRESHOLD

KUNDUCHI
35.

TIMBER SHELF

ABOVE SPRINGING

TYPICAL WALL NICHES
SONGO MNARA
43.

C. EXTERIOR

TIMBER FRAMES BUILT IN TO TAKE DOORS

C. INTERIOR

D. INTERIOR

D. EXTERIOR

MINOR DOOR

SUBSIDIARY DOOR

ABOVE SPRINGING

SONGO MNARA PALACE

ABOVE SPRINGING

Fig. 84

INDEX

Figure and Plate numbers are shown in heavy type.